India in 2050

India in 2050

Visions for a Superpower

Edited by

Karan Mehrishi

ink | OCCAM

ISBN: 978-93-92209-93-2

First published in India 2024
This edition published 2024

BluOne Ink Pvt. Ltd
A-76, 2nd Floor, Sector 136, Noida
Uttar Pradesh 201301
www.bluone.ink
publisher@bluone.ink

Printed and bound in Nutech Print Services - India

ink | OCCAM

To the forefathers and foremothers of the
Great Indian Civilization.

Contents

Introduction

Karan Mehrishi

'Freedom is not Free'
Korean War Memorial
MBTA Station, Natick, Massachusetts, US

Back in 2010, I was in China as a student. I took a direct flight from Frankfurt to Shanghai, so the 'system state' of my expectations was set in Western Europe.

Despite carrying a brown man's classic cynical demeanour, I could not distinguish my surroundings from those I had left behind a mere 12 hours earlier.

This was not true when I was travelling to my home country, as the differences were starker. Comparing how far China had come vis-à-vis India, I could not help but wonder where we went wrong.

Jealousy aside, I could not find a trace of communism oppressing the hoi polloi—the mental image seemed far-fetched. Common people seemed enterprising and, importantly, optimistic.

At the time, China was a $5.5 trillion economy, and it was not just the infrastructure that flabbergasted me and the accompanying Europeans, but the way Chinese people conducted themselves.

There was a sense of pride in whatever people were doing.

Unconvinced, I toured three Chinese cities and a few Chinese hinterlands, but the theme remained unchanged.

Everything pointed to the fact that the Chinese felt a sense of accomplishment and were convinced that they had arrived on the global stage!

During one of my excursions in Beijing, a local shopkeeper (apparently speaking flawless English) had a reflective explanation for the all-encompassing exuberance.

He believed that the Chinese have oriented themselves to a growth mindset as a collective society since the 1980s. When reforms happened, he said, they were not just about the evolution of industrial policies and infrastructure creation but also about the reprogramming of mindsets.

What the man was trying to say related to rational choices that would make Adam Smith proud. Since that trip, I have been convinced that nations make conscious choices to develop and succeed, and it is a collective effort. While it is the government's job to strategize the course of a country's evolution, civil society must desire socio-economic change even more so.

The nuances of the proactive role that the society embraces before a country takes off, breaching the middle-income threshold, was analysed by renowned economist Simon Kuznets in his legendry Kuznets Curve hypothesis.

As the Indian economy approaches the $5 trillion threshold, I see similar exuberance all around me.

The scale at which India is building its infrastructure is simply astounding, and businesses remain resilient despite macroeconomic and Black Swan events such as demonetization and COVID-19. Consumption, though taking the back seat recently, remains the backbone of India's growth story, and more is yet to come.

Moreover, India's geopolitical influence, especially after the successful organization of the G20 Summit in September 2023 in New Delhi, has significantly matured the country's global footprint.

Even though India continues to follow its tried-and-true philosophy, enshrined in the Non-Alignment Movement (NAM), we have indeed come a long way with version 2.0.

Gone are the days when India was a docile, reluctant military power, and a heightened sense of spirited self-assurance now appears to have a hallow effect on India's military adventurism.

Importantly, there is public buy-in to India's current military posturing.

Going by the showcasing of military equipment, replacing traditional memorabilia at public spaces, and the chauvinist chants at the conclusion of popular Indian military-themed movies, Indians now increasingly see themselves as victors and not victims.

This is a mindset change.

This also brings me to my own worldview in which I discuss my reasons for envisioning this book. I believe it is important for you as a reader to understand that as a journalist, I have designed this book to bring diverse perspectives with which I may or may not agree.

This is because, in my vision for India of 2050, free and fearless debate is the key. This does not mean that you agree with every opinion expressed in the following pages either. But as per my understanding, all these opinions must be carefully considered as they hold valuable lessons pivotal to India's future.

However, I would like to state that for me, as the editor of this book, economic planning and military strategy are two sides of the same coin. Therefore, when I talk about planning for India's economic prosperity, I want to talk about the need for aggressive military strategies in the same breath.

The reason why I intertwine my thoughts on economics with those of aggressive militarism is because history teaches us that no nation on earth has ever prospered economically without asserting its dominance militarily.

This makes business sense, too, given the importance of securing supply chains and exclusive economic zones in today's uncertain geopolitical environment.

With a very large economy, a need for innovation derived from defence-related research, and significant maritime borders, India cannot escape the moral dilemma pertaining to the dreaded choice between two alternatives:

- Peaceful co-existence with others and being 'imposed upon' by our enemies or
- Exert our 'unbridled dominance' and secure our interests at any cost.

A sweet spot exists, and India must decide its future course of action right now.

But before that, we must ask the following questions:

- Do we want to be one of the dominant forces of the world? or
- Are we prepared to continue existing as a docile, non-threatening nation?

The latter is safe, but the feasibility of the idea becomes inconsequential given the existence of two nuclear-armed neighbours (Pakistan and China) who threaten our sovereignty and work together to undo our economic strategies. Turkish Trojan horses in our backyard are yet another emerging problem that we must nip in the bud. A passive approach will not suffice amidst imminent threats.

What sense does economic focus make if our nationhood is at risk?

Furthermore, my worldview is influenced by the words of former commander-in-chief of the Indian Army, Field Marshall K.M. Cariappa, who once famously said, 'If the army is a nation's first line of defence, the industry is the second.'

As a nation-state or a bunch of nation-states within the larger Bhartiya framework (if you look at it with a Westphalian lens), India's historical humiliations at the hands of petty invaders was a direct outcome of its lack of focus on protecting its borders, despite its economic, scientific, and cultural achievements.

The collective suffering of our ancestors must rouse us with anger to realize our 'never again' moment. We must consequently guard against narrative builders who weaken our resolve to protect our sovereignty and our honour as Indians.

We must not forget that only a combination of military and economic might guarantee peace, and I cannot envision an India of 2050 that is compassionate towards other nations without securing its own interests first.

Therefore, I have no qualms in saying that my vision does not allow me to see India's sustained economic growth and prosperity without a clear focus on strong military-industrial complexes. Another mindset change that must encompass our civil society's collective aspirations as we plan for 2050.

I see this happening, too, especially after the consecration of the National War Memorial rightfully near the India Gate in New Delhi.

The monument signals not only our collective national reverence for our fallen heroes but also our collective national resolve to maintain our stand in defiance of our enemies.

In my opinion, this sets a great precedence for the future generations of Indians, who will be reminded of their rich military heritage and the collective sacrifices of their forefathers and foremothers.

India's economic aspirations must, therefore, be aligned with active militarism as a function of its further evolution as a nation-state until 2050. This pride will then naturally percolate into everything that we do as a nation today and tomorrow.

Getting back to the main business of this piece, the concept of this book manifested itself while reading about the Hainan Island incident of 2001, when an American and a Chinese military aircraft collided, leading to significant political escalations.

I believe the event was the first true progenitor of sorts when it comes to America's current view of China as an emergent power in the world. Even though, at the time, China would have been still emerging, it was defiant and self-assertingg.

Over the years, China has single-handedly reduced global inflation and driven American consumerism thanks to the economies of scale it has leveraged.

China's single-minded objectivity in building a world-beating manufacturing ecosystem oriented towards exports has allowed it to transform itself into a $19 trillion economy. It is also home to a burgeoning military-industrial complex that has tilted the balance of power in its favour in the East. Talking again about rational choices of a collective society.

Considering the timing of China's assertion of its economic and military might, I believe that India's moment has now arrived.

While it is different that China is using its newfound dominance against India's sovereignty, I believe that Indians must also accept their ascent and start hypothesizing the type of India they wish to see evolve over the next two decades.

At the same time, as a natural democratic ally of the US, India must also learn lessons from the former in building a resilient defence against Chinese aggression and a sustainable economic value chain, guaranteeing economic growth.

To be sure, in the larger scheme of things, twenty years is not a lot of time. While we know that India is moving in a certain direction, we do not yet know what kind of nation-state this country will evolve into.

Looking at the trends, India is expected to become a $25 trillion+ economy by 2050. With this size, India will be the world's second/third largest economic power and will enjoy unprecedented influence over the global rhetoric.

With its newfound influence, along with the US and China, India will be the third pillar of a tri-polar world of 2050.

So, India will be not only an economic and military superpower but also a dominant cultural power and a trendsetter.

India's rise to superpower status is already underway, and in less than a decade, the country will begin to assert its dominance in different realms of human life and culture worldwide.

Since the events will begin to unfold over the next decade, no attempts have been made to create a narrative about what kind of India Indians want to see.

The intention of this book is to introduce an intellectual corpus on India's organic evolution and present visions from leading Indians focusing on their chosen areas.

Hence, the book is a collection of these visions in the form of theme-based essays written by invited experts of different domains.

Certain aspects were originally on my agenda for this book, but time, contributor availability, and space constraints were not supportive. Chief among these is the 'rights to responsibility equation', which has become increasingly important today. Several factions in India still want rights without responsibility for nation-building.

Here, a change in mindset is an absolute necessity if we intend to move forward without friction. I give examples of South Korea's *Saemaul Undong* model in this context, but more of that can be found in my other works. Nevertheless, this remains an important topic for this book's next edition.

A majority of the contributors have, however, discussed demographics as a key aspect in India's future planning, and this is in line with my thinking as an India analyst. I have always believed that India's demographic dividend must be harnessed with a strategy in place. If we fail, we will lose a one-in-a-million opportunity to reach our potential.

I will, though, go one step further and say that all of us Indians must come together as a collective to transform our nation, even before we start planning for dividends and demographic directions.

Moving on, when you read this book, do not read it with preconceived notions—the fact of the matter is that this book cannot be put in a certain box or category.

I have organized this book as a kaleidoscope of diverse thought, much like the fundamental character of Indian democracy. As you turn the pages, you will see the free-flowing debate, representing diverse political leanings, religions, and social points of view.

Deliberately, the book includes views which might appear controversial, and even provocative, but I believe that there is no point in undertaking a project of this magnitude if multiple views are not represented.

We are fundamentally a secular democracy and must, therefore, accept opinions with which we might not necessarily agree. That is who we are as a nation, and our future depends on the preservation of this line of thinking.

According to American political scientist Jonathan Casper's words, 'the freedom to express varying and often opposing ideas is essential to variety of conceptions of democracy. If democracy is viewed as essentially a process...free expression is crucial to the openness of the process...', do the ultimate justice in this context.

Book Framework

In the following pages, I present twenty-five points of view on diverse and often opposing subjects. Consequently, the book is divided into seven sections, each dedicated to a certain macro-theme, and I have designed the content placement for an optimal reading experience.

Part I: Why India Matters

This section is important not only by virtue of precedence but also for setting the tone of this book. India matters and will matter even more in the coming years, and the lead authors of the section do justice to the theme. I will call India's rise a prophecy, a fallacy for an ancient continuous civilization. I believe that the time for India as a modern idea has come to fruition, nonetheless.

The theme continues with the overlapping concepts of economics, geopolitics, and finance and provides a glimpse of what is yet to come. Treat it like a preview of India on the move.

Yeshi Seli opens this section with her insightful piece on India's growing importance in world politics. India today is officially part of the big boys club, speaking figuratively, and Yeshi uses her experience as one of India's finest foreign affairs journalists to present a grand view of its rising clout.

Pankaj Murarka, one of the nation's most well-respected fund managers, writes on why India is irreplaceable in the grand scheme of things. He points out that India has been one of the world's wealthiest economies for much of its known history, and its size guarantees its accent, again. While discussing India's potential, Pankaj utilizes his profound expertise as a market mover and lists down his recommendations and reality checks. Pankaj is of the view that 'while the value addition in India is low at this point in time, gradual value increases over a period of time will help shift global supply chains to India. It must not be forgotten that China's manufacturing base was built over a forty-year period. If we get this right, India is likely to witness a manufacturing renaissance over the next two decades. Any global company not setting up its global manufacturing base in India will risk its global cost competitiveness in the future as India will emerge as the most cost-competitive manufacturing base, just like China, which witnessed this phase in the 1990s. Having said that, India needs to double down on this policy tool. Maybe go 4x on it because this is India's last opportunity to build a global manufacturing base, create jobs for its youth, and accelerate export-driven growth. With utmost urgency, we must be aware that there will not be any further ships anchoring this harbour, if we miss this one.

Part II: Imagining the Grand Strategy

When envisioning this book, my primary concern was to define the strategies that will make India a superpower. This is critical because this section forms the intermediate layer of this book and also its backbone. The grand strategy section builds on India's natural strengths as an economy, society, and demography. The belief here is that a successful country must identify what makes it tick and strategize its future prospects accordingly.

Lt Gen. Arun Sahni, former Indian army commander and a decorated military leader, argues that the armed forces and the other elements of national power will be shaped to facilitate national vision and safeguard India's security interests. This would necessitate a synergized military force that can be offensively employed either to protect territorial interests or for overseas engagements. In conclusion, Gen. Sahni states that 'the impetus of the farsighted measures initiated today has paved the way for the armed forces to be an effective instrument of national power, facilitating India's future vision. This, of course, comes with the rider that the current trend lines of an "all of nation" developmental approach will continue, for the vision to translate into reality.'

Seasoned macro trend watcher and one of India's veteran investors Ritesh Jain wonders whether India has what it takes to be a $30 trillion economy by 2050. In his insightful piece, Ritesh discusses the blueprint for India's transformation, and argues that it is economic dominance that India seeks ambitiously right now. He hypothesizes, 'Think about an economy which is more than ten times the size of the economy today is just twenty-five years from now—a $30 trillion economy by 2050!' Ritesh concludes, 'the likely contribution of India's growing population to its GDP growth would depend, on several factors including the size and growth rate of the total population and the addition that it makes towards the size of working age population, who are likely to become incorporated into the system through productive employment....The consumption is growing and it is growing across sectors and across income groups and will ultimately push manufacturing growth massively.'

Maneesh Dangi, one of India's most eminent fixed income fund managers and thought leaders, discusses India's inevitable convergence with the US and China. Maneesh is a mathematically inclined analyst and he astutely utilizes his prowess to dig deep and challenge conventions. Maneesh argues that 'by 2047, the Indian economy is expected to quadruple, though growth rates will moderate compared to the last two and a half decades. Some sectors may reach saturation, experiencing a slowdown, even as a trend of premiumization and upgrading continues. The burgeoning middle class will markedly elevate the standard of living, and the demographic shift will disproportionately favour premium sectors over mass-market ones. These dynamics signal a consumption upgrade similar to what China witnessed in the last twenty-five years, marked by shifts from two-wheelers to cars, smaller to larger homes, and a surge in luxury and electronic goods purchases.'

Chicago economist, development policy expert, and thought leader Krishna B. Kumar argues that human capital can continue to be India's superpower as the nation plans for 2050. Describing his thought process, Krishna states that the recurring theme in his essay has been the 'focus on the basics of development even if they are not glamorous or headline-grabbing. Whether or not India can achieve this inclusive growth will determine whether India will become a superpower that is economically, socially, and politically stable or a plutocracy that lacks the participatory power of large numbers of its people and the legitimacy that comes with it.' On point, Krishna concludes, 'superpower status is not claimed; it is bestowed by the world. A human-capital-centric path of growth and development will bestow this on India. Anything less would not do full justice to India's founding principles and its humanistic ideals.'

One of the nation's foremost political analysts, veteran business journalists, and master storyteller Sutanu Guru discusses his viewpoint on the importance of aspiration in India's growth story as it chases a $10 trillion dream. While aptly describing

India's evolution story, Guru states, 'One of the most beneficial fallouts of the rise of India will not just be a permanent escape from the "poverty-stricken third world country" trap; it will also be a permanent escape from the cage called "South Asia" where Western academics, institutions, and foreign policy establishments have confined India for decades.' Furthermore, says Guru, 'Till about a decade ago, Pakistan would automatically be added whenever there was a conversation or debate about India. Till the 1990s, the US foreign policy establishment routinely bracketed India with Pakistan in terms of geopolitics.... Part of that legacy lingers on in Washington as it pampers the Pakistan military when it suits its strategic interests. But, a convergence of national interests means India and the US are now strategic partners.'

Part III: Imagining the Priorities for India of 2050

History teaches us that nations must learn from their mistakes or else perish, remaining in a state of chaos and irrelevance.

Past inadequacies must be rectified, and mistakes must not be repeated. This is becoming even more important when it comes to a society's social cohesion and collectiveness. Caste, gender, religion, and traditions, therefore, play an important role, especially in a complex society like India's.

The section sets certain non-negotiable priorities for an India of 2050. As we plan for the next two decades, ignoring these priorities will be perilous for the survival of our nation-state.

Well-known academics and thought leaders Prerna Tambay and Pratap Tambe add an element of humanism to India's development story and argue that traditionally, 'oppressed-caste-thought-leaders focus more on problem thinking and hardly on solution thinking'. The authors have written their essays with great passion, thought, and sensitivity towards India's oppressed classes and women, a social situation that is peculiar to the country. Giving due importance to education, the duo argues that 'kick-starting the virtuous loop requires changing the priorities and increasing the governmental spending on the educational sector (primary, secondary, and tertiary). The business case for this investment to generate a more equitable distribution of education and economic growth among various caste groups is very strong. Essentially, this investment enables more and more oppressed caste students to pass through primary, secondary, and tertiary education and end up in the jobs best suited to their capabilities. This enables them to make their maximum contribution to India's economic growth and benefit from the same, reducing the differences in attainments between caste groups.'

International development and public policy practitioner Hemang Jani argues that India has a glorious history and tradition of respecting scientists and innovators. He says that the nation has always given very high significance to science and technology in its endeavour to improve the quality of life of its citizens. Jani rightly points out that scientists from ancient times, such as Aryabhata, Sushrut, Charak, or Patanjali, are still revered, and in contemporary times, scientists are held in very high respect. 'India's youthful demography aspires to be scientists and innovators and these aspirations are bound to prove India's greatest strength in the future.' Furthermore, Jani believes that these trends will accentuate further as India crosses the $5 trillion GDP threshold by 2027, becoming the third-largest economy in the world. 'There is a growing appreciation in India's leadership that the additional growth beyond $5 trillion will require significant innovation that can boost the productivity of land, labour, and capital,' he contends.

One of the nation's leading lawyers and opinion makers Nupur Sharma writes on the future of Indian women and policies supporting their cause. She writes, 'With the stage set, the affirmative action holding fort as the backdrop, the innumerable schemes and policies paving the stairway and the stricter penal provisions providing the necessary grip for a smooth climb to the top, I foresee 2050 welcoming the era of a woman's world, where we will no longer be asking, "Who runs the world?" The future of India is bright.'

Dynamic journalists Shweta Kothari and Kartik Malhotra discuss the role of media in India in 2050. Aptly titled, 'Government's Friend or Foe? How Media's Role Will Evolve,' their essay is a deep dive discussing the role of journalism in future India. While narrating their views under, Who Will Decide News? the authors write that 'by 2047—facts will be free, and comments will be the editorial distinction. That distinction will come at a premium that consumers of news will need to pay for. Why? Because that will be the only differentiator between what one publication publishes versus another.' Further, they state that 'true journalism will command a premium market price. But takers will be few. Richer countries with better education standards will lead to the demand for quality journalism. Countries like India, even as among the largest economies in the world, will still be grappling with low per-capita GDP, and hence the growth would not be equitable. In the threads of media control, from the Emergency to the speculated future of journalism, India stands at a crossroads. The lessons of the past echo warnings, urging a delicate balance between progress and press freedom. As we navigate the shifting sands of power, the role of a free and robust press becomes indispensable for realizing India's vision of a developed nation. In this intricate dance between the past, present, and future, the torchbearers of journalism must remain vigilant.'

Young academics Yashowardhan Tiwari and Shivani Badgaiyan write a brilliant narrative on religion and traditions in their essay titled 'Tradition as a Remedy to Religious Polarization'. Often ignored, the tyranny of sectarianism in India is the result of a lack of focus on pan-national traditions. In this context, the authors rightly argue that while religion remains a personal matter, culture is not. Citing the works of Prof. S.N. Balagangadhara over a period of four decades at the University of Ghent, Belgium, the authors are of the view that 'while scholars have traditionally provided varied interpretations of communal conflicts in India, most of them have emphasized their religious nature, rather than examining the cultural aspects. Ignoring the struggle of cultural paradigms has led to a partial understanding of the roots of such conflicts and a failure to provide amicable resolutions.'

Part IV: Imagining the Enablers of a Superpower in the Making

Obviously, without a steel framework, a nation-state cannot evolve. Infrastructure, housing, finance, banking, and environmental alignments are pivotal in this context. This section brings together leading Indians from core economic sectors that will define the next course of India's growth story. This section can be treated as a guardrail to India's growth and prosperity.

One of the nation's most prominent real estate developers and respected thought leaders Niranjan Hiranandani argues that in India's rise as a global economic superpower, the real estate, construction, and infrastructure sectors stand out as a key driving force. He is of the view that 'India has undergone multiple revolutions since independence, all aimed at promoting economic growth and enhancing its citizens' standard of living. From the green revolution to the textile revolution, the time is now ripe for a housing revolution.' After all, India has a housing deficit, so it is imperative to transform the housing landscape throughout the country. He estimates that the industry is expected to reach a market size of $1 trillion by 2030 and contribute 13 per cent to India's GDP by 2025.

Rajeev Pawar is one of India's leading fixed-income investors and economic thinkers. He writes his essay on the evolution of the banking space. Rajeev believes that 'one thing that is unlikely to change even in 2050 is the deposit model of banks. While on the asset side, there are multiple product and delivery options, the deposit model for liabilities is efficient and strong. While the whole concept of taking deposits from individuals, slowly building up current and savings accounts and convincing senior citizens to keep their life savings in a bank account sounds outdated, it actually works.' As he discusses the role of banks in the India of 2050, Rajeev states that 'for any bank to succeed, today or in the future, what it needs is an assurance that its deposit base will be there. India's high savings rate has enabled it to be well-positioned in this aspect. Twenty-five years from today, this will work even more in our favour. Our current demographic is under thirty, and they are more inclined to borrow and spend. But twenty-five years from now, they will be older and probably wealthier. At that point, they will again turn to banks for security. The tricky part is trying to connect these two seemingly different banks. The safe, secure, deposit-taking bank and the new age online loan dispensing bank.'

India's ratings industry veteran and sustainability champion Sankar Chakraborti argues that 'India's journey towards becoming a global power is uniquely defined by its rich cultural heritage, emphasizing sustainability and harmony with nature. In a world increasingly driven by environmental, social, and governance principles, India's ancient traditions offer vital lessons for sustainable development.' He is of the view that the journey to net zero is not just a policy goal but a reflection of

India's ancient ethos of living in harmony with nature, now being reimagined in the context of modern challenges.

Indian Railways veteran and one of its foremost engineers L.C. Trivedi reimagines the sector for 2050 and beyond. Trivedi is a railway pioneer and was one of the engineering leaders of the Vande Bharat Express project. He argues, 'Indian Railways, often dubbed as the lifeline of the nation, has played a pivotal role in shaping India's socio-economic landscape since its inception, and as we look ahead to the year 2050, envisioning the future of Indian Railways requires a comprehensive strategy that integrates technological advancements, sustainability measures, and enhanced passenger experience.' Trivedi's essay outlines a visionary road map for Indian Railways in 2050, focusing on innovation, efficiency, and inclusivity. The author is convinced that by 2050 'Indian Railways will have undergone a profound technological transformation, leveraging cutting-edge innovations to enhance its operational efficiency and safety standards'.

University of Florida–trained Indian economist and trade expert Sankalp Mathur envisions a strategy for India in a fragmented world trade order. He details the significance of the global trade project, why and if it is straying from an open trade world, and most importantly, 'what lies for India in a potentially new international trade structure'. Sankalp is of the view that redirecting economic policy towards the initial and final stages of the production process, where value is maximized, may offer a more promising avenue for growth, especially as services trade continues to expand amidst geopolitical uncertainties. Ultimately, Sankalp contends, 'India must pursue a leadership role in the ideals of global cooperation, dealing with global challenges.'

Amim Ahmed is one of India's leading marketing thinkers and I believe that his understanding of India's brand story is second to none. In his essay, Amim narrates that right from the Indus Valley Civilization to the modern world, India was universally referred to as '*sone ki chidiya*', a high-end brand for the world to understand, study, and gain. That was the power of brand India. Amim uses anecdotes describing the creation and success of local brands that built modern India and writes a compelling narrative. He is also mindful of the policy shortfalls and worries that in India's evolving brand story, we have become acquirers and not creators of brands despite a demonstrated capability. 'The point is that we are still running short of visionary leadership to create global consumer brands, despite the capacity to sustain them,' concludes Amim.

Part V: Safeguarding the Republic (Two Arguments)

For me, the security of our nation-state is paramount. Obviously, there are opinions and then some when a topic of this magnitude is discussed, but in my own opinion, there are no rights or wrongs here.

Each Indian, who is worth his/her salt, must proactively come forward and share his/her vision without hesitation. After all, this is about the future of our country, the continuation of our way of life, and our stand.

Domestic politics and geopolitics go together, and, therefore, I will argue that a discussion of this level must be free of any political correctness.

That is precisely why I am bringing together two 'counter-arguments' from two Indians to add diversity to this section.

The authors of these two arguments may inhabit two extremes of the political viewpoint spectrum, but their narrations are worthy additions to this volume. These writers are argumentative, straight to the point, and experts in their fields. Importantly, they write with a no-holds-barred attitude and with full conviction.

As opinions, these writings are their respective authors' personal views, but they indeed introduce debate and provoke thought. I believe that for readers, these opinions add a new paradigm—a fresh point of view on an important topic.

Therefore, there is an element of dynamism in this section. Read it with an open mind. After all, free debate must be encouraged.

Argument I: At his provocative best, India's prominent financial journalist Ben Kochuveedan dares to list twenty-three dreams for the Republic. He argues that we have twenty-three years to the 2047 destiny and believes that these twenty-three dreams can restore 'the constitutional, parliamentary, and democratic morality and sanctity, helping us regain institutional credibility and morality, reform our political discourse, reinvent the ethos and repose the trust of our teeming but hapless and hopeless youth who account for 66 per cent of the population.'

Ben may appear to be politically incorrect, but every word he writes comes from his profound understanding of India, which he has covered for decades as not only a journalist but also a man who has his ears to the ground.

Argument II: Debdeep Sengupta is not a military general, but if he were, I think he would have been a revolutionary. Without commenting too much here, I will leave you with just a segment from this piece. You have to read this hard-hitting, no-nonsense commentary to understand the nuances of statecraft. In the context of India's future planning, this is all you need to know from a strategic vantage point. In this essay, Debdeep introduces us to the concept of 'scope' in defence planning—a point that is often ignored in the traditional sense.

According to Debdeep, 'We are possibly the only major democracy and major economy in the world who are engaged in everyday warfare with our neighbours and their proxies, a warfare we cannot avoid as it has been thrust on us. Just like any sovereign nation, our military is an extension of our statecraft, in one small corner of the vast spectrum of engagement we share with other nations. Yet, India existed much, much before 1947, and the nature of aggression it faced has continuously changed with time. For a mathematically inclined nation, it is thus time to adopt a data-driven approach to what actually threatens us, and will threaten us, and to understand how we can respond to such developments by learning our history lessons.'

Part VI: Imagining the Future of the Republic through Indian Aspirations and Dreams

I believe that millennials bring a profound understanding of India today. People born in the 1980s and 1990s have witnessed the evolution of India like no other generation and have lived in an India of struggles and opportunities.

This section's purpose is to bring valuable perspectives of these young Indians who envision India of 2050 through their own aspirations and dreams.

Pallavi Nahata is one of India's well-known business journalists, covering the Indian economy with great enthusiasm. She received her training in finance at the King's College London and has established herself as an insightful journalist. Utilizing her journalistic skills, she writes her essay not just as her own opinion but also by taking into account the voices of other young Indians, who may never be heard. Pallavi argues, 'Beyond employment, crystal gazing into 2050, I envision not having to choose between passion and pay, affordable housing and healthcare, clean air and ease of commute.' She further states, 'The wish list can go on. But, at its core, a wish list is not too different from those before us. *Roti, kapda, kaam*, *aur makaan* continues to remain at the forefront of what young India wants.'

Roopak Gupta, a technologist and a Columbia MBA graduate, recounts his personal journey from Agra to New York. As an Indian kid growing up in the 1990s, Roopak narrates a tale of resilience, compassion, possibilities, and grit. Roopak is a man on a mission, and his journey is the story of India's digitization itself and what the future holds. He dreams, 'By 2050, India would stand on the precipice of a future where innovation is not an echo but a clarion call, and inclusive policies are not an afterthought but the blueprint of a society where technology serves all. Much like my youth's wooden box, the digital revolution must move to the commands of equity, ethics, and empowerment to truly bridge the divide.'

Sharmin Nisar Chougule is a Europe-based Indian lawyer and scholar. Hailing from the small town of Ratnagiri, Sharmin is today a PhD scholar in law and constitutional legality and researches distributed ledger technology (DLT) in smart contracts. In her essay, she writes, 'Looking ahead to the horizon of 2050, one envisions an India propelled by innovation, inclusivity, and sustainable growth. A nation where technological prowess converges with social equity, where educational excellence transcends barriers, and where governance reflects the aspirations of a burgeoning populace. It is a vision of India as a global leader, not just in economic terms but also in fostering a harmonious society grounded in democratic principles and cultural pluralism.'

Part VII: Sector Spotlights: Sectors Pivotal for a Self-Confident India of 2050

This section is dedicated to certain sectors, which are often ignored but remain pivotal to economic prosperity. Planning for

2050, after much deliberation, I have identified healthcare and reinsurance for this spotlight.

Vinay Singhal is a pioneer in India's healthcare space and has built and managed businesses over a career spanning several decades. Singhal has seen the Indian healthcare sector evolve into a major force to be reckoned with. In his essay, he argues that India should move to a larger 'wellness focus' from the current illness-centric approach. 'Advances in nutrition and enhanced societal focus on remaining fit will enable an enhanced focus on eating right, exercising right, meditating, and living a longer life. Science has made a lifespan of 100 possible for the largest population.' He also believes that there is a need to move towards the use of better medicines, better equipment, and digital support that will allow India to lead the world in this field as it has done by adopting digital systems in financial dealings, communications, and research. Importantly, Singhal is of the view that India should utilize large private hospitals for training new MBBS doctors by allowing them to attend medical colleges, for training more doctors.

Reinsurance practitioners Pratap Tambe and Rahul Ugile write on the role of reinsurance in India in 2050. Pratap actually convinced me about the sector's importance in India's future planning, and why it will play a critical role. Honestly, I was ignorant, and thanks to him, now aware of the sector's potential. Both these gentlemen are experts in their field and believe that India cannot ignore the criticality of reinsurance. The authors suggest that 'reinsurance enables the reduction of risk-bearing costs by selecting and pooling risks from multiple insurers to generate diversification benefits as well as leveraging its understanding of risks to work with insurers and businesses to keep risk within control limits. Insurers and reinsurers get to know a lot of things about the products and services as well as business practices of the businesses they insure. So, developing "skilled" reinsurance capital needed for its own economy is one of the most important strategic steps any superpower and aspiring superpower can take. Becoming less vulnerable to the flight of reinsurance capital from India is a strategic imperative for India. And as India grows its influence around the world, the capability to provide reinsurance to its allies will be strategic.'

As I conclude, my only request to fellow Indians is this:

Start believing in your country, and importantly, take ownership of your country. After all, India is our collective responsibility.

Part I
Why India Matters

1

Why India Matters to the World

Yeshi Seli

India has emerged as a country the world can no longer ignore. Geopolitics, Indo-Pacific, and the emergence of India as the fifth largest economy in the world have literally made it centre stage.

Countries like the US, Russia, France, the UK, and Germany, amongst others, are all its strategic partners. The credit, even if not entirely, largely goes to the popularity of Prime Minister Narendra Modi, who is considered as one of the most sought-after and influential leaders of the world. He has just been sworn in as the prime minister for a third consecutive term. He received phone calls and congratulatory messages from nearly all world leaders, including President Biden, Prime Minister Rishi Sunak, and President Vladimir Putin, amongst a host of others.

'Congratulations to PM Modi and the National Democratic Alliance on their victory and the nearly 650 million voters in this historic election. The friendship between our nations is only growing as we unlock a shared future of unlimited potential,' said President Biden.

In addition, foreign policy has received a much-needed push from India's eloquent external affairs minister Dr S. Jaishankar.

'Why is our presence in India important? Because it is a power at the heart of the reinvention of the world. We will meet the challenges of our century together,' said French president Emmanuel Macron. He was the chief guest of the seventy-fifth Republic Day, and his visit was marked by signing many agreements, which included manufacturing helicopters in India through a partnership between Tata and Airbus Helicopters.

'These helicopters and other spares can be used for further exports to friendly countries,' President Macron said.

France is also hoping to see 30,000 Indian students enrol in its universities and is offering incentives, including a long-duration Schengen visa for postgraduate students.

Well, it is not just France but all major countries across the globe that want to further deepen their ties with India.

US president Joe Biden called the US's partnership with India amongst the most consequential in the world. 'That is stronger, closer and more dynamic than any time in history.'

So, what makes India so special for most developed nations?

Let us examine recent developments and see where India stands globally. Leaders from across the world reach out to India when they make big decisions to seek humanitarian aid and development work and, most importantly, to have a strong ally in the Indo-Pacific that can counter China.

In this chapter, we will review most of India's feats, challenges, and increasing eminence in the world.

India's G20 Presidency

India successfully completed the G20 Presidency, and its conclusion during the summit saw world leaders including US president Joe Biden, French president Emmanuel Macron, British prime minister Rishi Sunak, Japanese prime minister Fumio Kishida, Australian prime minister Anthony Albanese, and German chancellor Olaf Scholz, amongst a host of others. Prime Minister Modi was meeting some of the leaders for the third or fourth time during the course of the year.

India hosted a virtual Voice of the Global South Summit before the commencement of meetings under the G20 Presidency, with the objective of making the platform more inclusive.

After successfully hosting the G20 Presidency with over 200 meetings held across all states and union territories of the country, India showcased foreign policy in a thematic and organized way.

People across India, from Srinagar in the north to Darjeeling in the east, which had seen no international events, became privy to something as large-scale as the G20. It generated employment, gave the local populace a sneak peek into what India did internationally, and eventually left a mark.

The G20 Tourism Working Group meeting in Srinagar was a landmark meeting. It was the first international meeting of this scale, attended by sixty delegates from twenty-seven countries. Even though there was thick security cover, even the locals were amazed at how quickly the strife-torn region was bouncing back to normalcy.

The Delhi Declaration, signed at the conclusion of the G20 Summit, was a landmark moment that most of the members had not anticipated. During all the previous meetings throughout the year and also during the G20 Summit in Bali, no joint declaration was made primarily because of the differences among the members, prompted by the conflict between Russia and Ukraine (which will mark its two-year anniversary on 24 February 2024).

In addition to the Delhi Declaration, India also got approval from the other members to include the African Union in the G20. This, too, was done with the objective of making G20 a more inclusive organization, unlike the UN, which is in dire need of reforms.

There were a few hiccups that had a snowballing effect during the conclusion of the G20 Summit, particularly the interaction between Prime Minister Narendra Modi and Canadian Prime Minister Justin Trudeau on the sidelines of the Summit, which led to a diplomatic row between India and Canada.

Non-Alignment Movement 2.0

India also participated in the Non-Aligned Movement (NAM) in Kampala this January 2024. However, after including the African Union in the G20 and also hosting a Voice of Global South Summit virtually before the main meetings of the G20 began in India, there will be a lot of overlap in this grouping.

'A multipolar world with a reformed United Nations at its core is key. Economic decentralization with greater regional production is so as well. But we must also press for cultural rebalancing where all heritage is mutually respected. By spearheading the African Union's membership, India showed during its G20 Presidency that change is possible. This should inspire reformed multilateralism,' said Dr Jaishankar.

India–Canada Diplomatic Row

It is learnt that Prime Minister Trudeau, during his interaction with Prime Minister Modi, said that the killing of pro-Khalistan separatist Hardeep Singh Nijjar in British Colombia was made with Indian agencies' involvement. Prime Minister Modi dismissed this as baseless.

However, when Prime Minister Trudeau returned to Canada after a delay of two days because of a snag in his aircraft, he spoke in the Canadian Parliament about India's involvement in the killing and also expelled an Indian diplomat from Canada.

India responded by expelling a Canadian diplomat and suspending visa services to Canadians. It also asked the

Canadian missions in India to downsize, which resulted in forty Canadian diplomats having to leave India.

'Canadian diplomats are in excess and are also seen to be interfering in India's domestic issues, hence under the Vienna Convention we are seeking diplomatic parity,' the external affairs ministry had said.

The diplomatic row continued for a few months, after which India gradually resumed visa services to Canada once it received assurance that its diplomats in Canada would be safe. Close on the heels of the diplomatic row between India and Canada, the US Department of Justice indicted an Indian man named Nikhil Gupta, accusing him of conspiring to kill Khalistan separatist leader Gurpatwant Singh Pannun. There were references to Nijjar's killing in the document released by the US justice department, suggesting a common thread.

India formed a high-level investigation committee to investigate the allegations in the case. Currently, Nikhil Gupta is in jail in Prague and the US is attempting to extradite him.

It is worth noting that despite these aberrations, India continues to be highly respected globally. So much so that India has taken independent stances on two major ongoing world conflicts, and the international community seems to have accepted these positions.

Russia–Ukraine Conflict

When the conflict between Russia and Ukraine began on 24 February 2022, Russian President Vladimir Putin called Prime Minister Narendra Modi to explain the circumstances leading to the conflict. This marked the first of many calls that took place between the two leaders, during which Prime Minister Modi always reaffirmed that dialogue and diplomacy were the only solutions to the conflict. Prime Minister Modi's statement 'this is no era for war' was also echoed in the Bali leaders' statements at the conclusion of the G20 Summit in 2020.

While the US, UK, France, and most of Europe supported Ukraine, India continued to refer to Russia as a friend. India also increased its oil imports from Russia from a mere 2 per cent to nearly 30 per cent, as it did not want to get embroiled in tackling inflation back home.

Leaders such as President Joe Biden and Chancellor Scholz conceded that India and Russia had long-term historical ties. Interestingly, India aligned with the West during the Israel-Hamas conflict.

Israel–Hamas Conflict

On 7 October 2023, Hamas attacked Israel and took over 300 people hostage. In response, Israel declared an all-out war, resulting in nearly 30,000 people deaths in Gaza. While India has been sending humanitarian assistance to Gaza, it has condemned the Hamas attack and reiterated that there is no room for terror.

Well, when we talk of strengths, we cannot ignore the challenges. India has had issues with China, especially regarding border disputes, and more recently, with neighbouring countries like the Maldives. In the extended neighbourhood, India contested a high-profile case in which eight naval veterans had been under detention in Doha since August 2022. Let us take a closer look at these countries.

China

India and China have been at a diplomatic low since the Galwan clashes in 2020. Despite having a bilateral trade of around $66 billion, regional issues continue to hinder the normalization of ties. China has expanded its influence in India's neighbouring countries, including Pakistan, Bangladesh, Sri Lanka, Maldives, Nepal, Myanmar, and Bhutan, through its Belt and Road Initiative. However, whenever these nations face a crisis, they often seek assistance from India.

In 2022, Sri Lanka suffered bankruptcy and India stepped in to help by providing a Line of Credit, which allowed Sri Lanka to purchase essential items such as fuel, food, and medicines from India. Similar Lines of Credit have been extended to Bangladesh, Nepal, Bhutan, and the Maldives by India.

Maldives

The historical ties between India and the Maldives have been strong, with India providing assistance during COVID-19 and supporting the development of critical infrastructure. However, all this changed in November 2023 after the new president Dr Mohamad Muizzu asked the Indian military, consisting of eighty-eight personnel, to leave the Maldives.

The deadline for the personnel to depart was set for 15 March 2024. These personnel were primarily in operating one helicopter and two Dornier aircraft used for humanitarian relief and rescue operations. Unfortunately, due to the announcement of the deadline, there was a delay in getting clearance for a teenage child to be airlifted, resulting in the child's death.

As a result of these developments, the Maldivian government is facing considerable turbulence, and there are also pro-Indian leaders who do not want the country's association with India to be weakened in favour of China.

Qatar

In recent times, India faced one of the biggest challenges regarding the case of eight naval veterans in Qatar. These eight naval veterans were employed by an Omani firm, Dhara

Consultancies, for naval exercises in Doha. On 30 August 2022, around midnight, Qatar's Ministry of Interior picked them under the guise of participating in an exercise but, instead, were kept in detention centres.

They were placed in solitary confinement for over eight months, after which they were clubbed in pairs. Charges that had not been made public were framed against them, and the death penalty was announced in October 2023. However, later, this death penalty was commuted to varying jail terms for each individual.

The Indian government made significant efforts to repatriate these veterans. There was optimism that political goodwill would make it happen before April, and finally, these men were granted their freedom.

India's Humanitarian Assistance

Irrespective of the challenges India faces within its own space, it consistently provides help to countries in need. India has extended humanitarian aid to Ukraine, Afghanistan, Turkey, and Sri Lanka, and it continues to do so whenever it sees a nation facing a crisis. The only exception is Pakistan due to strained diplomatic relations between the two countries and Pakistan's habit of raising India's internal issues on public platforms. This has made it difficult for the two countries to improve their relationship.

What Lies Ahead

India will continue to strengthen its position on the diplomatic front. Many countries across the world are having elections this year, including India, which went through the polls in May this year. Despite this, the international community is eager to collaborate with India on all fronts. The Indo-Pacific region is of particular importance, with countries like the US and France seeking to collaborate with India to counter China and fortify their positions in the Pacific.

France has a strong interest in the Indo-Pacific region because it is home to over 2 million French people, with 1.65 million living in French territories. Additionally, there are over 7,000 French troops permanently stationed in the region for sovereignty missions and other purposes.

French territories in the Indo-Pacific include Mayotte, La Reunion, the Scattered Islands, and the French southern and Antarctic territories in the Indian Ocean, as well as New Caledonia, Wallis and Futuna, French Polynesia, and Clipperton Island in the Pacific.

France considers itself an island state in the Indo-Pacific. Therefore, fortifying its position with India at this juncture is pragmatic as it will enhance the accessibility of French territories in the Indo-Pacific.

President Macron and Prime Minister Modi reiterated their commitment to further strengthen the long-standing partnership between the two nations based on their common vision for the Indo-Pacific. They emphasized the significance of the regions for their respective sovereign and strategic interests. This was stated in a joint statement following the bilateral meeting between the two leaders on January 25 in Jaipur.

Defence and security partnerships have been the cornerstone of India's and France's partnership in the Indo-Pacific, which includes a number of bilateral and regional initiatives in the Indian Ocean region.

President Macron and Prime Minister Modi also discussed the early launch of the Indo-Pacific Triangular Development Cooperation Fund to promote the growth of green technologies being developed in the region.

'The two leaders agreed to explore opportunities for coordinating economic projects and programmes in the Pacific and also acknowledged projects being carried out by the French Development Agency in India,' the statement added.

Meanwhile, in a bid to reaffirm France's commitment to India, President Macron has spared no opportunity to support India in its desire to host the Olympics to COP33 in 2028.

France is the current host of the Olympics, and in conversation with President Draupadi Murmu, President Macron said, 'We will be delighted to build a stronger cooperation on sports with India and will support India's intention to organize the Olympic Games in India for the future.'

In a bid to appease India and strengthen its bilateral relations, France is offering sops to prospective Indian students. As a value-add, French universities are offering courses and subjects to Indian students with the hope of attracting more Indian students to study in France.

As a part of this effort, Indian students pursuing a Master's degree in France will be granted a five-year Schengen visa.

In addition, France is also supporting India's candidacy for the International Energy Agency, and the French president was among the world leaders who called to congratulate Prime Minister Modi on his third term.

Meanwhile, it is important to note India's increasing clout in West Asia. India and Saudi Arabia have forged a strong partnership. Recently, a historic moment took place in Madinah when an Indian delegation led by a non-Muslim woman, minister Smriti Irani, was welcomed without any mandatory outfit. This reflects the growing friendship between the two nations that goes beyond just trade and diplomacy.

Similarly, the president of UAE, Mohammad bin Zayed Al Nahyan, visited Ahmedabad to attend the Vibrant Gujarat Summit and addressed the audience. These examples demonstrate how India has become a nation that everyone wants to be associated with diplomatically.

US and Russia

When it comes to India's relations with the world's two major powers, the country will continue to maintain a balance between its relations with the US and Russia in the years ahead.

It has become clear that both nations have accepted India's partnerships with each of them individually. Consequently, India's foreign policy will continue to be driven by its own interests, its surging economy, and its position in the Indo-Pacific.

The future looks promising as India aims to become the third-largest economy globally in the years to come. It is for these reasons and more that India will continue to remain significant on the world stage!

2

India, the Irreplaceable Giant: Serendipities Leading the Way

Pankaj Murarka

According to well-regarded British economist Angus Madisson, at the beginning of the eighteenth century, India controlled almost a quarter of the global gross domestic product (GDP) in terms of purchasing power parity (PPP). This means that at the dawn of the modern era, India was the world's largest economy and its people one of the most prosperous.

Similar to today's export-oriented economies of China, Germany, and Japan, India was a major trading nation that exported textiles, engineering items, ships, precious ornaments, and spices and accumulated massive gold resources in return.

Looted and plundered by the British colonialists, the Indian economy was reduced to a mere 4 per cent of the global GDP by the time it gained independence in 1947. The India that emerged from the quagmire was not only devoid of capital and infrastructure but also a nation with very little experience in capitalism-led industrialization and the conduct of trade on Bretton Woods principles.

Recording a literacy rate below 5 per cent, India also had access to very little talent and management expertise required for the spawning of modern enterprise. By 1950, India had become a perfect example of a ravaged client state that depended on the alms of a master state, in this case, Britain.

India missed the bus due to its status as a captive colony and never really enjoyed the fruits of the Industrial Revolution. Relegated to third-world backwaters, thanks to further isolationist policies brought about by the non-alignment movement, the nation could not compete with Asian tigers such as South Korea, Taiwan, constituents of ASEAN, and then China.

The country, as a result, continued with its infamous 'Hindu rate of growth'[1], experiencing massive wealth inequalities and food insufficiencies in the process.

The Emergence of a New India

Despite having no head start, India's contribution to the global GDP (PPP) is over 8 per cent today. As we start 2024, India is relentlessly expanding its economic capacities at an unprecedented rate.

Thanks to liberalization and the unwavering grit of the Indian people, India has today successfully spawned some of the most sophisticated industries in the world, including software services, automobiles, space tech, and pharmaceuticals.

As India stands at the cusp and begins its superpower journey culminating sometime in the 2040s, the India story has begun to unfold once again. Considering the current trends, India is well on its way to attaining the $10 trillion GDP mark by 2033 and will be only the third country to do so.

The expectation is that by this time, India will be a middle-income country, with a per capita income somewhere around $6,700. Importantly, however, in terms of PPP, an average Indian will have a per capita income in excess of $24,000.

While this may appear low when compared to the Organisation for Economic Co-operation and Development levels, one must consider that these will be the per capita incomes of 1.5 billion people, on average! Given these realities, India will generate massive consumption power, acting as a magnate for the global economic forces.

This will allow the Indian consumer classes to exert significant influence over the global economy, making India an irreplaceable market for any company worth its salt.

So, what would these modalities translate for India? Simply put, the world will be here, irrespective of what naysayers think.

Emulating the Japanese and Chinese Miracles

Similar to India, present-day Japan and China are also products of Western exploitation and humiliation.

Pre-Miji Japan was a resource-poor nation with fairly insignificant trade relations with the outside world. Primarily an agrarian society, imperial Japan remained a closed society run by Daimyo fiefdoms and Shogunates.

After several setbacks due to its lack of influence over global trade and constant bullying by Western powers, Japan was ready to change itself for good. It was only after Emperor Meiji-led restoration that Japan started to emulate Western standards and techniques by actively hiring European and American mercenaries, engineers, and architects.

Such was Japan's zeal to rebuild itself into a modern nation that in less than forty years since the start of the Meiji restoration, Japan became a major global economy and military power.

By the 1930s, Imperial Japan began to impose itself on the world and dealt with Western powers as their equal. After its defeat in the Second World War, Japan aligned itself with the US. By taking advantage of favourable US trade policies under the

Marshal Plan, Japan re-established itself as a major economic force worldwide.

By the 1980s, Japan was already the world's second-largest economy and was well on its way to claiming the top spot. But that was not to be, and the nation faltered due to a combination of factors, including falling birth rates and an out-of-turn devaluation of the US dollar (Plaza Accord).

Nevertheless, by the turn of the century, in less than 100 years of its transformation, Japan established itself as one of the world's foremost economies, boasting the highest standards in technological evolution, high per capita income, and best business practices. Japan today is home to forty-one Global Fortune 500 companies, operating in the most sophisticated and high-tech sectors.

China, on the other hand, started at the same time as India. During the Second World War and later, the Chinese Civil War ravaged its economy, and the current People's Republic of China only came into existence in 1949.

Under communist leader Mao, China was largely an agrarian economy, with pockets of industrialization and high poverty levels. So many similarities existed with neighbouring India that until 1980, both countries were neck-to-neck in levels of development and per capita incomes.

It was only after Deng Xiaoping led the Chinese Communist Party to accept the 'decision on the reform of the economic system' that China opened its economy to foreign investment, technology, and management.

By aligning its banking, businesses, and governance while focusing on special economic zones (SEZs) strategically located around the eastern ports, China rapidly transformed itself into a global manufacturing powerhouse.

Real growth happened from 1990 onwards, when the Chinese economy grew at a turbocharged rate of 9–10 per cent in real terms for almost two decades. China also secured favourable trade terms with Western powers such as the US, Europe, and Japan and attracted significant foreign direct investment, leading to its garnering an over 28 per cent share in global manufacturing output.

China also built world-class infrastructure by investing trillions of dollars through an innovative concoction of debt and hybrid instruments. The nation also focused on the education and training of its masses, an exercise that spawned a well-trained and job-ready labour force. Today, China has emerged as the world's second-largest economy, worth almost $18 trillion in nominal terms and boasting a per capita income of over $13,000.

At the same time, given its status as the factory of the world, China's annual exports amount to a gargantuan $3.3 trillion, helping it enjoy a current account surplus of almost $0.8 trillion annually.

The India Opportunity

The Japanese and Chinese miracles have had their times, and demographics are no longer supporting their ascent anymore. Further economic growth for these countries will come from efficiencies already achieved and innovation.

While these countries will continue to dominate the global economic order for the foreseeable future, with China expected to record positive growth numbers for at least a decade more likely, both countries will not represent the next big opportunity.

The trouble with these nations is that despite boasting a well-developed infrastructure and socially responsible and trained labour force, their status as a magnate for global talent is unthinkable.

Interestingly, unfavourable demography is not the only reason.

Often ignored reasons include their cultural exclusivity and inherent distinctions from Western cultures. Therefore, this lack of inclusivity will be perhaps the most significant Achilli's heel, as the next course of their evolution will depend on the acquisition of foreign specialist talent.

The US's ability to attract global talent through the development of an inclusive society is perhaps its biggest trump card, allowing the nation to continue its economic dominance in the global system unabated.

India is probably the only country in the world that can compete with the US for global talent primarily because of its pluralistic society, widespread use of English as a medium of communication, and status as a functional democracy.

As luck would have it, India has evolved into a nation that is not only dynamically similar to American democracy but has also built a robust institutional system over the years. India's democracy combined with the aforementioned institutional set-up, which in turn is not only independent but also under an elaborate judicial system, provides both businesses and citizens a virtual guarantee of fairness and the rule of law.

Despite its problems with low enrolment rates and a labour force that is majorly underqualified for quality jobs, India is also today a leading feeder of engineers and technocrats through a focus on STEM-based education.

In fact, by supplying 5.5 million engineers to the world's engineering talent pool, India is today known as the software engineering capital of the world. It is expected that by 2033, Indian engineering talent will be 10 million strong and contribute to almost 30 per cent of the world's talent pool in this segment.

Not to mention, because of this software engineering prowess, India has spawned an enviable software industry with an annual export revenue of almost $200 billion. It is rapidly moving towards the $500 billion target, which will be achievable in less than a decade.

This is India's advantage that no country can emulate, at least in the foreseeable future. India's top talent today not only leads fast-growing high-tech companies at home but has also gone on to become CEOs of some of the world's largest software and technology companies.

Further evolution, surplus, and relatively cheap talent have also helped India emerge as a global research and development (R&D) hub. Almost all major Fortune 500 companies have an R&D centre in India, and it is said that such activity cannot happen without Indian talent.

All said, Indian talent can now be considered the implementors of global technology, while technology's evolution has been concentrated within a handful of countries.

These advantages exist for India in addition to its already well-established engineering prowess pertaining to its over $250 billion and $45 billion automobile and pharmaceutical industries, respectively.

Challenges

Challenges do exist for India, given its hostile neighbourhood consisting of two nuclear-powered states, along with its lack of focus on human resource development.

As things stand, despite its service prowess, India seems to have no dedicated plan to develop a robust talent-feeding system that draws from varied demographics and regions.

The dichotomy here is that the country will be the largest supplier of labour to the world, contributing to 22 per cent of the total global labour supply over the next two decades. The fact is that India will have 1 million people joining its workforce every month for the next twenty years, effectively adding 240 million people to its labour force over the next two decades. Consequently, the country has the most favourable population dynamic available anywhere in the world.

With the majority of its population now below the age of thirty-five, India has a runway of at least two decades of uninterrupted supply of relatively cheap and abundant labour. If India can harness this human capital and play its cards well, the Indian economy can be 8–10x its current size over the next twenty-five years before its demography peaks and it regains its past glory after almost 300 years.

If this opportunity is wasted, India will not only miss the Fourth Industrial Revolution but also find itself stuck in the infamous 'middle-income trap'—a disaster of sorts for the young nation.

India just needs to plan its human resources with a strategic intent and orientation. For Indian policymakers, perhaps now is the time to ask what kind of India they wish to see: the next America or the next China.

Additionally, India must remain aware of the prevailing ground realities regarding capital and reserve accumulation for its own good. The US is home to the reserve currency, which has played a crucial role in its economic and military dominance of the world.

Post-Bretton Woods, every other country that achieved economic prosperity after the Second World War had to build dollar reserves through exports to US/Western allies and achieve a strong currency.

The People's Bank of China, which has dollar reserves of over $3 trillion, and the Bank of Japan, which is the largest creditor to the US and the world, while having a dollar reserve of $1.1 trillion, are good examples to consider. These examples must be studied in detail if India wants to build a sustainable and resilient economy that can tide over economic shocks. All these reserves have been dominantly built through current account surpluses and not capital inflows alone.

The ship left the shore long ago as far as India's opportunity to build an export-oriented economy is concerned. The result is that today, Bangladesh's textile exports are higher than that of India, Vietnam beats India in electronic exports, and Thailand does more auto-ancillary exports than India.

All these countries are a tiny fraction of India in terms of size and scale. But they have been focused and have used their strategic advantages for the best of their economic growth and development.

From Figure 2.1, it seems ironic that while India and China have a similar share of the global labour force (~20 per cent), India's share in global exports is a mere 2 per cent compared to China's 14 per cent.

Even smaller countries with a much smaller labour force have a much higher share of global exports than India.

Figure 2.1: India's opportunity to make a mark on world exports

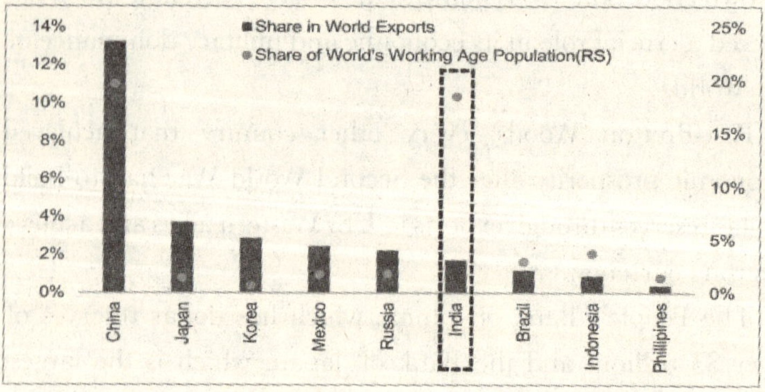

Source: Renaissance Investment Managers

Planning the Next Phase

While India's efforts to build an export-oriented economy have failed, another window of opportunity has emerged in the post-COVID-19 world.

Today, over 90 per cent of the world's complex manufacturing supply chains are linked to China. During COVID-19, multiple disruptions were faced due to severe lockdowns in various countries, leading to massive imbalances in the supply of goods to different parts of the world.

These supply chains are extremely complex in nature and have been built over the last forty years to adjust to 'just in time' manufacturing practices, which ensure very lean inventory in the warehouses and efficient use of capital.

In the post-COVID-19 world order, the global Fortune 2000 companies want to diversify their supply chain and reduce their dependence on China, given the risk of geographical concentration exposed by COVID-19–driven lockdowns.

Additionally, the subtle geopolitical realignment of the world has accelerated in the last few years with the ongoing trade war between the US and China and the Russia-Ukraine war.

Consequently, global corporations must urgently reduce their dependence on China as a manufacturing hub. Nevertheless, given China's dominance in global supply chains, marginalizing China from the global manufacturing supply chain for at least the next quarter century is virtually impossible.

As a result, China+1 has become an essential toolkit for every CEO of Fortune 2000 companies, and the challenge is to develop an additional manufacturing base similar to it.

The strategic advantage that led to China's emergence as the world's manufacturing capital through the cheap and abundant supply of labour has ceased to exist. At $7 per hour, China's labour cost is no longer cheap and Chinese labour is not willing to migrate to urban production hubs anymore due to the high cost of living.

Taking advantage, the Government of India has seized the global opportunity by rolling out manufacturing subsidies in the form of production-linked incentives (PLI) for entities setting up new manufacturing units in India for exports and also giving a concessional direct tax rate of 15 per cent on new manufacturing units.

Due to its large population base, India has an abundant supply of cheap labour, which can be deployed on a large scale with the right policy.

No other country can supply the labour force at a scale and cheap cost than India. Foxconn, Apple's largest vendor, employs over 1 million people in China alone. Therefore, if Foxconn and Apple want to build a second manufacturing base outside of China, there is no better option than India.

Perhaps the greatest example is that of Apple, the single largest-selling consumer product line in the world. With a Bill of Materials of $100 billion annually, Apple had zero manufacturing in India in 2020 when COVID-19 struck.

In 2024, about 14 per cent of Apple's global manufacturing will be done in India, and it has a strategic plan to make it 25 per cent of its global production by 2026. Every other global corporation will follow suit.

Therefore, the PLI scheme has become a strategic policy tool for India to attract new manufacturing, drive export growth, and create manufacturing jobs. Through the scheme, the country has already committed $30 billion in incentives to domestic and foreign companies setting up new manufacturing units in the country.

While the value addition is low at this point in time, gradual value increases over a period of time will help shift global supply chains to India. It must not be forgotten that China's manufacturing base was built over a forty-year period.

If we get this right, India is likely to witness a manufacturing renaissance over the next two decades. Any global company not setting up its global manufacturing base in India will risk its global cost competitiveness in the future, as India will emerge as the most cost-competitive manufacturing base, just like China, which witnessed this phase in the 1990s.

Having said that, India needs to double down on this policy tool. Maybe go 4x on it because this is India's last opportunity to build a global manufacturing base, create jobs for its youth, and accelerate export-driven growth.

With utmost urgency, we must be aware that there will not be any further ships anchoring this harbour, if we miss this one.

Part II
Imagining the Grand Strategy

3

The Indian Armed Forces in 2047: A Credible Instrument

Lt Gen. Arun Sahni

The world today is currently experiencing a transition due to a unique interplay of complexities. Indicators point towards a multipolar polycentric world order, with the US still as the major power, China in contestation, and countries like India as 'leading powers' in different geographic spaces. Therefore, India in 2047 would be a middle-income nation and a leading power in the Asia-Pacific region. The country's armed forces and the other elements of national power will be shaped to facilitate national vision and safeguard its security interests. This would necessitate a synergized military force that can be offensively employed either to protect territorial interests or for overseas engagements.

The rationale for this assessment is based on the strong foundation being laid continuously brick by brick by a resolute national leadership. Their vision and social mobilization have led to action in the form of path-breaking policies, inclusive initiatives, and external outreach to harness the opportunities being created in a world under transition. The focus on self-reliance/Atmanirbharta in critical sectors, including defence, instilling national pride by embracing India's rich civilizational heritage and economic empowerment through path-breaking financial-cum-digital initiatives, innovative social security schemes, and emotional connectivity across different sections of the society and focus on improving governance, has paved the path for this glorious future. The clarion call of Prime Minister Modi for India to become a leading power by 2047 is based on a sound understanding of factors that constitute national power. India holds great strategic and economic significance due to its central location in the Indian Ocean and proximity to major global economic centres in South Asia, Southeast Asia, East Asia, and China. It also possesses valuable natural resources, a large and young population, strong leadership, good governance, economic development, industrial capacity, technology, military strength, diplomatic influence, and a national character influenced by its rich cultural heritage. Additionally, its liberal democratic credentials align with those of the US and other developed nations.

To crystal gaze on the shape of the armed forces at the macro level, it is necessary to assess the security scenario and its future role. Threat assessment itself will have a wider canvas of challenges from cyber, space, and ever-evolving disruptive technologies with fast-paced changes by generative AI and climate-related disasters. This will be in addition to the legacy threats of unresolved land and maritime borders. The territorial estrangement with both our neighbours, China and Pakistan, will diminish in intensity but is not likely to be resolved in light of the larger geopolitical subtleties. China will continue to be a major threat, with the land borders still unresolved and increasing challenges in the maritime domain.

The exclusive economic zone (EEZ) and the development of the 'blue economy', the future 'engine of growth' for the world, will create contestation and strife in the maritime space of the

Indo-Pacific, necessitating a strong and effective navy. China's war-waging arsenal, including missile and long-range vectors, disruptive weapon platforms, and space and cyber capabilities, will give it an asymmetrical edge against India. But our own growth trajectory with built-in deterrence will stymie any major aggressive adventurism by this adversary. However, this will not obviate the probability of skirmishes and conflicts restricted in space, with no end in sight. Pakistan will still be an 'irritating thorn', with nuisance value, both in supporting terrorist activities and in being a proxy of China. However, the threat of terrorism, fundamentalism, and radicalization will continue to be a challenge, with changing faces repeatedly. These activities will be supported with the tacit support of a frail Pakistan and steered by 'non-state actors', with their roots embedded in the Levant and Middle East.

Technological advancements have led to a disproportionate increase in the capability, quality, and accuracy of surveillance sensors, while space-based intelligence, surveillance, and reconnaissance (ISR) assets have provided real-time transparency of the area of interest or battlespace. Artificial intelligence and machine learning have revolutionized the processing of information, replacing human interfaces in gleaning intelligence. This has led to a quantitative reduction in human resources in the land forces, which has offset the desired increase in naval combat power and troops in the specialist cadres that utilize high technology systems. At the apex level, suitable structures will be put in place to optimize the use of space and cyber domains while safeguarding and facilitating national security imperatives. India's interests and security challenges will also extend beyond the territorial and maritime borders. In addition to being the preferred security provider in the near and extended neighbourhood, India will require a strong military capability to safeguard its security interests and support its larger aspiration as a regional power.

The growing importance and willingness of India to steer global discourse, underscored by the success of its G20 Presidency, are indicators of a more assertive foreign policy and aspirations to be a global player. India is thus likely to assume the mantle of a 'system shaper' and the preferred partner for addressing unforeseen challenges faced by the developed and developing nations. Climate change will increase the frequency and intensity of natural disasters, with catastrophic impacts on the stability of the smaller nations in the Indian Ocean/Indo-Pacific region. Apropos, the armed forces will have to be prepared for offensive employment for 'out of area contingencies' for not only humanitarian assistance and disaster relief missions but active interventions in the smaller littoral states of the Indian Ocean.

The armed forces will, at that stage, comprise five major services: army, navy, airforce, cyber, and space forces. Additionally, the special forces agency will be structured to execute missions of strategic intelligence in conjunction with national intelligence agencies. The forces within the mandated existing strength will have suitably qualified manpower to optimally exploit high technology systems, especially those manning the cyber and space commands. The technical qualifications and 'terms of service' of this specialized human resource would have been suitably amended.

The armed forces would have been restructured into 'joint theatre commands' and placed under the operational control of the Comprehensive Defence Strategy (CDS). At that stage, the service chiefs would be responsible for the foundation pillars of their respective services, that is raise, train, and sustain. The space and cyber commands would continue to function under the integrated headquarters. Its elements would have been suitably meshed in at different levels within the theatre commands.

For the effective functioning of the armed forces, there would be two new organizational staff structures at the military-strategic and operational-strategic levels for optimizing the planning, conduct, and execution of joint plans by the CDS and theatre commanders. In addition to the operational aspects, this integrated staff would also be responsible for space and cyber operations. There will be suitable horizontal linkages, with other national structures undertaking missions in space and cyber domains at different hierarchical levels of the organizations. This will ensure synergy and complementarity of effort for critical national outcomes.

The CDS would also be looking at influence operations, which by then would be an integrated function at the national level. This would entail not only setting or implementing narratives and counter-narratives, in conjunction with similar national initiatives that address different facets of national concern and morale but also suitable strategic communication initiatives. Promoting interoperability with partnership countries will be a special area of focus. Ensuring real-time intelligence/information from groupings like Five Eyes and other similar initiatives will be a priority. As India's regional and global outreach increases, military diplomacy will be a new area for the armed forces to explore. To address these multiple new dimensions, internal restructuring would have to be carried out within the organization at various strategic and operational levels. Also, due to changed dispensations in the command-and-control functioning within the armed forces, suitable modulations will be made in the nation's higher defence organization, steered by the National Security Advisor (NSA). Aspects related to effective oversight and coordination amongst multiple agencies responsible for security will continue to be a key function of the National Security Council Secretariat (NSCS).

Force structuring of the respective services will ensure retention of the technological-modernization edge, with an equipment profile in the ratio of 30:40:30. It means the service-specific inventory will comprise 30 per cent advanced systems, 40 per cent current generation equipment, and 30 per cent platforms that are nearing obsolescence. Special provisions for the induction of high-technology systems and disruptive weapon platforms would be in vogue. Drones and an array of unmanned autonomous weapon platforms would be in the inventory of respective military services. Developments based on new-age technologies of generative artificial intelligence (AI), machine learning (ML), augmented reality (AR), and virtual reality (VR) would be used for upgrading the in-service legacy weapon platforms and ISR inputs from multiple sensors.

The developed indigenous capability in defence, an outcome of Atmanirbharta's drive, would empower the armed forces to acquire 'state-of-the-art' capabilities in time and be in tune, if not ahead of the technology curve. Another aspect that would be in keeping with the enhanced role of India in the mid-twenty-first century, is to have built-in organizational flexibility to constitute a special grouping of forces for offensive/'out of India' employment. Towards this, the army will have dual-tasked formations that are trained and equipped for undertaking amphibious and airborne operations. Meanwhile, the air force/navy will have suitable platforms in their respective inventories for undertaking joint operations as and when the need arises.

The land forces will be structured to retain a fine balance between manpower and employment of technologically advanced systems without diluting their tactical-cum-operational responsibility. The army will be networked, with a resilient early warning-cum-monitoring system (ISR), terrain-specific mobility, robust and seamless communication linkages, and battlefield survivability against adversaries' long-range vectors and disruptive weapon platforms. The tactical groupings will have suitably integrated drone/counter-drone employment, loiter munitions, and electronic warfare (EW) systems. Smart border management with multiple sensor inputs and mobile reserve forces will ensure dynamic response astride at the Line of Control and Line of Actual Control. The army will be restructured selectively for both offensive employment and out-of-India operations. Towards this, there would be brigade/division quick reaction forces (QRF) that would be dual tasked for short-notice employment within and outside India's territorial boundaries. These QRFs would be for terrain specific employment and with the capability to be the first responder in the case of natural disasters.

Blue-water navy will have an increased and diverse combination of modern naval platforms. In addition, it would have two to three carrier groups to not only protect but dominate the exclusive economic zone while safeguarding critical sea lines of communications in the Indian Ocean. To support responsive and effective sea domination/sea denial operations, it has a globally linked maritime domain awareness (MDA) system. This centre is seamlessly linked with similar nodes across the globe, with selective representatives from like-minded countries. Towards 'collaborative security' initiatives and to promote interoperability, joint training exercises with navies of partnership countries like QUAD and other Western nations will remain a priority.

The air force would be equipped with its desired complement of aircraft squadrons and sufficient resources to handle 'two front threats' as well as perform strategic, operational, and tactical tasks. Additionally, the air force would also lead the service in exploiting the assets in space. Its fleet would at that stage be looking at transitioning to MUMT (manned unmanned teaming) in a high-density environment and for deep strike missions. The cyber command will ensure cyber deterrence by defensive and offensive exploitation of cyberspace, in conjunction with other national security agencies responsible for cyber operations, such as National Technical Research Organization (NTRO), Intelligence Bureau (IB), and National Investigative Agency (NIA).

Space exploitation for seamless strategic and operational communication links and real-time surveillance/intelligence functions will enhance resilience and promote dexterity in the armed forces. Stringent joint training will ensure that these singularly separate services function like a well-oiled synergized machine and have time-tested standard operating procedures for optimizing efficiency. The security mandarins and apex political leadership will have to ensure meaningful strategic deterrence. This requires periodic evaluation and upgradation of nuclear deterrence, especially to counter China's dramatic expansion of its power projection abilities and constantly enhance its nuclear arsenal.

In conclusion, it is reiterated that the impetus of the farsighted measures initiated today has paved the way for the armed forces to be an effective instrument of national power, facilitating India's future vision. Of course, this comes with the rider that the current trend lines of an 'all-of-nation' developmental approach will continue for the vision to translate into reality.

4

Does India Have What It Takes to Be a $30 Trillion Economy by 2050

Ritesh Jain

The International Monetary Fund (IMF) has projected that India will become a $5 trillion economy and have the third-largest gross domestic product (GDP) in 2027–28.[1] India is looking at $30 trillion in GDP by 2050, with a per capita income of $21,000.[2] Although it may seem very overly optimistic, India is currently experiencing several structural changes and growth that make this goal achievable.

India's soft power is now widely recognized, allowing the country to have better and wider international relations. India is now better connected with a greater number of countries than Russia, the US, or even China. None of the nations is threatened by India.[3] India's festivals, spiritualism, art and culture, culinary varieties, dance forms, music, yoga, and more have fascinated people from all across the globe for centuries, driving and promoting the tourism industry in India. This is not to say that the country is not capable of handling tactical situations that require the involvement of defence forces, as demonstrated by its ability to manage anti-pirate activities in the Persian Gulf region.[4]

So far, the Indian growth story has primarily been service-led. Unlike middle- and high-income countries of East Asia that took to globalization through manufacturing-led activities, South Asian countries, especially India, took the service-led path to globalization and growth.[5]

Figure 4.1: Declining urban unemployment rate indicates higher job creation by India Inc.[6]

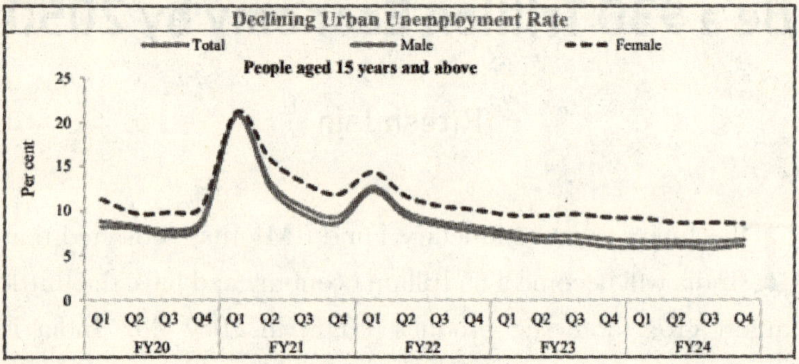

Source: Government of India Monthly Economic Review, April 2024

Although services play a significant role in the economy, they alone cannot catapult the nation to the next level due to the low employment rate they generate. Between 2005 and 2015, the manufacturing sector's contribution to the Indian economy remained stagnant at about 16 per cent (varying between 14.7 per cent and 16.7 per cent), while the share of services had grown and was close to 50 per cent[7] during the same period. See Figure 4.1. However, without manufacturing, the economy cannot reach the $30 trillion target because generating jobs from manufacturing is five times more than what services can offer, and, hence, most low-income countries initially focus on manufacturing before transitioning to services when they attain middle-income status.

India has faced challenges in increasing the share of its manufacturing sector in its economy. Employment is a crucial factor that drives a nation's growth process by creating the necessary base for increased consumption. However, the global pandemic has set back the manufacturing sector by several years. The sector is yet to fully recover from the dual lockdowns in 2020 and 2021, and optimal capacity utilization is still a prerequisite before additional labour and capital can be employed.[8] Physical infrastructure is vital for the growth of the manufacturing sector, which is a necessary condition for the Indian economy to develop into a $30 trillion economy. Going forward, it is expected that manufacturing will contribute to 25 per cent of India's GDP.

India's Journey to a $30 Trillion Economy by 2050: A Blueprint for Transformation

India is currently aiming for economic dominance. The goal is to have an economy more than ten times larger than its current size within the next twenty-five years, with a target of reaching a $30 trillion economy by 2050. To achieve this, India is shifting its focus from a predominantly service-led economy to manufacturing, implementing policy reforms, and taking a proactive approach to emerging global challenges. Let us delve into the key elements shaping India's trajectory and the underlying strategies that promise to reshape its economic landscape.

Population: Boon or Bane?

According to The Mad King,[9] India's demographic story is very different from other countries. India has about thirty years or so before it crosses the crucial age-dependency threshold. This presents a unique opportunity as the odds are in India's favour. In contrast, China will cross the line in 2027, the US crossed it in 2023, Europe in 2006, and Japan in 1994. Due to higher mortality rates, the base for the countries has narrowed between 1960 and 2020, but the top has widened, which is a common pattern for the young population. India is poised for exponential economic growth in the coming twenty years as the majority of its population belongs to the 20–45 age group (see Figure 4.2). This age group is characterized by high levels of consumption driven by major life events such as purchasing the first car, buying the first home, getting married, and having kids, all of which create significant opportunities for consumption and manufacturing-led growth.[10]

Figure 4.2: India's population percentage (by age): 1960 versus 2020

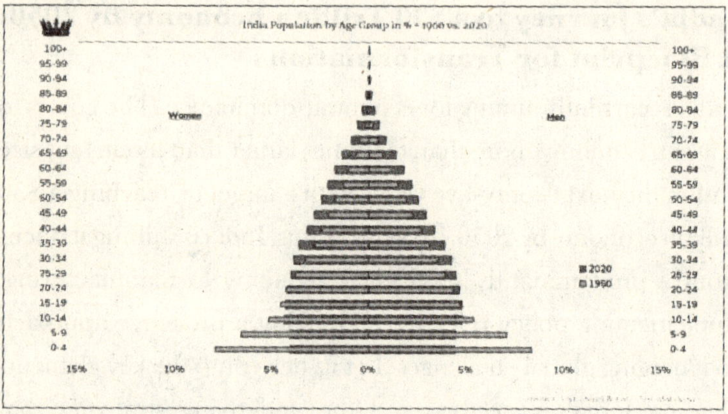

Chart Courtesy: Grant Williams

In terms of India's population, there is a shift from it being a bane to being a boon. An ageing population would have resulted in more pressure on the country's resources, including higher spending on social security, pension schemes, and health services. This would have led to lower consumption, which eventually will slow down the GDP growth rate, as has happened in the West. The West has a higher age-dependency ratio (the number of dependents per 100 of the working-age population). India, on the other hand, has remained insulated from this phenomenon, with the age-dependency ratio gradually decreasing from

53 per cent in 2013 to 47.5 per cent in 2022.[11] The working-age population as a proportion of the total Indian population (refer to Figure 4.3) is set to reach its pinnacle at 68.9 per cent by 2030, with the age-dependency ratio touching its lowest level at 31.2 per cent during the same period.[12]

Figure 4.3: India's population

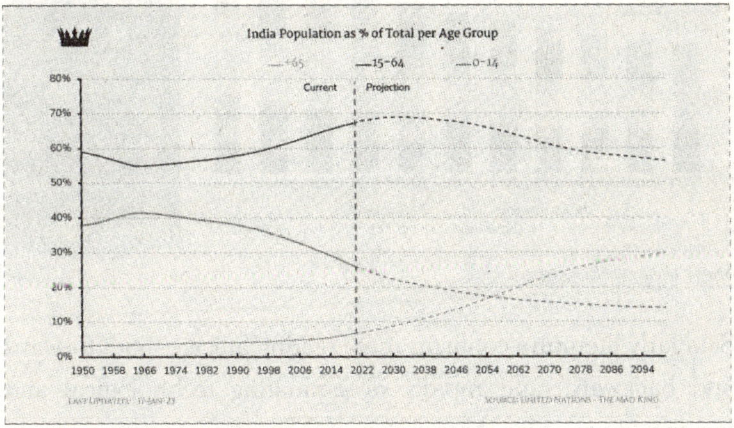

Chart Courtesy: The Mad King: From Babies to Boomers

Manufacturing: Key Growth Engine

India's economic growth is largely driven by its manufacturing sector. By 2050, manufacturing is projected to contribute a significant 25 per cent to India's GDP, with electronics manufacturing alone expected to constitute 6 per cent of the GDP, doubling its current share by 2030. This growth is not merely a statistic but a testament to India's commitment to industrial development and self-sufficiency.

The India Cellular and Electronics Association (ICEA) estimates that the electronics manufacturing sector is expected to see 15 per cent growth to reach $115 billion in FY24 alone.[13] This growth is largely due to the impressive performance of mobile phones, which are expected to contribute over $50 billion to the overall revenue in the current fiscal year.[14] Refer to Figure 4.4.

Figure 4.4: Indian consumer goods industry[15]

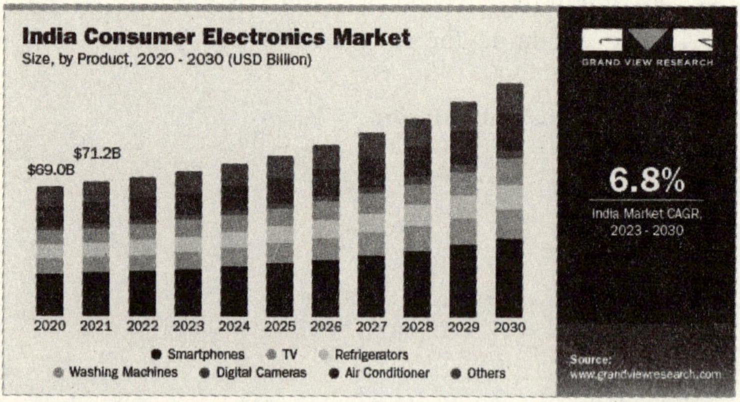

Source: www.grandviewresearch.com

Scholarly literature confirms that creating linkage (both forward and backward) and rapidly disseminating technological and technical knowledge through 'training on the job' can stimulate growth in the manufacturing sector.[16]

The make-in-India initiative has led to the approval of the Electronic Development Fund Policy. The key objective behind this scheme was the rationalization of the present duty structure. Furthermore, the introduction of the Modified Special Incentive Package Scheme (M-SIPS) is aimed at providing approximately 15–20 per cent capital expenditure. In the next few years, manufacturers of consumer electronics will increase investments in research and development (R&D), distribution, and production. Organized retail has increasingly grown in significance with the development of robust retail chains, including e-retailers such as E Zone, Reliance Digital, and Tata Croma.[17]

We already have visibility for the next ten years and can see one success story in the form of electronics manufacturing (see Figure 4.5).

Figure 4.5: India's electronics domestic production

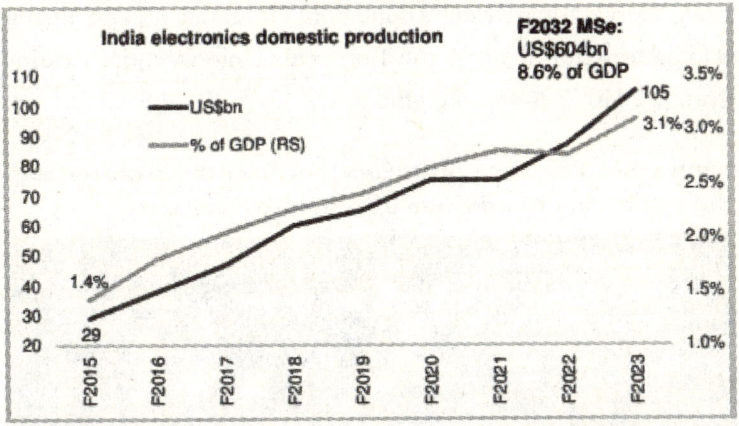

Source: Ministry of Electronics and Information Technology, Morgan Stanley India Industrials Research

Accelerated Manufacturing Growth

India has set an ambitious manufacturing goal of propelling manufacturing growth at a rate twice that of the overall GDP. This accelerated pace is envisioned to create unprecedented job opportunities across the country, providing a substantial boost to employment. With the Chinese system breaking down, India plans to increase its manufacturing capacity in-house without entering tie-ups with neighbouring countries such as Bangladesh, Myanmar, and Pakistan.[18] Any quality issues that may arise can be taken care of by the world's most populous country.

Electricity Demand

In order for the manufacturing sector to achieve the necessary growth, the most important thing is electricity generation. The industrial sector consumes more electricity than any other sector. The progress of manufacturing is reliant on a steady supply of power, which can be achieved by means of electrification, as the country strives to move away from fossil fuels. The demand for electricity also remains buoyant due to the growing demand from the ever-increasing population. 'In India, it also means adding an equivalent of the European Union's entire existing grid by 2040.'[19] Refer to Figure 4.6.

Figure 4.6: The huge difference between the required and the actual rate of addition of renewable capacity

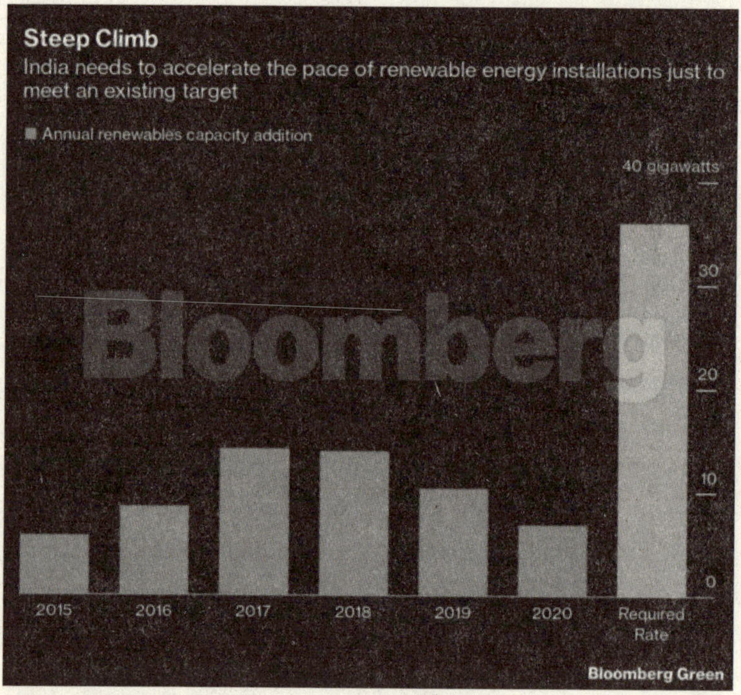

Source: Central Electricity Authority

Energy Security and Transition

Recognizing the pivotal role of energy in economic transformation, India places a strong emphasis on energy security and transition. Electrification is deemed indispensable for achieving its manufacturing goals and signifies a commitment to sustainable and efficient energy sources.

India being an emerging market with the largest population in the world[20] faces a challenging task in transitioning to a net-zero carbon emissions country. The 2030 target has now been pushed to 2070. However, India is on track to reach both its short-term and long-term targets delineated in the Panchamrit action plan. These are as follows:

- Achieving a non-fossil fuel energy capacity of 500 GW by 2030.
- Meeting at least 50 per cent of the energy needs using renewable energy by 2030.
- Reducing CO_2 emissions by a billion tonnes by 2030.
- Reducing carbon intensity to less than 45 per cent by 2030.

India has set a goal of achieving a net zero emission target by 2070. Achieving this stated objective will warrant, among other things, a substantial, if not mammoth, development that will result in replacing coal with alternative and renewable sources of electricity as well as replacing petroleum with renewable power for transportation. As of 2022, coal, natural gas, and oil accounted for 75 per cent of India's energy use.[21] However, in 2023, the share of fossil fuels in electricity generation has decreased to 56.8 per cent.[22]

India has announced plans to gradually reduce its reliance on non-fossil fuel as a power generation source, ultimately restricting its use to 50 per cent of its electricity supply by 2030. Achieving this target will require a massive investment to the tune of $363 billion during 2020–29 in novel power projects and batteries providing significant investment opportunities for both national and international investors. India has proven to be resilient even during the most challenging energy crisis seen in the global arena since the oil crisis of 1973 buoyed by the energy security strategy that it adopted. The four-pronged strategy involves the following:

- Diversification of supplies to the energy sector.
- Expanding the footprint of its exploration and production.
- Exploring and implementing alternate sources of energy and achieving energy transition by transitioning to a gas-based economy.
- Implementation of green hydrogen and electric vehicles.

India has expanded its crude oil suppliers from 27 countries in FY07 to 39 in FY22. This expansion was achieved by adding new suppliers such as Russia, Guinea, Libya, Columbia, Equatorial, and Gabon. At the same time, India has strengthened its international ties with countries like the US and Russia.[23]

Import Substitution and Low-End Manufacturing

India aspires to increase its GDP per capita by adopting a strategic approach that involves import substitution and low-end manufacturing until the GDP per capita reaches $10,000. This strategic approach aims to fortify economic foundations before transitioning to more advanced manufacturing processes. Through the import substitution route of industrialization, India is striving to reduce its dependence on imports and build its own industries to boost economic growth. The Make in India initiative is a clear step in that direction.

Import Substitution and Inflation Dynamics

While import substitution forms a core strategy, it is recognized that this could result in higher inflation in the short term. The challenge lies in carefully managing these inflationary pressures while also ensuring the long-term benefits of self-reliance and economic resilience.

Embracing the Chaebol Business Model

Inspired by the South Korean model, India envisions nurturing its own chaebols—large business conglomerates that become global champions. This model is characterized by family-controlled enterprises and aims to drive economic dynamism and global competitiveness, akin to the success stories of other Asian economies. Progressively aligned with the Indian government's key concerns, about six to seven mega-firms, including the Adani Group and Reliance Industries, controlled by two of Asia's richest tycoons, have acquired a strong foothold in their respective industries. They are perfectly capable of raising significantly huge sums of funds to finance their operations, research and development, growth, and expansion. These firms have extreme experience and solid political connections that help them navigate India's complex bureaucratic obstacles. They are exploiting various avenues, such as the government's privatization plans and subsidies, to successfully execute their ongoing projects and plan for future ones at a speed and on a scale that had hitherto remained elusive to the country.[24]

Friendshoring Opportunities

As global dynamics shift, India sees the opportunity of friendshoring—positioning itself as an alternative to China. With a large and diverse market, India seeks to attract capital leaving China and presenting a significant opportunity for economic growth.

Collaborating at the international level with various business organizations can open up multiple opportunities, especially pertaining to such areas as knowledge exchange and technology transfer. Indian entrepreneurs, both domestic manufacturers and exporters, have the opportunity to take advantage of cutting-edge manufacturing techniques, build fulfilling partnerships for endeavours in research and development, and gain access to the most sophisticated technologies. The US recognizes India as an indispensable ally in building global supply chain resilience.[25]

Exponential Growth in Tourism

Tourism is a significant contributor to India's economy, accounting for over 7.5 per cent of GDP as of 2021.[26] According to projections, the Indian tourism and hospitality industry will generate more than $59 billion in revenue by 2028, with foreign tourist arrivals (FTAs) expected to cross 30 million. The Indian government envisages a forex inflow of approximately $56 billion and is expected to create nearly 140 million jobs in the tourism industry by 2030, with a focus on inclusive growth and high-value areas such as adventure tourism, ecotourism, and cruise tourism.[27] Spiritual tourism is also emerging as a new growth driver, with Ayodhya, a place of religious, historical, mythological, and cultural significance, being transformed into a spiritual tourism hub that attracts a large number of tourists and tourism entrepreneurs.[28]

In India, the transportation and communication infrastructure has developed rapidly, playing a vital role in advancing the sector. As of FY23, nearly Rs 10 billion has been invested in developing tourism infrastructure in India. This has led to a significant improvement in India's roads and airways network, resulting in substantially reduced travel time for long distances, making travel more affordable for the masses, and increasing accessibility.[29] The number of operational airports in the country has doubled from 74 in 2014 to 148 in 2023.[30] The primary focus has been on technological integration, with a special emphasis on sustainability and innovation. This has created an environment conducive to propelling the growth of the travel industry in a manner that can contribute significantly to the economic future of the country.

Insights from Key Figures

Insights from notable figures, such as HDFC Bank chairman Atanu Chakraborty, provide valuable perspectives on India's growth trajectory. Projections indicate that if the current pace of growth continues, India could reach the $30 trillion mark by 2045–50, with a per capita income of $21,000.

While the International Monetary Fund has expressed concern about growing public debt, it will be less of a concern if it grows at a rate lower than the rate at which nominal GDP is increasing. As long as India can continue to have 12–13 per cent nominal GDP growth (6 per cent real+6 per cent inflation) then there is no need to worry about IMF concerns. The debt can be inflated away as long as the denominator (GDP) is growing faster than the numerator (public debt). India only gets into a debt trap when it stops growing its GDP by 5–6 per cent.

Challenges and Risks

Despite the optimism, challenges loom on the horizon. Rising debt, potential inflation, and the ever-present risks associated with geopolitical tensions, especially in the Middle East, pose significant challenges to India's economic aspirations.

Conclusion

In this chapter, we have examined India's detailed plan to achieve a $30 trillion economy by 2050. From manufacturing resurgence and the embrace of global business models to managing inflation and navigating geopolitical risks, India's journey is fraught with challenges and opportunities. As the nation propels itself into a new economic era, the resilience and adaptability of its strategies will be paramount in realizing this ambitious vision.

The likely contribution of India's growing population to its GDP growth would depend on several factors, such as the overall population size and growth rate, as well as the number of people who are of working age and can contribute positively to the country's economy. With a relatively young population, India has a competitive advantage in sectors like services and manufacturing, and this demographic has started to flex its purchasing power and attitude towards discretionary expenditure. Consumption is on the rise across different income groups and sectors, which should ultimately lead to increased manufacturing growth. When combined with other factors discussed above, India is expected to reach $30 trillion by 2050.

5

India's Inevitable Convergence: Reflections from the US and China

Maneesh Dangi

Forecasting a nation's gross domestic product (GDP) in twenty-five years is a complex task. However, by delving into the country's historical growth, identifying potential risks, and drawing comparisons with similar nations in terms of income and demographics, we can gain valuable insights into the future trajectory of its economy. While this method is not foolproof, it provides a solid foundation for our predictions.

In simple terms, GDP equals the number of workers times their average output. Considering workers are usually aged 20–59, the size of this group in India will grow by 50 per cent in the next twenty-five years. Additionally, each worker's output will likely increase 2.5-fold, growing at 3.5–4 per cent per year. This is a promising trajectory, more or less the same rate at which it grew during 1998–2018. During the same time, the US workers' output grew at just ~1 per cent annually.

The significance of India's workers' output growing at a faster rate than their US counterparts cannot be overstated. Currently, our workers produce only a tenth of what an American worker does. This substantial gap presents a significant opportunity for growth. If we can effectively train our workforce and avoid major setbacks, we are poised to continue our rapid economic expansion.

Having estimated the labour force and per-worker output growth, understanding the economy's future size in the US dollar also requires considering potential currency fluctuations over time.

Anyone who has visited the US or Europe knows the cost of living there is much higher. For instance, a monthly wi-fi subscription costs about $100 in the US, compared to just $10 in India.

Over long periods, the price differentials across economies should reduce. Because Indian prices are so low, it is fair to assume that they will converge, slowly but surely, with the US. This convergence is a testament to India's economic strength and potential.

Should India's prices by 2047 mirror China's current levels, expect a 3 per cent annual real appreciation of our currency. It is crucial to note the significance of 'real' in this context: if our inflation rates are 3 per cent higher, our currency's value effectively remains unchanged. Drawing from past trends, a more cautious projection would be a 1.5 per cent annual real increase in currency real value.

To project India's GDP growth in the US dollar, we sum the growth rates of the worker population, per worker output, and currency adjustments. This approach suggests that India's economy could reach a size of $14–20 trillion, slightly below but comparable to China's and the US's current economic scale.

It is important to recognize that the growth rate of our worker population is expected to decelerate significantly compared to the past twenty-five years. That will chop off our growth over the next twenty-five years by approximately 1–1.5 per cent. Therefore, this period is the last opportunity to leverage our demographic dividend, as both the overall population and the workers are likely to decline thereafter. See Table 5.1.

Table 5.1: Estimating the size of major economies in 2047

1998–2018					
US inflation	2.2%				
	Real Per wroker GDP growth	Price converg_ ence (Curr effect)	Worker growth	GDP Growth in USD	GDP 2022 in USD (trln)
China	7.3%	3.5%	0.8%	11.6%	18
India	3.8%	1.5%	2.2%	7.4%	3
US	1.1%	0.0%	0.9%	2.0%	25
2022–2047					
US inflation	2.2%				
	Real Per wroker GDP Growth	Price converg- ence (Curr effect)	Worker Growth	GDP Growth in USD	GDP in 2047
China base case	2.6%	1.0%	-0.9%	2.8%	35.39
China Good case	4.8%	2.1%	-0.9%	6.1%	78.01
India base case	3.6%	1.5%	0.7%	5.8%	13.70
India good case	3.8%	3.0%	0.7%	7.5%	20.40
US	1.1%	0.0%	0.3%	1.4%	35.60

**China worker output's range is 1 per cent higher or lower vis a vis India. The past real currency appreciation in China has been more rapid. At 2 per cent real appreciation, Chinese prices will be equal to that of the US in twenty-five years. Do observe that the worker effect (growth in working age group) itself means India's GDP will grow at 1.5 per cent faster than China's at the same level of per-worker output growth.*

Population Structure of 2023's India Is Akin to 1998's China

Over the next twenty-five years, our populations will age, growth will slow sharply, and we will have fewer babies, similar-sized younger workers, and many older workers—a transition to a population structure that happened in China over the past twenty-five years. A striking similarity in both the structure and the evolution of the population gives us valuable insights into how India's macroeconomic landscape and consumption patterns might evolve, drawing parallels from China's experience over the past two decades. See Table 5.2.

Table 5.2: Population distribution and change in China and India

Population distribution					Population Change	
	China	China	India	India	India	China
	1998	2022	2022	2047	2022–2047	1998–2022
Children	34%	23%	35%	25%	14%	−25%
Youth	35%	28%	33%	28%	0%	−11%
Old workers	21%	31%	22%	28%	53%	69%
Elderly	10%	19%	10%	19%	129%	121%
Dependents	44%	41%	45%	45%	19%	14%

The ratio of youth to children doubled in China from 1973 to 1998, from 0.5 to 1, aiding improved parenting, education, and general care for the younger generation. This—more than anything else—paved the way for a more productive workforce and growth boom in China over the past forty-five years.

India's ratio of youth to kids reached China's in 1998. So, if you are impressed by China's educational and sports outcomes, patent filing, and its rise in high tech, there is a distinct possibility that India will witness similar trends over the next twenty-five years. Reason: There will be fewer babies per family in 2022, leading to better health and educational outcomes for the new working class over the next twenty-five years. See Table 5.3.

Table 5.3: Size of population of China and India

Size of population (in cr)								
	China				India			
	1973	1998	2022	2047	1973	1998	2022	2047
Children	45	43	32	20	30	47	49	42
Youth	24	44	39	**29**	16	32	46	46
Old workers	14	26	44	**36**	9	17	30	46
Elderly	6	12	27	49	4	7	14	32
Total	89	125	142	134	59	102	139	166
Youth/kids	0.5	1.0	1.2	1.5	0.5	0.7	0.9	1.1
Growth in Total population		41%	**14%**	-5%		75%	36%	**19%**

China's population increased by 60 per cent in the past seventy-five years, while India's grew by 140 per cent. Such a rapid rise in population meant that Indian infra, state, and utilities could not keep pace with the population growth and that is the key reason for haphazard growth and a weak state. Finally, Indian population growth has slowed and will likely grow at only 10–20 per cent over the next twenty-five years, somewhat similar to what China saw in 1998–2022 (13 per cent). This is the key reason why Indian public services, including infra, will improve dramatically over the next twenty-five years, as all incremental spending will improve the per-capita availability of the same.

Fewer Children and Stagnating Youth Population over the Next Twenty-five Years

You might find it surprising, but the number of babies born in India has been decreasing each year since 2004. In the next twenty-five years, the total number of children in our country is expected to be 15 per cent lower than it is today. Pretty much similar to the trend that China saw from 1998 to 2023.

Even the youth population aged 20–39 will stagnate in India. This group spends a lot on higher education and training, enters the workforce and buys a bicycle, a motorcycle, or a small car, rents or purchases its first home, and is a major consumer of home furnishing, beverages, fashionable clothing, footwear, and accessories. It is a peak spending age. With saturation in this group, India will have past-peak weddings very soon. If you are selling talcum powder, soap or cheap footwear, there exists a secular stagnation for your products. Unless, of course, you upgrade your products and preimmunize them!

Suppose you are currently benefiting from the services of migrant workers, whether as drivers or live-in maids, it is worth appreciating this affordability while it lasts. Over the next twenty-five years, these services are likely to become more expensive. This change will be driven not just by the evolving aspirations of the 20–40-year-old Indian workforce, who are increasingly seeking different employment opportunities, but also due to the slowing growth rate of this young working population. This phenomenon is not unique to India. About a century ago, countries like Britain and the United States enjoyed similar periods where such services were relatively inexpensive. No more.

Also, because both children and the youth population are collectively declining, this is a structural force that will stay for very long. If you are an analyst wondering why many of our FMCG firms are showing lacklustre volume growth, do not be surprised if this situation worsens in the next many years! There is a reason why many of the consumer stable goods firms trade at single-digit multiples in China.

Premiumization

Presently, less than 4 per cent of Indian households earn $10,000 annually. With equitable growth, around 40 per cent of families could reach this income bracket by 2047, representing what we currently define as the upper-middle class and rich. Consequently, about 30–40 per cent of Indian consumers in 2047 may emulate the spending patterns of today's top 5 per cent. That means 8–10x growth in durable goods, jewellery, ready-made food, and services in healthcare, education, and tourism.

Viewing India's economic progression through another lens, as the nation's income approaches today's Chinese levels, consumption patterns are likely to align similarly. Consequently, sectors such as leisure, recreation, and hospitality could witness exponential growth, potentially twenty times current levels, even when many 'bread, butter, and Parle-G' businesses struggle.

Because of the significant growth in the size of the upper-middle class, there exist substantial opportunities for premiumization and growth in sectors yet to reach saturation. Take the example of quality education; even though the student population has declined secularly now, the cost of good quality education will soar. International school costs about Rs 3 lakh in Mumbai, same costs Rs 22 lakh per annum in Beijing. In twenty-five years, the cost of premium education and many other premium services will likely converge with today's Chinese costs. The key lesson for most businesses catering to the basic needs of the younger population is to upgrade the product in terms of quality and features. Everything premium will see significant growth. But if you are selling uniforms to kids or tiffin boxes or primary school study material or run-off-the-mill pens or pencils, you may stare at stagnant times!

Rise of Middle-aged Ones: The Older Workers

The third group of people, the middle-aged or older workers, from age 20–59, will see significant growth in population in India (about 50 per cent). Unlike the younger demographic, which focuses on physical assets such as homes and durable goods, middle-aged individuals tend to lean towards financial savings as they prepare for retirement. This phase of life is also characterized by an upgrade cycle in consumption: purchasing larger homes, investing in better home furnishings, and upgrading from two-wheelers to small cars and then to larger vehicles. This group is typically more productive and spends less, making them the peak savers. China experienced rapid growth in this group of people from 1998 to 2022, which led to fast productivity growth, low inflation, improved current account balances, and a significant boom in financial wealth.

As the middle-aged cohort builds significant financial savings, those financial savings will have to be rerouted into the economy by banks and others as debt to the younger population to help them purchase cars, houses, and durables and for corporations to build newer capacities. Currently, India's private debt stands at only 50 per cent of GDP and has been relatively stagnant for nearly a decade, in contrast to the US (150 per cent of GDP), China (190 per cent), and Europe (83 per cent). Considering a typical pattern observed at this stage of the economic cycle, it is likely that India's debt will grow rapidly, becoming 75–100 per cent of GDP in the coming twenty-five years. Though much of the financing is likely to happen on large bank balance sheets, opportunities for niche players catering to unique businesses will also grow rapidly—especially in low-ticket business finance, microfinance, real estate, CV, and loan against property financing. Banks will incrementally retrench from project finance and firms will have to rely on non-banking financial companies and alternate pools of capital to fund these projects.

This demographic shift towards middle age group will likely influence culture and politics as well, with more films featuring middle-aged protagonists, reflecting their experiences and interests. Additionally, there will be a notable shift in consumption patterns towards quality, with a growing demand for healthier, premium food options like organic cereals, vegetables, and better-quality milk. With enormous wealth and numbers, this group will remain the most dominant in forcing its biases on politics, too.

Finance

In the early 2000s, Mutual Fund Assets Under Management (MF AUM) in India were approximately 10 per cent of bank deposits, a figure that has risen to about 25 per cent today. This places India's current state akin to where the US mutual fund industry was in the late 1980s. Since then, in the US, mutual fund assets as a percentage of GDP have risen to over 125 per cent. If India continues to see a flow of funds equivalent to 1 per cent of its GDP into mutual funds, and assuming markets deliver even run-off-the-mill returns, it is likely that MF AUM as a percentage of GDP could double to 50 per cent by 2047. This growth trajectory would mean that mutual funds and similar wealth products grow at 12–14 per cent over the next twenty-five years and would account for about half of bank deposits in the coming period.

Wealth and Luxury Goods

India's current total wealth stands at approximately $15 trillion, in contrast to China's $85 trillion and the United States' $125 trillion. As the Indian economy's size converges with today's China, its wealth, too, will do so.

In India, an intriguing aspect of wealth is the very high level of promoter shareholding across businesses. Since 2001, promoters have maintained an average shareholding of around 50 per cent, a stark contrast to Europe and other Asian regions, where it is closer to 20 per cent. Unlike East Asian economies, where dual structure ownership or crossholdings are common for maintaining control, Indian promoters often prefer direct majority control in their firms. Given this, the top 2,000 families, who hold a disproportionate share of wealth today, will continue to dominate. This concentration of wealth suggests that India will likely have billionaires, surpassing current numbers in the US (750) and China (1,000). Even the tally of those with $100 million in wealth will match the US's current 10,000.

This wealth concentration will significantly impact luxury sectors worldwide, including travel, wellness, exclusive education, private jets, luxury cars, yachts, and fine arts. Indian rich will continue to fund grand temples and community places but will also likely start to help institutes such as IITs to upgrade their infra and research facilities. Concurrently, the growth in private wealth management businesses will be unparalleled as Indian capital begins to increasingly fund new or riskier ventures through venture capital, private debt, and venture debts.

Rapid Rise of Old Population

Finally, the elderly population, those aged sixty and over, is projected to increase by 2.7 times by 2047. Since ageing and healthcare spending correlate well, a substantial opportunity for healthcare businesses catering to teeth, eyes, knees, and many such areas, along with tertiary care for major ailments, exists. In the near future, significant changes are expected in China, where the population is projected to double to 37 per cent of the total population, compared to 19 per cent in India (from the current 10 per cent). This suggests that the impact China has had on commodities and infrastructure over the past twenty-five years will likely have a similar effect on elder care.

Urbanization

Apart from the demographic transition, India will have another fundamental transition, from a predominantly rural and agrarian society to an urban and working-class one. It is likely that about half of the population will reside in urban areas in twenty-five years (from the current 30 per cent). With a dense population, many rural areas near urban centres will undergo suburbanization, leading to approximately three-quarters of the population adopting an urban lifestyle. So businesses engaged in fashion and home furnishing, fast food, mobility, tourism, and delivery will grow rapidly.

Welfare State

Our country's political commitment to capitalism and property rights remains high, which means we will continue to have very high wealth and income inequality. This will give birth to a welfare state at a very low level of per capita income. We will continue to have some of the largest government welfare programmes in the world, spanning from food security to health and education. Unlike the US, where these sectors are more privatized, the Indian state will continue to provide services in the education, finance, and health sectors. As it is, the trend of adopting welfare policies, particularly those prevalent in South India, seems to be gaining traction at the national level.

Indian Goods Manufacturing Will Grow, but the Real Magic Will Happen in Services

Since many Western firms are being forced to review their China-only manufacturing policies due to rising hostility and an increasingly expensive labour pool, India may benefit. India will likely develop a decent ecosystem to build its own defence wares and electronics. But all of that is unlikely to aid India in displacing China as a dominant supplier of goods. Despite a lot of efforts—both micro and macro—Indian non-oil exports have crawled at 3 per cent per annum growth in the last decade, and today it is at 9.70 per cent of GDP, a level last seen in 2004. The reverse is true for China, whose hegemony has risen secularly over this period, and the current trends suggest that China's dominance in global exports will grow further given its dominance in renewable echo systems (electric vehicles, solar panels) and as it continues to march ahead in terms of productivity growth. Given all of it, even though India will begin to matter to commodities such as crude, where its consumption will be almost 7–8 per cent of the global consumption, double of today, its role in nonferrous commodities will remain peripheral.

Because of India's diaspora, English language skills, and cultural advantages—our people will remain key exports to the rest of the world—earning us cumulatively 7 per cent of GDP through service exports and remittances. This number has grown by 10 per cent over the past two decades. India already has net exports of $150 billion worth of software services. That number as percentage of GDP used to be negligible in the 1990s, rose to 1 per cent in 2004 and is now 4 per cent. The software services growth will likely continue to rise at 7–8 per cent over the next twenty-five years, making it a trillion-dollar industry by 2047. This will benefit cities like Bangalore and Hyderabad, amongst others, which supply knowledge labour to the world. Indian office space is still cheap even though the talent arbitrage has been reducing over the years. Expect 10s of REITs (Real Estate Investment Trusts) springing up across the country and a rise of wealth managers who will cater to invest in such instruments.

Rates and Currency

India has historically faced a current account deficit, often exacerbated by rising crude oil prices, leading to a steady depreciation of the Indian rupee over the years. This depreciation has kept Indian wages significantly lower in dollar terms compared to the West. However, as India's demographic profile evolves, with a decline in its youth population and a rise in a more productive middle-aged population, the country's current account deficit will likely be half of the last twenty-five years' average. That will reduce pressure on the currency and aid a long-term price convergence process with the West and China.

Our vibrant democratic system has kept a lid on inflation, which is why we have never had hyperinflation—a recurrent feature in most developing countries. Our inflation has averaged 7.70 per cent for the past fifty years, 6.50 per cent over twenty years, and 6 per cent over ten years. But given the changes in demographic profile, we are likely to see the inflation rate move to 4 per cent over the next decade and thereafter converge further to the Western and Chinese levels of 2–3 per cent.

The combination of lower inflation and a reduced current account deficit will positively impact the Indian rupee, which has depreciated at an average rate of 3 per cent over the past twenty-five years. Given that our inflation differential is likely to be at least 2 per cent lower compared to the past quarter-century, and the current account deficit (CAD) is likely to be about half of what it was during this period, it is plausible to imagine a stable rupee over long periods. My base case scenario is an annual depreciation of the currency by about 1 per cent.

Stable or slowly depreciating currency will have significant implications on interest rates in India. Mirroring the trend seen in China, where interest rates converged with those in the developed world over the past quarter century, something similar may play out in India. Considering this, an Indian thirty-year bond at 7.5 per cent is not a bad deal for long-term investors for both locals and foreigners. I expect more substantial flows in Indian bonds from foreign investors over this period relative to equities. The Indian public finance will continue to benefit from interest rates that remain lower than the nominal GDP growth, aiding in more sustainable fiscal management.

Stocks

Our corporate return on equity is higher than almost all the emerging markets across time frames. A median Indian corporation, amongst the top 100 that you are likely to invest in, earns a return on equity (RoE) of 16 per cent, distributes about 30 per cent as dividends, and grows its earnings at 11 per cent. A median corporation in the US is likely to earn about 2 per cent less and grow at 3 per cent less. Do you know China's listed firms' RoE will be less than 10 per cent? This is why our stocks have always remained expensive relative to most of the other stock markets.

As the size of the economy grows, expect a steady decline in RoEs. Indian earnings have grown at 7 per cent in US dollars over the past twenty-five years. But markets delivered significantly better because of two reasons: our currency depreciated by 3 per cent annually and our stocks got repriced quite sharply. As I expect the currency to depreciate at a lower rate and stocks to have little room to reprice higher, the returns will be lower over the next twenty-five years. More like 10–11 per cent. If bond yields converge to the Western world, the return could be higher. But purely from the point of view of risk premium, it is at 3 per cent over sovereign bonds.

With the expected slowdown in the depreciation of the Indian rupee, foreign investors stand to gain as their returns in local currency will translate more favourably into US dollar returns. Conversely, for local Indian investors, the incentive to diversify investments outside India may be reduced for the same reasons.

Real Estate

India, for being so big and dense, its big cities will continue to remain very expensive. The only other place to compare the Indian real estate price trajectory is that of China. The growth boom, lack of space, rapid urbanization, and vertical growth meant that Chinese properties became very expensive over the past 15–20 years. A 1000-sq-ft apartment in Beijing costs Rs 7 crore. About 2.25x of Mumbai (Rs 30,000 per sq ft versus Rs 67,000 odd in Beijing, away from the city centre). If our per-capita income and property prices converge with China's in twenty-five years, our properties will deliver a 3 per cent real return. Add to this 3–4 per cent inflation and 2.5 per cent rental yield, you will receive a decent 9 per cent annualized return.

Real estate in cities like Bangalore and Hyderabad are likely to perform better, both because their economic prospects are better and the current price point is much lower than that of Mumbai (Bangalore is about 35 per cent lower, on average, outside of city centres, and about half near the city centres). Those expecting Indian property markets to align with Western price-to-income ratios will be disappointed. India's unique population structure and density suggest a trajectory more akin to China's, rather than that of the US.

But Not Everything Will Get Better in India

The stark contrast between the cleanliness, aesthetic charm, and advanced road infrastructure of Western and East Asian nations often leaves us in awe. Despite significant strides in infrastructure over the past quarter-century and matching per capita income with nations like Thailand, India's public spaces still fall short in cleanliness and aesthetic appeal. While improvements are hoped for, reaching the standards we admire abroad might remain elusive.

Moreover, concerns like high AQI levels are expected to escalate. Persistent pollution from industrial emissions will continue to contaminate air and groundwater, and climate change is set to exacerbate issues with increasing heat and humidity. This grim environmental backdrop contributes to the struggle against malnutrition and stunted growth among millions, potentially worsening health outcomes. Given the dense population and the growing number of vehicles, urban woes such as traffic congestion are also predicted to intensify. Tragically, India's prominence as a hub for diabetes and cancer is likely to strengthen.

If China chooses to remain antagonistic towards us, we may face threats from both sides of Kashmir. Our labour participation rate continues to remain puzzlingly depressed and has not recovered since a secular fall began in 2006. While the future holds promise, these challenges underscore the complexity of India's journey towards progress.

In summary, by 2047, the Indian economy is expected to quadruple, though growth rates will moderate compared to the last two and a half decades. Some sectors may reach saturation, experiencing a slowdown, even as a trend of premiumization and upgrading continues. The burgeoning middle class will markedly elevate the standard of living, and the demographic shift will disproportionately favour premium sectors over mass-market ones. These dynamics signal a consumption upgrade similar to what China witnessed in the last twenty-five years, marked by shifts from two-wheelers to cars, smaller to larger homes, and a surge in luxury and electronic goods purchases.

6

Human Capital Can Continue to Be India's Superpower

Krishna B. Kumar

The mention of the word superpower conjures images of gleaming skyscrapers, a mighty military, and bullet trains. While some of these become highly visible and even inevitable trappings of a superpower, India's superpower has always been its people. Ensuring the flourishing of its people whose potential is fully realized in the social, economic, and political arenas will ensure that a superpower status would be more durable and inclusive. The collective human wealth indicative of such flourishing is what we broadly mean by 'human capital'.

While the term 'capital' often brings to mind tangible assets like machines and infrastructure, or the finances used to acquire them, it is important to recognize that human capital is equally, if not more, crucial for economic growth and development. In fact, human capital often complements and even creates physical capital. However, the visibility of physical capital can sometimes lead to disproportionate investment, overshadowing the importance of human capital.

It is hard to miss the towering skyscape of many an emerging power, projecting prestige[1] on the global stage, even when such investments have portended financial trouble.[2] Broad investment in human capital might be less visible or glamorous, but it is the bedrock on which many successful development stories have been built.

Engaging in an exercise on what kind of a superpower India should be is not an idle one based on fantasy but one rooted in relevance. Between 1990—the year before it undertook large-scale economic reforms necessitated by a financial emergency—to 2022, India's real per capita gross domestic product or GDP (adjusted for inflation) has nearly quadrupled;[3] unadjusted increases are higher but would be misleading. In 2022–23, India's GDP was the fifth highest[4] in the world in dollar terms and adjusted for purchasing power parity (to account for what a dollar really buys), it was the third largest.[5]

India also made strides in broader development. While the poverty rate in India has been a subject of much debate[6] (with recent estimates of extreme poverty ranging from 0 to 10 per cent), there is little doubt that hundreds of millions of people have been lifted out of poverty since the 1991 liberalization. A recent study estimates[7] that 415 million Indians left poverty in the last fifteen years alone. Over 400 million Indians are in the middle class—nearly a third of the population—with that percentage expected[8] to double over the next two decades.

India has emerged from the back-to-back shocks of COVID-19, high inflation created by the pandemic-induced stimulus, and global conflicts as the fastest-growing major economy: 7.6 per cent in the second quarter of 2023, compared to 6.3 per cent for China and almost twice[9] the average for emerging economies. This speaks to the Indian economy's strength and resilience.

On the geopolitical front, too, India's stature and participation in global initiatives have increased tremendously. Its role in the Quadrilateral Security Dialogue (Quad) appears to be solidifying. It is an eponymous member of BRICS,[10] and it is part of the more recent and US-initiated I2U2[11] partnership and Indo-Pacific Economic Framework for Prosperity.[12] Its leadership of G20 and hosting of the group's summit in New Delhi in September 2023 cemented not only its global standing but also its stature as a voice of the Global South.[13]

In geopolitics, size matters. Varying combinations of a large geographical area, population,[14] and GDP allow a country to defend itself, amortize the high costs of public research and development and infrastructure over its many citizens (India's Digital Public Infrastructure[15] being an excellent example of both), and more easily obtain a seat at the table of most important global forums. India can now lay claim to all the above factors, further lending credibility to its superpower aspirations.

Especially when it comes to people, India has the most of them, having surpassed[16] China's population during the first half of 2023. And this population is young. India's median age[17] is less than thirty, while it is approaching forty in China and the United States and is even higher in Europe and East Asia. This youthfulness can be a huge strategic and competitive advantage for India, especially in the face of China's declining labour force and population.

India has a solid track record and continues building a human capital-centric strategy. To give just a few examples, India produces the most STEM graduates in the world. India has 5 million software developers (second only to China's 7 million), and the number continues to grow. Inside and outside the country's borders, Indians have always distinguished themselves in science and technology, arts, business, and, increasingly, politics.

Indeed, human capital has long been a major Indian export. Nearly 18 million Indians live abroad, making it the world's biggest diaspora. Thanks to this diaspora, India received $125 billion in remittances,[18] again the largest in the world. Indicative of the divide that exists in Indian human capital, a quarter of Silicon Valley start-ups are managed[19] by people of Indian origin, while millions[20] of construction workers have contributed to the construction boom in Gulf countries.

What challenges remain for India in further nurturing this enviable human wealth? The potential to capitalize on abundant labour when fertility rates are declining is referred to as the 'demographic dividend', but to cash in on this dividend, India will have to continue investing in its people's education, health, and socio-economic participation.

The impressive accomplishments listed above have been uneven. Less than a quarter of Indians 25–64 years of age have upper secondary attainment, and only around a third of 25–34-year-old Indians, a group crucial to realizing the above-mentioned dividend, have it. Unsurprisingly, India ranked a lowly 116 out of 174 countries in the World Bank's 2020 ranking of human capital.

The percentage of value added by the agriculture sector[21] in India has been declining and will be 15 per cent in 2023. A decline in this percentage is inevitable with economic development as the industrial and service sectors grow. But 44 per cent of India's labour force is in agriculture—the most in any sector—resulting in a low value added per unit of farm labour.

In contrast, only 24 per cent of the Chinese labour force is in agriculture, evidence of a more robust process of agricultural transformation.[22] While India's technology sector is a great pride of the country and is fuelled by the highly educated, the agriculture and low-end manufacturing[23] sectors have not served the less educated well in providing comparable improvements in the standard of living.

Indian development has also been lagging on the gender dimension. While India ranked 132 out of 191 countries in the UN's Human Development Index, in the Gender Development Index, which distils the gender gap in life expectancy, education, and income, it ranks even lower.[24]

Upper secondary attainment among women 25–34 years old is 18 per cent, less than half[25] the value for men. And post education outcomes are not encouraging for women either. Despite a recent uptick, the steady decline of already low participation of Indian women in the labour force has been a key concern[26] of the last fifteen years.

Disparities in the various dimensions discussed above inevitably manifest themselves in high inequality,[27] with the top 10 per cent of the population getting 57 per cent of the national income. Conquering the moon[28] coexists with one of the worst rates[29] of child malnutrition and stunting, with the Global Hunger Index ranking India 107 out of 121 countries.

Given these challenges, some have despaired that India cannot[30] be an economic superpower. Dwelling on these uncomfortable statistics need not derail India's aspirations to become a superpower but can rather clarify the tasks ahead.

Ensuring productive livelihoods and fostering a more even development of human capital can lead to economic, competitive, and strategic (both in terms of hard and soft power) advantages. Continued lack of opportunities, especially for the young, could lead to conflicts and chaos.

India's youth unemployment rate has hovered[31] around 22 per cent. The Arab Spring uprisings[32] of 2011—sparked and spread in large part by discontented youth—continue to be a reminder for countries that do not create meaningful economic and political opportunities for their young.

Moreover, India aspires to be a voice and inspiration for the Global South, and addressing human needs and generating broad-based development within the country will give India the moral authority to do so. Mahatma Gandhi's metric for development is still relevant in this regard: 'The true measure of any society can be found in how it treats its most vulnerable members.'

What can India do to become a superpower grounded in human capital? Narayana Murthy, the doyen of India's tech industry, said two decades ago: 'If you want to eradicate poverty, you don't do it by redistributing existing wealth; you have to create more wealth.'[33]

His advice still rings true as India moves to the next stage of development, going beyond the minimal standards of surpassing abject poverty and aiming for human thriving at a large scale. Augmenting India's human wealth can be the route to create more wealth for the country.

Political will, rather than a huge amount of resources or technical know-how, is needed to accomplish this. For a country that has mastered rocket science, the policy options should seem straightforward and centre around increasing human capital and productive opportunities for the many.

While the percentage of Indian GDP spent on education has been increasing after it hit a low[34] of around 3 per cent in 2006, it falls short of the 6 per cent previous commissions have recommended and is lower than the percentage spent by many developed and emerging economies. Investment in secondary education is lagging, and while primary education is universal, quality is lacking.[35]

Increased focus on access to secondary education, improving the quality of teachers, holding them accountable, and creatively using technologies can help address these problems. India's expenditure[36] on health, another crucial component of human capital, has also languished between 2 per cent and 3 per cent of GDP, half the value of China and the lowest among BRICS nations.

Vocational education[37] and training have always received second-grade treatment compared to general and higher education in India and, indeed, the world, both from the government and the public. The obsession with worthless[38] college degrees has resulted in the education system churning out graduates with unemployable skills, which not only short-changes the economy but also creates resentment among the youth who cannot find jobs.

The stated aim[39] of the National Education Policy of 2020 to take vocational education seriously is, therefore, welcome news. Fostering the growth of low-end manufacturing[40] (through improvements in infrastructure[41] and politically difficult labour reforms) that can absorb those without a college degree and those toiling in lower productivity agriculture and services, encouraging entrepreneurship at all levels to further enable inclusive growth, and doing all this while ensuring incentives at the high-end, growth-driving sectors do not suffer would be sound strategies to pursue.

Globalization played a big role in India's economic rise and poverty eradication.[42] Openness did not destroy domestic companies but made them stronger and less monopolistic. Imports[43] and FDI did not represent a new form of colonialism but diversified the country's input and industrial base. It is, therefore, important for India to remain open and increase investment in trade with other emerging economies.

The aim should be to ensure that the benefits of globalization are spread more evenly, which the human-capital-centric approach discussed here can facilitate. Being open is how India can care for the world, including addressing climate change and viewing openness as an opportunity to create jobs and new industrial sectors rather than as an impediment to development. The *Vasudhaiva Kutumbakam* (the world is one family) motto India adopted for the G20 meetings should inspire such a global stance.

While this has been said many times before, it now truly seems that India is at a crossroads. It can continue to grow at dizzying rates in an aggregate sense, and this growth will continue to eradicate abject poverty as it has in the last few decades. However, only inclusive growth—growth that is broad-based rather than concentrated in certain sectors, education levels and geographic areas—will lead to large-scale flourishing and improved well-being of large numbers of people.

The recurring theme in this essay has been to focus on the basics of development, even if they are not glamorous or headline-grabbing. Whether or not India can achieve this inclusive growth will determine whether it will become an economically, socially, and politically stable superpower or a plutocracy that lacks the participatory power of large numbers of its people and the legitimacy that comes with it.

Superpower status is not claimed; the world bestows it. India will receive this if it follows a human-capital-centric path of growth and development. Anything less would not do justice to India's founding principles and humanistic ideals.

7

Aspirational India Chases a $10 Trillion Dream

Sutanu Guru

Sometimes, anecdotal data can be as compelling as verifiable data. This one is about the driver employed by the author. Sanjay is paid Rs 20,000 a month. His wife Geeta spent more than a year honing her skills in a beauty parlour where she was paid a pittance. Now she works for Urban Clap, the online aggregator, and earns more than Rs 30,000 a month without breaking a sweat. Sanjay's father is a security guard in a mall and earns Rs 12,000 a month, while his mother works as a domestic help and earns about Rs 14,000 a month. Despite not having completed senior school, the family earns a combined monthly income of about Rs 75,000. Sanjay and Geeta have two sons who attend a 'convent' school and have already learnt to code. The family has no pretensions of being a middle class, but they are saving a significant amount of money.

Aspirational Indians

No doubt, this anecdotal example is not representative of all Indians. However, it does indicate two important things: first, except for some isolated rural areas, India now offers enough opportunities to even illiterate citizens and their families to permanently escape poverty. Second, for aspirational Indians acquiring skills and not being fixated on 'stable government or white-collar jobs' is the way forward as the economy targets to exceed the $10 trillion gross domestic product (GDP) mark by 2035. India was once a victim of a vicious cycle of low growth and high poverty. However, the country has now entered a virtuous cycle of high growth and low poverty. In fact, the term 'low poverty' is a misnomer. Independent organizations like the World Bank have released[1] data indicating that less than 15 per cent of Indians are poor. In 1991, when economic reforms were initiated, more than 50 per cent of Indians were classified as poor. By 2035, only about 3 per cent of Indians are expected to be categorized as poor.

Let us break it down into actual numbers. Anyone earning less than $2 a day is categorized as poor. Per capita income refers to the income of an Indian in a year. An Indian family (except for the educated and affluent elite minority) still consists of five members. So, a family is poor if their daily income is $10 per day. In other words, if a family earns less than Rs 800 a day or Rs 24,000 a month is poor. Effectively, as per the World Bank, about 90 per cent of Indians are no longer poor. The author would call a big majority of them aspirational Indians; citizens and families who have broken through poverty but still do not earn enough to be sure of future financial well-being. Almost all of them work in the so-called 'informal sector' or even as 'gig workers'. Many of them still do not earn enough to ensure a 'pension' when they leave the workforce. But, as they say in colloquial slang, they are getting there. By 2035, the per capita income of India in purchasing power parity terms will be about $15,000. The anecdotal example of driver Sanjay and his family shows how that will happen. India may never reach the levels of economic prosperity that the United States has achieved, nor can it match the sheer size of China's economy in the foreseeable future. Yet, given those two caveats, what India will achieve by 2035 will be remarkable and transform not just India but also the entire world.

Escape from South Asia

One of the most beneficial fallouts of the rise of India will not just be a permanent escape from the 'poverty-stricken third world country' trap; it will also be a permanent escape from the cage called 'South Asia' where Western academics, institutions, and foreign policy establishments have historically placed India. Till about a decade ago, whenever there was a conversation or debate about India, Pakistan would automatically be added. Till the 1990s, the US foreign policy establishment routinely bracketed India with Pakistan in terms of geopolitics. In fact, there were occasions when the US state department officials like the notorious Robin Raphael would hector India and even go on to claim that the accession of Jammu and Kashmir to India is disputed. Part of that legacy remains in Washington as it pampers the Pakistan military when it suits the strategic interests of Uncle Sam. However, a convergence of national interests means India and the US are now strategic partners. As the accompanying chart shows, Pakistan is rapidly becoming irrelevant to India. By the end of 2022, the value of exports from India was more than double the entire GDP of Pakistan. Although Pakistan will continue to try and bleed India with terror attacks, there is little that it can do to stop or even delay the rise of India towards a $10 trillion economy by 2035 (see Figure 7.1).

Figure 7.1: India's export versus Pakistan's GDP

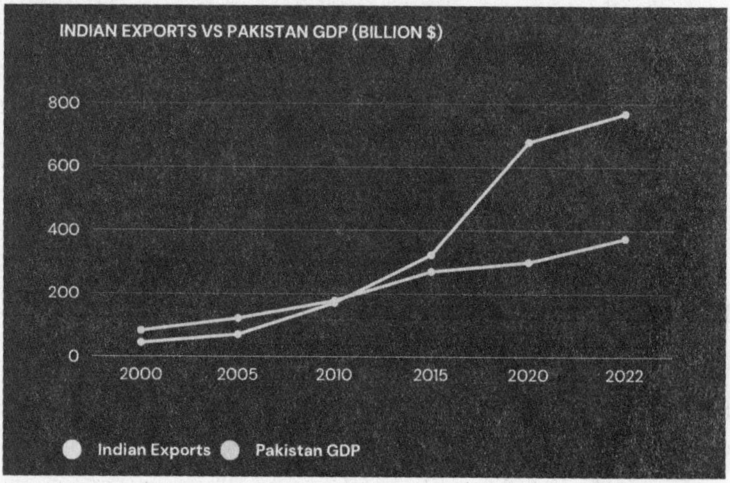

Pakistan will indeed become a pesky irritant. But make no mistake, China will remain a strategic threat and often a menace. Over the last seven decades, China has made it abundantly clear that it does not want friendship with India. Even when it was an extremely poor country, China nursed ambitions of being the sole dominant power in Asia, both economically and militarily. It has never shied away from 'putting India in its place', including the military humiliation in 1962.

Perhaps the only factor that can prevent or delay India's emergence as a $10 trillion economy by 2035 is a military conflict with China. To forestall that, India need not go on a military spending binge. Indian policymakers just need to send a message across to the autocratic regime in Beijing that a war with India will also be ruinous for the Chinese economy.

Over the last decade or so, the Indian establishment has, by and large, succeeded in sending that message. After all, no matter how autocratic and ambitious the rulers of China are, they do happen to be pragmatic and hard-nosed and would not risk calamity for a strategic aim that may not be achieved. India and China are not destined to be friends, but perhaps they can learn to live and let live.

Taxes and Poverty

As mentioned earlier, it is now widely believed that India has permanently left behind the vicious cycle of low growth and high poverty. The slogan 'Garibi Hatao' was once used to inspire hope for poverty reduction, but it ultimately proved to be empty. We should not forget that when the government led by the then prime minister P.V. Narasimha Rao dismantled the stifling socialist-cum-communist command and control structure of the Indian economy, more than 50 per cent of Indians lived in absolute poverty.

Although there was some change, it was not immediately visible for another decade or so. Since the times of Jawaharlal Nehru, governments have tried to implement policies to ameliorate poverty, mostly without success. One cannot doubt their intent, though questions on their competence do arise in hindsight. So, what has changed in the last three decades besides a more favourable policy environment for entrepreneurs to pursue their dreams?

Figure 7.2: Total central collection from 2000 to 2023

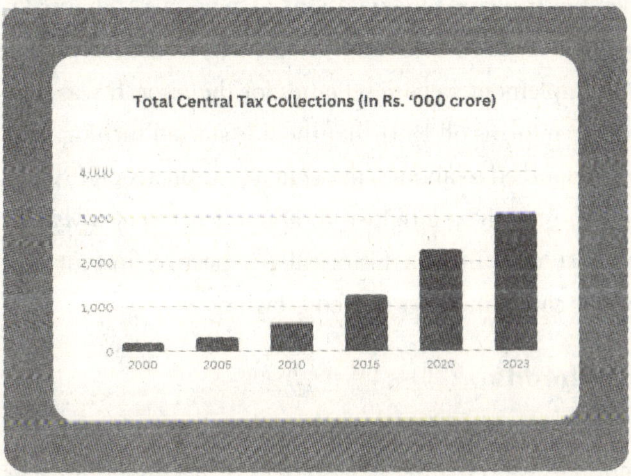

Source: Ministry of Finance

As Figure 7.2 indicates, it is all about money, or rather the government's tax revenues. Even if Indira Gandhi, who gave the call for 'Garibi Hatao', wanted to, her regime simply did not have the resources to help the poor through the empowering welfare schemes that we see nowadays in such abundance.

This was mainly due to a cycle of low growth and low income, which resulted in empty coffers for successive governments. Some governments tried to deficit finance their way to welfare, but this made things worse by creating high inflation and balance of payments issues. However, after the liberalization in 1991, the government coffers started swelling, and finally, there was money for welfare schemes.

It is important to keep one thing in mind here. Growing tax revenues are not the sole reason why poverty in India started declining at an accelerated pace in the last three decades. The reason is simple mathematics created by enabling policies. For decades after independence, GDP grew at an average 'Hindu rate of growth' of 3 per cent while the population too grew at an average rate of more than 3 per cent.

In effect, there was simply no growth in per capita income; a fact that condemned Indians to generations of poverty. Additionally, low GDP growth rates also implied a lack of resources (tax revenues) to implement welfare schemes for the poor. It was only post-economic reforms of 1991 that the tide started turning. The GDP growth doubled to about 6 per cent a year on average, while the population growth rate dipped to about 2 per cent a year or less. The effect was, from a historical perspective, instant and magical as per capita incomes started growing.

New Livelihoods

The real impact that enabling and liberal policies of the government had was creating new sources of livelihood for tens of millions of Indians. Just one example will show how powerful and transformational this impact has been. At the moment, Shreya Ghosal and Sunidhi Chauhan have become superstars when it comes to playback singing and live performances across the world. But no one would have heard of them were it not for private television channels, sponsored by corporate clients, promoting talent hunt shows that captured the imagination of tens of millions of viewers in the country.

Shreya and Sunidhi earn eight figures and more and can, by no stretch of the imagination, be touted as representative examples of the entertainment industry in India. But hundreds of thousands earn relatively stable and comfortable livelihoods thanks to the boom in the entertainment industry.

Prior to 1991, Indian families had very limited access to entertainment and news beyond what was offered by the government-run monopoly, Doordarshan, for whatever little entertainment and news it provided. In the 1980s, the government monopoly telecasted a host of popular shows made by private entrepreneurs that became immensely popular. But the number of stable livelihoods that were created by these popular shows was extremely limited, numbering maybe a few thousand in a country with a population of 600 million.

In 1991, the arrival of satellite TV in India changed the country's media landscape. Affluent Indians could access global channels like CNN, which broadcast live the aftermath of the Iraq invasion of Kuwait and the subsequent military action by a United States-led alliance.

But it was not until 1992 when Star TV Network entered India and triggered an explosion in cable TV viewership. Across every neighbourhood in India, small-time entrepreneurs raced to connect households with a cable TV connection at Rs 100 a month. Many were killed in turf wars that followed.

But eventually, cable TV became a stable industry with massive revenues. Livelihoods suddenly became a reality at two levels. The first was at the distribution end, where hundreds of thousands earned their livelihood by servicing tens of millions of cable-connected households (these would also become the first to offer wi-fi connections at home when the internet revolution arrived).

Then, there were hundreds of thousands of livelihoods generated in the production and supply of entertainment content. Within a few years, there were dozens of channels not just in Hindi, but also in a whole array of Indian languages. All of them had voracious and seemingly insatiable appetites for new content. Competition was fierce as consumers now had choices and were no longer solely dependent on the government-monopolized Doordarshan. This created not just avenues for Sunidhi and Shreya but also for hundreds of thousands of technicians, artists-cum-actors, make-up professionals, light and sound experts, singers, canteen and transport suppliers, insurance agents, and much more.

These professionals did not become millionaires. But they became the first of the newly rising breed called aspirational Indians who had grabbed the opportunities offered in a new India to permanently escape poverty. So much of new business also meant more tax revenue for the government. That helped the state finance welfare schemes that would help the unfortunate poor who could not benefit from all the new opportunities being created.

However, this path of economic growth and improved livelihood opportunities in India did have a big weakness. Almost all the new livelihood opportunities came from the services sector, which could not be enough to fulfil the job aspirations of such a large workforce that populates India. For a variety of reasons, mostly related to legacy and lingering aftereffects of a bureaucratic mindset, India was not blessed by a manufacturing revolution of the kind East Asian economies had gone through.

Make In India

If we take a quick look at the history of development over the last century or so, we can see a clear trend: when countries move from low-income to high-income, they transition from dependence on agriculture to manufacturing and then, eventually, services. This pattern has been observed in almost every successful country that has made the transition from poverty to prosperity. India is, perhaps, a unique country that has experienced a services sector evolution without achieving the same level of success in manufacturing.

Figure 7.3: India's rising clout in mobile phone manufacturing

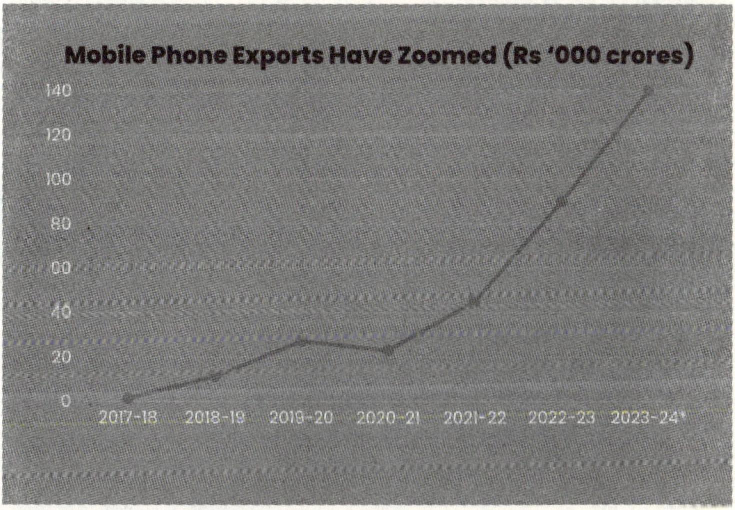

*Source: MOSPI. *2023–24 Projected.*

As mentioned earlier, one reason India has struggled to attract global investors to set up large manufacturing bases is due to legacy factors such as land and labour laws. Another reason is the virtually dysfunctional judicial system in which even simple matters like commercial arbitration can take almost a decade to resolve.

Not surprisingly, even Bangladesh has ready-made garments exports that are higher than India. Furthermore, Vietnam has emerged as the top choice for global investors as they seek to reduce their supply chain dependence on China. However, India has not completely failed at manufacturing, and there are isolated pockets of globally competitive excellence. For instance, India has, without doubt, emerged as one of the many manufacturing hubs for the automobile and auto components sector in the world, thanks to enabling policies. The key to success lies in the active encouragement and promotion of domestic entrepreneurs and companies by the state, which includes incentives such as tax breaks, cheap loans, and subsidized land. All countries that have succeeded in manufacturing have followed this approach, starting with Japan in the 1950s.

It is only in the last decade or so that policymakers in India have realized the value and power of domestic manufacturing. To promote and incentivize domestic manufacturing, the government has launched a production-linked incentive (PLI) scheme. There have been many critics of this policy. Yet, the government has persisted in its efforts. As students of economics would know, it takes about a decade at least for a manufacturing ecosystem to become established, stable, and thriving. Against that backdrop, the chart on exports of mobile phones manufactured in India clearly shows that success is possible (see Figure 7.3).

In the second decade of this century, there were just two factories manufacturing and assembling mobile phones in India.

Currently, there are more than 200 such factories. These factories not only generate direct jobs but also create an entire ecosystem of ancillary and support units, which provide livelihoods for many Indians.

The government has identified fourteen sectors to promote the PLI scheme. There is little doubt that these sectors will play a big role in India becoming a $10 trillion economy by 2035 and beyond. It is not necessary for all the fourteen identified sectors to become more successful than China in capturing global markets. What is more important is for them to become globally competitive. Exports will help, no doubt, as they will inevitably grow, as the example of mobile phones indicates. But India itself is the second-largest consumer market in the world. It would be a win-win if Indian companies that manufacture in India offer them to Indian consumers at globally competitive prices.

A Mindset Change

As pointed out, governments indeed play a vital role in pushing an economy towards relative prosperity. They implement enabling policies that have transformed India into a $4 trillion economy with a per capita income of about $8,000 in terms of purchasing power parity. As the economy has reached a path of a sustained annual GDP growth rate of 6 per cent to 7 per cent, the $10 trillion target for 2035 does not look elusive. But governments can do only so much. When nations transform, societies and social mores, too, need to transform.

One abiding obsession of Indians since independence has been getting a government job. Even now, more than a hundred thousand, including postgraduates, apply when jobs for peons in a government office are advertised. One reason for this is the stability of income that a government job offers.

The other reason has been the lucrative possibility of making a lot of money through bribes. However, both these reasons are changing. At the net level, government jobs are not growing. Besides, fiscal compulsions mean that even government employees now have to pay for their pensions, just like people in the private sector. The digital and internet revolutions also mean that the scope for 'bribes' is becoming lower with each passing year. In such a scenario, Indian families need to let go of this obsession with government jobs.

There is another reason for the urgent need to change mindsets. The digital revolution, big data, robotics, and AI are the next wave of the future, and they are intrinsically interlinked with 'unstable' jobs. Gig work will become increasingly more prevalent and widespread.

The traditional concepts of stable jobs will disappear except for a tiny fraction of the workforce. In such an event, the challenge for young Indians is to focus on skills that will enhance livelihood opportunities. To put it differently, Geeta, the wife of the author's driver, earns more as an Urban Clap self-employed professional than many MBAs. When India becomes a $10 trillion economy, those who understand this will flourish the most.

Part III

Imagining Priorities for India of 2050

8

Role of Caste and Gender in India's Economic Growth till 2050

Prerna Tambay and Pratap Tambe

India aims to become a superpower by 2050. To achieve this goal, the country must take various actions to ensure it becomes the best it can be from different perspectives. One such perspective is caste and gender. Caste is a uniquely Indian institution closely linked to gender, which has some specific Indian features but also shares multiple features with other countries. According to Dr Ambedkar, caste endogamy originated and is sustained through control over the marriage choices of women.

The citizens of oppressed castes include both men and women, while those who suffer from gender oppression are predominantly women. Empowering and enabling all women to progress will help reduce the influence of caste on the Indian economy and culture by providing them with more choices in marriage. In this essay, we will explore how caste affects India's progress towards becoming a global superpower and how this journey will impact both caste-oppressed and gender-oppressed individuals. We will provide recommendations that apply to both groups and discuss the intersectional nature of caste and gender. Finally, we will conclude with our suggestions for the way forward.

When some people in India talk about the country's glorious past as one of the wealthiest nations in the world, they often overlook the fact that this wealth and high-quality standard of living were not uniformly distributed. A vast underclass of people produced high-value goods and services that primarily benefited the rich and powerful rather than themselves. In contrast to the underclasses in Western nations, who rebelled and brought about revolutions and renaissances, the Indian underclass never rebelled, and there has never been a true Indian renaissance.

In India, the underclass had been conditioned to believe in the theory of karma since birth. This has rendered them incapable of rebelling against their fate. They believe that their current fate is the result of their past actions, and by doing good karma in their present life, they will be delivered in their next birth. On the other hand, the privileged believe that their current fate is the result of their past good karma. Although there have been a few attempts at rebellion and renaissance, caste is still a defining feature of what it means to be Indian or of Indian origin. It is correlated with many things in India and is an unfortunate reality of the country's past.

Although caste originally originated in Hinduism, it has now become deeply rooted among all Indians and Indian-origin people of all religions, irrespective of where they are currently based. Caste differences can be seen in various aspects such as house locations, clothes, language, beliefs, practices, food habits, behaviours, festivals, or saints. The underclass mentioned above mostly refers to the Shudra castes, and outcastes (including Tribals) are referred to as oppressed castes. In contrast, the Vaishyas castes, Kshatriya castes, and Brahmin castes are referred to as privileged castes. When we envision India's glorious future of India as a superpower, it is natural to question whether we will return to becoming a prosperous but unequal nation. India's current trajectory is raising concerns about this issue.

What are the alternatives to a caste-based unequal socio-economic system in a prosperous Indian superpower?

Communism of the purest kind was tried in Russia and China, but they have since transitioned to 'somewhat capitalistic' societies. Since 1991, India has been following a capitalist path. The broad consensus seems that markets are better in most areas, and democratic governments are needed where markets fail. While there may be local imperfections and no perfect solutions, many countries, including India, have a combination of capitalism and democracy. India's increasing liberalization, privatization, and globalization are likely to continue.

Although it is uncertain whether a rollback will continue, the chances of it happening are low despite the efforts of the Naxalites and a significant number of socialist-leaning voters in parts of India. So, we will not engage with those possibilities and instead focus on the impact of caste and gender in an economy and country governed by democratic governments overseeing markets.

Let us explore how caste affects democracy and markets, how democracy and markets affect caste, and what this means for India as a potential superpower. The two-tumbler system in rural tea stalls, still prevalent in many parts of India, illustrates the cost burden that caste generates for businesses in an economy. Through means like this, caste causes cost burdens for all goods and services in India because caste norms and networks significantly affect individual (and potentially business-level) economic decisions and outcomes in India.

Caste-based social networks can have both positive and negative influences on social mobility. After India gained independence, reservations aided by caste networks have helped to reduce disparities in education, occupation, income, and access to public resources among different caste groups. When these differences drop dramatically towards a statistical zero, the inefficiencies that caste causes in the Indian economy will decrease to a statistical zero. Until this happens, one can be sure that caste will continue constraining India's economic growth. Based on the empirical evidence, there is still a long distance to travel before India reaches this happy destination.

So, the question we need to ask is, what policies do we need to create to reduce the differences in attainments between caste groups to almost a statistical zero, assuming that talent is equally distributed across them? This is achievable by enabling and developing each caste group's talent to its fullest potential. Reservations supported by caste networks can help in this process. Reservation in undergraduate and postgraduate education in publicly funded institutions has reduced the differences in attainments between caste groups. However, resistance to reservations still exists in some specialized courses/institutions and research courses/institutions, as reservation is considered a zero-sum game.

If we increase the number of reservations for the oppressed caste, it will reduce the number of seats available for the privileged unless we create more seats. However, creating additional seats requires investment. Therefore, to address the impact of caste on India's economic growth, we need to attract investors, including the government, to invest in high-quality educational institutions and seats. These investors must be open to reservations because there is strong resistance to reservations in privately funded institutions.

Despite pledging to increase the allocations to education to 6 per cent before the 2014 elections, the Modi government has only been able to allocate an average of 0.44 per cent to the education sector since then. This has resulted in significant pressure on publicly funded academic institutions to raise money through consultancy, alumni, and public donations, as well as monetizing research. The institutions are being forced to increase the number of seats without a commensurate increase in governmental funding. This pressure is having a direct and indirect impact on the mental health of both staff and students and has led to a rise in the number of student suicides. There is a high degree of pressure on educational staff to generate more funds, and students from oppressed caste backgrounds face prejudice to finance their education and complete their courses on time.

The challenges faced by oppressed caste students in academic institutions are already high, and prejudice and pressure only exacerbate them further. These students struggle to compete for grades, internships, jobs, etc. Increasing public funding can help reduce the pressure and make it sustainable to increase the number of available seats. However, the Indian government cannot invest without growth in tax collection, which requires economic growth in India. If the Indian economy continues to grow over the coming decades due to the deployment of the Indian demographic dividend to value-generating sectors, it is feasible to expect that the government will be able to invest in creating more high-quality and high-quantity educational institutions and seats. This will help deploy the demographic dividend to high value-generating ends and create a virtuous loop. Although this is one of the most critical recommendations, it is not the easiest to implement.

To initiate a virtuous loop requires changing the priorities and increasing the governmental spending on the educational sector (primary, secondary, and tertiary). The business case for this investment to generate a more equitable distribution of education and economic growth among various caste groups is very strong. This investment will enable more students from oppressed castes to complete their primary, secondary, and tertiary education and secure jobs that match their capabilities. This will allow them to make their maximum contribution to

India's economic growth and reap the benefits of it, ultimately narrowing the achievement gap between different caste groups.

Before discussing the business case for the broader economy, let us discuss the business case for the educational sector. Governments have increased the number of seats for oppressed castes in the past few decades, but they have not prioritized investments to reduce the number of dropouts among them. Investing in improving the student experience by implementing solid policies and actions against caste discrimination on campus, improving teaching-learning methodologies and management, providing scholarships and loans, and enhancing academic and non-academic support through mentoring and online support from alumni can have a strong business case. Improving the mental health of all students, including oppressed caste students, through an all-encompassing approach like the UK University Mental Health Charter can also be beneficial. At the very least, these investments can help improve outcomes like on-time course completion, average grades, getting jobs after completion, and performing well in those jobs. At the most, they can unleash the creativity and motivation of oppressed caste students to deploy their unique lived experiences and perspectives in classrooms and campuses to improve the quality of thinking and research and improve campus life in general. Some of these improvements are of direct material value to the management of academic institutions. Although improving campus diversity takes effort, it generates value.

It is essential to reduce the number of students dropping out of school and committing suicide, particularly among the marginalized and oppressed castes. It is equally crucial to support talented students from diverse backgrounds who face various challenges in acquiring high-quality primary, secondary, and tertiary education and help them acquire respected positions in government, public, and private sectors. This is necessary for several reasons, including inspiring other students to persist despite the prejudice and pressure and providing good role models who demonstrate the feasibility of breaking away from the respective circles of common fate.

Parents often push their children and support them to achieve great success in life. This is especially true if they believe in their children's abilities to make it big. In order to become a better superpower, India needs to increase upward social mobility. To achieve this goal, talented students from oppressed castes should receive more attention than they are currently getting. Their success is a vital metric of India's transformation towards becoming a more equitable superpower. Moreover, these students think differently, ask different questions, and generate unique values that others cannot develop. Therefore, it is important to increase the diversity of campuses to generate richer student experiences and help India become a better country. On campuses, we have had too much of the same thinking for far too long. Connections forged across caste groups on campuses can persist beyond the campus and generate value across lives and careers. Talented students from oppressed castes can create new value in the government, public, and private sectors.

As the two-tumbler example illustrates, the Indian government, public, and private sectors serve some castes better than others. Caste strongly correlates with consumption patterns and many different economic dimensions in India. The business models, products/services, and distribution strategies targeting specific caste groups differ from those targeting multiple/all caste groups. Improving the caste diversity of employees enables corporates to serve different caste groups better and helps enhance the design of products/services and distribution strategies to meet the needs of varying caste groups. This is true in physical/intangible products and services, including insurance and finance. As more and more talented oppressed caste students join jobs and start new businesses, they will help meet the needs of Indians better than a less caste-diverse set of employees and employers can.

Improving caste diversity at all levels in the government, public, and private sectors can lead to sustainable economic growth. However, this will enhance sustainable economic growth. But this is simply the base level of value that talented oppressed caste students can generate if given an opportunity. The first generation of beneficiaries of reservation managed to make significant progress and give better education to their children, many of whom have done well, even in the private sector and at senior levels. Some second-generation beneficiaries hide their caste, which prevents the role model benefits, but others have been open about their caste identities, creating positive role models. The third-generation beneficiaries are more optimistic and ambitious, with high expectations for themselves. As someone well-connected to talented, oppressed caste people everywhere, I am very happy to see this. I have a friend who I presented an award for topping his university and who founded a company that sold for 150 million GBP.

He now invests some of his money to support other oppressed caste entrepreneurs. The increasing number of second- and third-generation entrepreneurs and the quality of their enterprises indicate that India is moving in the right direction. Based on personal experience, I know that oppressed caste professionals and entrepreneurs have different values, priorities, questions, and propositions. They often face rejection and a lack of opportunities, which naturally gravitates them towards more challenging opportunities. They are better suited to greenfield, disruptive businesses. While literature suggests there is a survival bias among them, those who succeed well in professions and business tend to be more resilient and sustain at senior levels longer than others. Oppressed caste-owned businesses that survive the initial few years tend to maintain and grow well.

Herein lies my final and most crucial prescription for India. Find and invest in the best talent among the oppressed castes. Find them young, coach them, and prepare them for academia, professions, and business. By selecting and managing the best talent effectively, we can produce many award-winning academics, professionals, and entrepreneurs. In fact, if we even develop a few billionaires among them, that will pay for India's investments. This is because oppressed caste professionals and entrepreneurs typically invest their wealth in helping others from their community. They will also pay more taxes, which will help kickstart the virtuous cycle of growth. To achieve this, we need to promote organizations like the Karta and Eklavya. Impact investors should also invest in long-duration accelerators that can help identify and invest in talented individuals from oppressed castes, enabling them to actualize their full potential and create value for India.

If this is not done, we will continue to see many talented individuals not reach their potential. It is important to create better policies and investment sources, such as venture capital and project finance, to allow oppressed caste professionals and entrepreneurs to build large businesses in disruptive technology areas, where they often have natural advantages. This is the best way to accelerate India's journey to becoming a more equal society where everyone has the opportunity to succeed.

We have focused on caste, which is an institution that affects both men and women. Now, we will reflect on the role of gender oppression in India's journey to becoming a good superpower from a gender-oppressed perspective. In recent decades, the participation of women in education, employment, and enterprise has increased but there is still room for improvement.

The reservation system offered to women in India reflects the global consensus on improving gender representation in all sectors. Indian women continue to break new ground every year.

An increasing number of laws, policies, and practices are being put in place to enable and recognize the importance of women's role in the Indian economy, including and beyond housework, childcare, and caregiving. Despite the progress made in gender-specific facilities to enhance the degrees of freedom experienced by women in education, employment, and enterprise, significant constraints still apply to Indian women. Each woman must navigate through complex contexts in families, workplaces, and marketplaces to actualize her potential freedom and progress. The interactional aspect of caste and gender is particularly important since it offers a way to transform India rapidly.

Inter-caste marriages between people from different castes have increased over the years and reflect the growing freedom of women across caste groups. Caste is an institution sustained through endogamy. Increasing inter-caste marriages between men and women of similar attainments weaken caste and strengthen cross-caste group bonds. Such couples tend to work harder and be more successful since they tend to have weaker caste ties on both sides. This is better for Indian economic growth on its own as well as through reducing the burden that the two-tumbler type of systems causes to the Indian economy.

Unfortunately, many thought leaders from oppressed castes tend to focus more on identifying problems rather than coming up with practical solutions, as this essay attempts to do so. There are numerous articles, columns, and books that highlight the issues faced by the oppressed castes, but rarely do they offer concrete and practical solutions. Moreover, when solutions are proposed, they often require government intervention and funding to help the oppressed castes. However, none of these proposals discuss where the necessary funds will come from, especially as the role of government is expected to shrink while the role of markets increases.

It is necessary for thought leaders from oppressed castes to find ways like those proposed in this essay to achieve the development of oppressed caste people while generating tangible new value for India. If more talented individuals from oppressed castes embrace this type of thinking and are given opportunities to solve problems using their unique viewpoints, India will rapidly become a much stronger global superpower.

9

Role of Science, Technology, and Innovation in India's Development at 2047

Hemang Jani

'Science, technology, and innovation are not merely words for us; they are the very lifeblood of a New India.'

—Prime Minister Narendra Modi

Bharat has a glorious history and tradition of respecting scientists and innovators. India has always given very high significance to science and technology in its endeavour to improve the quality of life of its citizens. Scientists from ancient times, such as Aryabhata, Sushrut, Charak, or Patanjali, are still revered, and in contemporary times, scientists are held in very high respect in the country. India's youthful demography aspires to be scientists and innovators and these aspirations are bound to prove India's greatest strength in the future.

The above trend will accentuate further as India crosses the $5 trillion gross domestic product (GDP) mark by 2027 to become the third-largest economy in the world. There is a growing appreciation in India's leadership that the additional growth beyond $5 trillion will require significant innovation to boost the productivity of land, labour, and capital. Prime Minister Modi is guiding this push for innovation by continuously encouraging, motivating, and easing innovation in India. Leading from the front, he has always consulted scientists in all discussions, including those on the fight against COVID-19, food security, new education policy, 5G launch, green hydrogen mission, fintech, and many more. No day goes without him meeting at least one scientist or an innovator at his office. India's modern leadership, respectful and aware of the importance of scientific development, is ready to seize opportunities to further India's march to become a technology powerhouse.

As India's economy grows, so will its importance as a geopolitical player. However, India's national power and ability to project power beyond its borders will depend on its science, technology, and innovation leadership. Global technology giants such as Google, Apple, Microsoft, ASML, TSMC, Samsung, and Huawei have provided unparalleled global influence to their respective host countries. India's innovators and scientists have global reputations, and most technology companies hire talent from India. Indian scientists have worked on large inter-governmental projects such as CERN, ITER, and LIGO. In the future, India will surely leverage its international cooperation and diplomacy to further its scientific goals.

Every nation strives to improve the lives of its citizens. Since the Industrial era, nations with higher levels of technology have been able to do so. Science, technology, and innovation (STI) play a major role in any nation's economic and social growth. They directly or indirectly affect every sector of the economy and help create a healthy, educated, and prosperous society. India is no exception.

In the history of independent India until recently, the most notable science- and technology-backed growth experience was the 'Green Revolution', which transformed the agriculture and animal husbandry sector in the country, ensuring the much-needed food security at that time. Similarly, the recent achievement by India putting 'Chandrayan' on the moon also traces its roots back to India's space programme, which started in the 1960s. Since then, India has achieved much progress in various sectors, such as pharmaceutical and chemicals, biotechnology, and information technologies.

Currently, we are living in the age of artificial intelligence. Since the middle of the twentieth century, scientists have been improving machines to mimic humans in every task. Humans thought and machines executed at the beginning of the twentieth century; machines will think, and humans will execute by the end of the century. This will also change how nations plan and improve the lives of their citizen. Artificial intelligence will have an exponentially bigger impact than the invention of the steam engine had on the Industrial era! It will affect every aspect of life in ways one cannot imagine. With its huge talent in computer programming, India is ideally situated to take full advantage of this revolution.

India's national science, technology, and innovation strategy will play an important role in improving the lives of its citizens as well as its global position during the twenty-first century. India's economic growth was propelled by the opening of the economy in 1991. However, it also provided impetus to a silent technology revolution in the area of information technology services. India became the factory of first transcriptions and servicing and later coding and programming for the West. This has set the foundation for the country's next phase of technology-led growth.

However, the road ahead is not as easy as it was until now. It requires more than the human capital involved in the IT era growth; it requires better planning, broader vision, and deeper investment. So far, human intelligence has created technology, and now technology is creating human intelligence and technology! Almost every facet of life will be redefined by the advent of artificial intelligence. Only those nations that have invested in it early on will be able to drive the growth of their economy and the prosperity of people; the rest will have to follow suit. In this era, an ecosystem approach to creating an innovative society would be advantageous. India will need to continue to evolve its education policy, upgrade its bureaucracy to continuously improve ease of innovation, maintain and further deepen aspirations in its youth for technical education, improve ease of doing business to assist commercialization of technology, and continuously support a harmonious external environment to maintain its access to technology. India needs BEST (Bharat's Ecosystem for Science and Technology) as it aspires for the best for its citizens and the world.

If one surveys the current landscape of India's science and technology ecosystem, three aspects stand out: people, infrastructure, and policy. As far as people are concerned, India has a comparative advantage, given its population's sheer size and the investments it made in science, technology, engineering, and mathematics (STEM) education. India today produces 25 per cent of the world's STEM talent. It produces the largest number of engineers, particularly software engineers, in the world. More than 260 medical colleges have been opened from 2014 to 2022. To quote the prime minister, 'In the last eight years, one university and two colleges have been opened every week in the country.' A large number of Indian students further pursue STEM education outside India, particularly in the US, Canada, Australia, and other advanced countries. Overall, India has a considerable advantage as far as the available talent is concerned, and this advantage is bound to grow with increasing investments in education under the new education policy and continued positive demographic trends.

India also enjoys a reasonably robust science and technology infrastructure. According to some studies, India has about 450 centrally funded laboratories that conduct research in diverse areas such as space, nuclear energy, biotechnology, earth science, and agriculture. Above these, there are innumerable laboratories operated by state governments and academia. The output of these laboratories has been improving over time, and some, such as those in nuclear and space, have surely added to the national strength and prestige. While India boasts of a robust public sector research and development (R&D) ecosystem, its private sector has traditionally been reluctant to invest in R&D due to the long gestation period required for commercially advantageous outcomes. This, fortunately, is changing, and certain sectors such as Pharma, IT, electronics, and automobiles have been seeing increasing private sector investments in R&D. Prime Minister Modi has taken a particular interest in increasing budgets allotted to R&D and all the major scientific ministries, including the Department of Atomic Energy, Department of Space, Department of Science and Technology, have upgraded laboratory infrastructure in the facilities managed by them.

India has also done relatively well in terms of upgrading its policies on innovation in various sectors. Last year, a new space policy was announced, making India one of the most liberalized jurisdictions to research outer space activities. Similarly, India has upgraded its policies to improve the ease of researching areas such as telecom, unmanned aerial vehicles, autonomous vehicles, AI, defence, and geospatial. The government has also been encouraging the capacity building of India's senior bureaucracy to understand technology-related policymaking better through a capacity-building commission. Overall, India is no longer lagging behind advanced nations in the ease of doing research and innovation and in some sectors, it even has a lead. From Chandrayaan-2 etching India's name on the lunar surface to our prowess in developing vaccines during the pandemic, science and technology have powered our national aspirations. They have woven a web of 5G connectivity, propelled us into the digital age, and fuelled our march towards becoming a $5 trillion economy by 2026–27.

But our journey does not end here. In a world poised on the cusp of non-linear growth, fuelled by artificial intelligence, biotechnology, and renewable energy, the true heroes will be those who embrace science, technology, and innovation. We must move beyond linear progress, forging new pathways for development that are inclusive, sustainable, and responsive to global challenges like climate change and healthcare disparities.

This future hinges on nurturing young minds, fostering a culture of entrepreneurship, and ensuring equitable access to the fruits of these advancements. Let us empower every child, every village, and every corner of our nation to tap into this vibrant innovation ecosystem. Remember, it is not just about building rockets; it is about building a brighter tomorrow for all.

Let us leverage the power of science, technology, and innovation to rewrite the world order, not with dominance but with collaboration and compassion. Let us become stewards of a future where prosperity is shared and progress knows no bounds. Together, let us propel India and, with it, the world towards a truly incredible future.

This age of technology is parallel to India's growth story and opportunity ready to be tapped into. Let us seize it with both hands, guided by the light of science, the spark of technology, and the spirit of boundless innovation. The path that unfolds before us is paved with the remarkable strides we have made in the past decade. Just ten years ago, our mobile internet penetration was a mere 8 per cent; today, it stands at over 70 per cent. We have launched 104 satellites, placing us among the top four spacefaring nations. Our start-up ecosystem, once nascent, now boasts over 80,000 unicorns, with innovations reaching the farthest corners of the country. Remember the darkness of COVID-19? In record time, we developed two indigenous vaccines and administered over 2 billion doses, showcasing our strength in medical research. We have also tripled our solar power capacity in renewable energy, establishing ourselves as a global leader in solar panel production. Our prowess in IT and software services is unrivalled, making us the world's back office.

However, challenges remain. Bridging the digital divide, fostering deeper research in cutting-edge fields like quantum computing, and nurturing scientific talent requires unwavering focus. To achieve this, we must prioritize public-private partnerships, encourage cross-disciplinary research, and create an environment where every innovator feels empowered to take flight. The future's horizon beckons. We are developing indigenous fighter jets, aiming for a manned space mission, and paving the way for self-driving cars. Imagine telemedicine reaching the remotest villages, precision agriculture boosting farmer incomes, and artificial intelligence-powered solutions tackling our environmental challenges. This potential ignites our spirit, the promise that propels us forward.

As the clock strikes midnight on 15 August 2047, India will not just be a nation draped in the golden cloak of independence; she will be a vibrant kaleidoscope, each facet gleaming with the brilliance of scientific prowess and boundless innovation. Imagine lunar footprints etched by Indian boots, a testament to a nation audacious enough to waltz with the stars. In this cosmic ballet, let us not forget the tireless steps of ISRO, our vanguard in space exploration, who will now dance with private partners and young stargazers.

Picture cities humming with the silent symphony of intelligent infrastructure, where self-driving cars glide along data-woven roads, and homes morph into havens of comfort, seamlessly synced with technological whispers. This vibrant orchestra extends to satellites dancing in the celestial waltz, launched not just by ISRO's mighty hand but by the nimble steps of agile start-ups, fuelled by the agency's knowledge and a shared dream of conquering the cosmos.

Healthcare will transcend its current form, embracing the magic of CRISPR to rewrite the very code of life and artificial intelligence to diagnose maladies before they flicker into existence. Here, too, ISRO's role remains pivotal, partnering with healthcare giants to beam down telemedicine to remote villages, bridging the digital divide and ensuring the healing touch of technology reaches every corner of our nation. Classrooms will become vibrant with the thrill of personalized learning, nurtured by immersive platforms and AI tutors, who tailor education to the unique tapestry of each mind. And here, ISRO's satellites will become celestial teachers, beaming down educational content to the farthest corners, ensuring every child gets a chance to reach for the stars, both metaphorical and literal.

This vision is not a sterile playground of technology; it is the soul of Prime Minister Modi's *panchpran* woven into the fabric of society. *Sabka saath*, the inclusivity, ensures the fruits of progress reach every corner, every life. ISRO, once a bastion of state-owned marvels, now opens its doors to private innovators, ensuring every dreamer can contribute to the nation's spacefaring saga. *Sabka vikas*, the development, is measured not just in GDP graphs but in the smiles of empowered farmers, women's confident strides, and every child's boundless potential.

ISRO, with its weather and agricultural data satellites, will guide farmers towards bountiful harvests, ensuring food security and prosperity for all.

This journey will not be without its challenges. Resource mobilization must be strategic, ethical considerations addressed with foresight, and the potential displacement of jobs navigated with compassion. But with each obstacle overcome, our resolve will only harden, and our spirit will only brighten. For in 2047, India will not just be a nation of a billion dreams; it will be an orchestra of those dreams taking flight, powered by the engines of science, technology, and innovation. It will be a new India, not just built on the echoes of freedom but on the promise of a future where every life, every corner, and every aspiration shines with the brilliance of a thousand suns.

This symphony of progress will require every citizen to be a conductor, composing a future where prosperity is shared and progress knows no bounds. Together, we will propel India and, with it, the world towards a truly incredible future. This is not just a vision; it is a clarion call, a thunderous echo urging our nation to reach beyond the stars and build a tomorrow worthy of our boundless potential.

Let the engines roar, let the innovation blaze, and let the future unfold. The time to dream is now, the time to build is upon us. Welcome to new India, a nation where science, technology, and innovation are not just words but the very heartbeat of a glorious future. And in this vibrant tapestry, ISRO will remain a constant thread, weaving together the dreams of seasoned scientists and young start-up visionaries, propelling our nation towards an era where the sky is not the limit but the launchpad.

The tapestry of India's future is woven in every lab, classroom, and start-up garage. Let us be the generation that weaves it with the golden threads of science, the silver threads of technology, and the vibrant threads of innovation. So let the symphony begin, let the constellations be our audience, and let the dance of progress, fuelled by collaboration and shared ambition, lead us to a future brighter than a thousand supernovas!

India's start-up ecosystem has been growing at a dizzying pace, although not uniformly across all sectors. There is a need for additional focus on emerging areas such as quantum and artificial intelligence, wherein other countries have progressed quite well over the last two decades. The top five nations generally have a significantly larger number of start-ups and higher total funding across most sectors compared to India. However, India has shown strong performance in sectors like clean energy, food security, and agriculture, with many start-ups and significant funding. Continued support for renewable energy, energy efficiency, and clean technology start-ups can further accelerate India's transition to a low-carbon economy. On the other hand, sectors like artificial intelligence, quantum computing, and robotics in India have room for significant growth in both start-up numbers and funding.

While India's current number of start-ups and funding in quantum computing is relatively small, the global market for quantum computing is projected to reach $1 trillion by 2030. India could capitalize on its strong STEM talent and research base to lead in this emerging field. India's National Quantum Mission is a right and timely step in this direction. Although India has a growing number of artificial-intelligence start-ups, the sector still has significant potential for further growth. Funding can be directed towards specific sub-sectors such as healthcare artificial intelligence, agricultural artificial intelligence, and artificial intelligence for manufacturing to address India's specific needs. Similarly, the Indian robotics market is expected to reach $7 billion by 2025, driven by automation in manufacturing, healthcare, and agriculture. Increased funding could support the development of robots tailored to India's unique challenges and opportunities. India's growing digital economy and increasing cyber threats make cybersecurity a crucial sector. More start-ups focusing on innovative security solutions for critical infrastructure, financial services, and healthcare can be encouraged. Food security and agriculture are crucial for India's food security and rural development. Funding start-ups developing innovative solutions for sustainable agriculture, precision farming, and post-harvest management can enhance the country's food security and create rural livelihoods.

Riding on the success of Startup India 1.0, Startup India 2.0 could focus on fostering more collaboration between start-ups, investors, research institutions, and government agencies to create a vibrant and supportive ecosystem for innovation. Encourage start-ups that address India's specific challenges and opportunities, such as healthcare access, education infrastructure, and financial inclusion. Provide funding and mentorship to early-stage start-ups to overcome the 'valley of death' and increase the chances of success, an area that remains under-addressed and often abused by big funders to squeeze the valuations. STEM education and training programmes need immediate focus on creating a skilled workforce for the emerging technology sectors. Unlike the dot com era, the efforts required by the industry to reskill or upskill the young workforce will be significantly higher if not addressed through the education ecosystem.

India's research and development scene boasts a promising outlook fuelled by significant investments and a balanced sectoral focus. Ranking eighth globally in gross expenditure on research and development (GERD) spending, India pours resources into crucial areas such as natural sciences, engineering and technology, and agricultural sciences. This diversified approach translates to advancements in healthcare, infrastructure, and food security, the cornerstones of national progress. Notably, private sector participation is burgeoning, with its share in GERD funding on the rise (see Table 9.1). This growing confidence in India's research ecosystem bodes well for future innovation and economic growth. However, bridging the gap between public and private funding remains challenging, and targeted incentives could unlock even greater potential in India's R&D landscape.

Table 9.1: Top ten GERD countries

Rank	Country	GERD ($ billion)	% of GDP
1	United States	765	3.11%
2	China	572	2.40%
3	Japan	429	3.22%
4	Germany	390	3.19%
5	South Korea	251	4.40%
6	United Kingdom	201	2.47%
7	France	190	2.54%
8	**India**	**162**	**2.62%**
9	Italy	145	1.45%
10	Canada	131	1.84%

While public funding remains dominant, the private sector's share in GERD funding is steadily increasing. This indicates growing private sector interest and confidence in India's research ecosystem. Encouraging further private sector investment through incentives and collaborative research programmes could be beneficial. Converting research advancements into commercial applications remains a significant challenge in the public sector. More focus on bridging the gap between research and industry could create innovative products and services, boosting economic growth. While India's sectoral focus is diverse, further strengthening areas such as information and communication technologies (ICT), social sciences, and humanities could be valuable. These sectors are crucial for addressing contemporary challenges and fostering social progress. See Table 9.2.

Table 9.2: GERD by sectors and share of public versus private share

Rank	Country	GERD ($ billion)	Top sectors (%)	Public share (%)	Private share (%)
1	USA (NSF data)	811.5	Health sciences: 27.9%	32.5	67.5
			Natural sciences: 26.4%	18.2	81.8
			Engineering and technology: 22.1%	12.3	87.7
2	China (limited data)	491.2	Natural sciences: 32.5%	70.2	29.8
			Engineering and technology: 30.3%	58.6	41.4
			Social sciences and humanities: 15.2%	86.4	13.6
3	Japan (RISTEX data)	312.2	Natural sciences: 34.4%	34.1	65.9
			Engineering and technology: 33.5%	18.6	81.4
			Health sciences: 16.8%	42.5	57.5
4	Germany (BMWF data)	151.5	Engineering and technology: 29.5%	27.8	72.2
			Natural sciences: 27.2%	33.5	66.5
			Life sciences: 18.5%	43.2	56.8
5	South Korea (NSTI data)	101.2	Engineering and technology: 34.4%	25.4	74.6
			Natural sciences: 25.9%	32.1	67.9
			Information and communication technologies: 16.9%	11.8	88.2

Rank	Country	GERD ($ billion)	Top sectors (%)	Public share (%)	Private share (%)
6	United Kingdom (BEIS data)	86.4	Health sciences: 28.9%	38.7	61.3
			Natural sciences: 23.7%	25.4	74.6
			Engineering and technology: 19.5%	19.2	80.8
7	France (ANR Data)	81.6	Health sciences: 27.5%	35.2	64.8
			Natural sciences: 24.0%	28.7	71.3
			Engineering and technology: 17.3%	19.8	80.2
8	**India (DST Data)**	**76.5**	**Natural sciences: 32.5%**	**60.2**	**39.8**
			Engineering and technology: 29.2%	**44.1**	**55.9**
			Agricultural sciences: 17.6%	**81.3**	**18.7**
9	Italy (ISTAT data)	58.5	Natural sciences: 29.7%	35.7	64.3
			Engineering and technology: 24.4%	24.6	75.4
			Life sciences: 17.2%	40.5	59.5
10	Canada (STC Data)	53.6	Health sciences: 30.3%	35.9	64.1
			Natural sciences: 27.8%	28.3	71.7
			Engineering and technology: 24.0%	20.3	

To match the private sector's GERD spending of the top nations, India needs a strategic approach to R&D investments This approach should be two-pronged: first, direct investment in sectors of high importance and second, building a supporting ecosystem that allows the private sector to grow its R&D systems.

India already has a strong IT sector, but further investment in areas like artificial intelligence, machine learning, cybersecurity, and quantum computing could unlock significant potential. India's pharmaceutical industry is robust, but domestic R&D needs a boost to compete globally. Investment in areas such as drug discovery, precision medicine, and biopharmaceuticals could be crucial. India's manufacturing sector is growing but needs to upgrade to compete in advanced manufacturing and adopt technologies like robotics, automation, and additive manufacturing. India's ambitious clean energy goals require further R&D in renewable energy sources such as solar, wind, and hydrogen, along with energy storage and grid technologies. India's large agricultural sector faces challenges like climate change and resource scarcity. Investing in precision agriculture, genetic engineering, and sustainable agricultural practices could be critical. While focusing on applied research for immediate economic benefits, India should not neglect basic research in fundamental sciences, which provides the foundation for future innovations.

Offering tax breaks, subsidies, and other financial incentives can encourage private companies to invest more in R&D. Developing a skilled workforce in STEM fields and attracting global talent through initiatives such as research fellowships and talent visa programmes are crucial. Ensuring robust IP protection fosters innovation and attracts private investment. Simplifying regulations and approval processes for R&D projects can reduce bureaucracy and encourage private participation. Building strong collaboration between universities, research institutions, and private companies can create a synergistic ecosystem for R&D. Encouraging start-ups and creating a vibrant innovation ecosystem can drive private sector R&D and generate new ideas. Investing in research infrastructure, including labs, equipment, and data centres, is crucial to support the R&D activities of the private sector.

Numerous studies have found a positive correlation between GERD and GDP in the long term. Increased R&D investment leads to technological advancements, innovation, and productivity gains, which can drive economic growth. Several confounding factors affect the relationship between GERD and GDP. Economic growth can also increase R&D spending, creating a two-way relationship. While factors like education levels, infrastructure, and institutional quality also play significant roles in economic growth, making it hard to isolate the impact of GERD alone. The type of R&D is key to growth. Investments in basic research may not have immediate economic benefits but can lay the foundation for future innovations. Conversely, applied research and development directly focused on commercial applications can have a more immediate impact on GDP. See Table 9.3.

Table 9.3: Author's calculations of potential increase in India's GERD if it were to grow at the average rate of the top five countries and reverse the ratio of public to private investments by 2047

Country	GERD year 2022 ($ billion)	Moderate growth scenario year 2047	High growth scenario year 2047
USA	765	1.8–2 trillion	3–4 trillion
China	572	1.2–1.4 trillion	2–3 trillion
Japan	429	600–700 billion	800–900 billion
Germany	390	550–600 billion	700–800 billion
South Korea	251	500–600 billion	700–800 billion
UK	201	400–500 billion	600–700 billion
France	190	350–450 billion	500–600 billion
India	162	500–700 billion	800–1 trillion

Focusing on R&D in sectors with high economic potential, like information technology or renewable energy, can lead to stronger correlations with GDP growth. Focusing on specific technology sectors through strategic GERD investment can undeniably strengthen India's economic potential and place it on a path towards becoming a global leader!

10

Women in 2050

Nupur Sharma

In January 2014, ahead of the 16th Lok Sabha (Parliamentary) elections, the then Gujarat chief minister and Bharatiya Janta Party's potential prime ministerial candidate, Shri Narendra Modi, emphasized the need for greater women's participation in the democratic processes and India's economy.

This, however, was not a hollow statement, as he had administered the uber-prosperous state of Gujarat for over a decade and was proud of heading a state that churned out a staggering 117 women *crorepatis* from a small Gujarat village of Khoraj (near Sanand) itself. In 2024, after transforming the lives of 10 crore women via self-help groups (SHGs) and making 1 crore '*lakhpati didis*', Prime Minister Modi has vowed to make an additional 3 crore (or 30 million) women '*lakhpati didis*'.

As the chief minister of Gujarat, he had implemented several women-centric schemes, including E-Mamata, Mission Mangalam Yojana, Chiranjeevi Yojana, and the PM's Excellence Award-winning flagship training scheme Kaushalya Vikas Kendra. These policies made him popular with female voters and bolstered his reach to the clear majority mark in the 2014 Parliamentary Elections, a first for the Bharatiya Janata Party.

This mission to empower women across the rural-urban Indian landscape has been successful. During his speech in Parliament during the 16th Lok Sabha, the honourable prime minister emphasized the need to have a skilled workforce beyond conventional college diplomas and degrees. His focus on not limiting our populace's options to becoming job seekers but encouraging entrepreneurship and affirmatively and adequately backing the citizens to become job creators instead was spelled out in the policies and schemes he introduced as the prime minister of India.

Not surprisingly, women have taken full advantage of the opportunities presented to them, with 69 per cent of loans under Pradhan Mantri Mudra Yojana and 84 per cent of the loans under Stand-Up India having been sanctioned to womenfolk alone as of 2023. According to the Periodic Labour Force Survey (PLFS) Report (2022–23), there has been a 4.2 per cent increase in the female labour force participation rate to 37 per cent in 2023 from an abysmally low 23.3 per cent in 2017–18 and 20.2 per cent in 2012 (as per International Labour Organization).

Why is India still lagging in its development even after seven decades of independence? This is a question that we must demand an answer to from the previous governments. After all, during the Congress period, India saw the longest-serving woman prime minister in the world Mrs Indira Gandhi, and a female leader as the ruling UPA chairperson Mrs Sonia Gandhi who was at the helm of all governmental affairs for almost a decade.

The answer lies in the political will and intent (or perhaps a lack thereof) to encourage greater economic participation by women in the country and to provide an environment conducive to the same. To promote entrepreneurship, Prime Minister Modi introduced the very basic but essential Jan Dhan Yojana in 2014. This programme allowed citizens from all backgrounds to open zero-balance bank accounts. Its main goal was to bring the economically weaker sections into the fold of India's formal economy and to ensure minimal to no leakages in direct benefit transfer. These accounts had a debit card and a guaranteed contingency insurance policy of Rs 1 lakh.

By 2023, over 50 crore Jan Dhan accounts had been opened, 56 per cent of which belonged to women. Additionally, 67 per cent of these accounts were opened in rural or semi-urban areas. Of course, this begs the question of why almost 30 crore women went without bank accounts for these many years! And why has nobody ever thought about it before?

The Government of India, led by Prime Minister Modi, provides several benefits to women, including insurance, services, maternity benefits, extended maternity leave, and health schemes for pregnant and lactating mothers. These schemes are available to women from all walks of life. According to government statistics, a whopping 141 health benefit packages under the health insurance schemes are exclusively earmarked for women and they also account for nearly 49 per cent of Ayushman Bharat card recipients making use of the popular Rs 5 lakh per family health insurance scheme.

As per the guidelines of the National Food Security Act, the Pradhan Mantri Matru Vandana Yojana offers financial aid of Rs 5,000 to first-time pregnant and lactating mothers and Rs 6,000 to second-time mothers with an annual income of less than Rs 8 lakh per family. It is worth noting that the benefits are not limited to pregnant or expecting women only.

The biggest beneficiaries of the Swachh Bharat Mission have been women. The provision of basics such as toilets has not only made our country 100 per cent open defecation-free but has also gone a long way in ensuring the safety, hygiene, health, and protection of our sisters' modesty.

Similarly, the target behind the highly successful Ujjwala Yojana was to reduce the health hazards caused to women due to traditional cooking methods. This scheme has provided approximately 10.27 crore connections and has been supported by the government by extending the subsidies for up to 12 LPG refills.

The government has made enabling decisions to create a safe environment for women. It has criminalized the act of 'triple talaq' and introduced the death penalty for the rape of minor girls. Additionally, it has amended the Juvenile Justice Act in the aftermath of the dastardly Nirbhaya rape case and set up One-Stop Centres in every district to provide assistance to women in crisis. Overall, the government seems dedicated to ensuring women's safety and well-being.

The Indian government has implemented various schemes, such as Beti Bachao, Beti Padhao, Sukanya Samriddhi Yojana, and Janani Suraksha Yojana, with the aim of ensuring the survival and prosperity of girls and women in the country. As a result of these initiatives, the Directorate General of Civil Aviation declared in 2023 that India had the highest number of female pilots at 15 per cent, three times higher than the global average of 5 per cent. This achievement is commendable in itself.

Now, let us talk about the representation of women in Indian politics. During Prime Minister Modi's first term, 50 per cent of the Indian Cabinet Committee on Security consisted of women, a historic achievement. In his second term, the 17th Lok Sabha had the highest number of women members of Parliament in the history of the Indian Parliament. Additionally, the Women's Reservation Bill, which caused much debate and opposition, was finally passed under the Modi-led government in 2023. These are significant accomplishments for women's representation in Indian politics.

A closer examination of the policies, schemes, and decisions of the Indian government led by Prime Minister Modi, which particularly and strongly benefit women, provides a clear insight into his thoughts, roadmap, political will, and intentions. He has consistently delivered impressive electoral victories and to commemorate India's 100 years of independence with a developed India, the government is making every effort to promote women's participation in the economy whilst making it easier for them to maintain a work-life balance. The question is, are we willing to accept this opportunity?

An administratively experienced, decisive, and dynamic orator, who belongs to a political party now famous for fulfilling its manifesto promises, is expected to deliver a bonanza when he announces his third term. This, in turn, will spawn a new chapter in the rise of women's power.

After all, we are the only largest democratic country that prays to goddesses, including those in human form. So does our prime minister, and we must take him literally.

With the stage set, affirmative actions, holding fort as the backdrop, innumerable schemes and policies paving the stairway, and stricter penal provisions providing the necessary grip for a smooth climb to the top, I foresee 2050 welcoming the era of a Woman's World, where we will no longer be asking, 'Who Runs the World?'

The future of India is bright.

11

Is Government Friend or Foe? How Media's Role Will Evolve By 2047

Shweta Kothari and Kartik Malhotra

Introduction

Kuldeep Nayar was the Editor of the *Indian Express* in 1975 when Indira Gandhi declared the Emergency. Nayar was close to Gandhi, by his admission. So much so that when the late prime minister once cut her hair short, she asked Nayar how she looked. 'Even more beautiful now,' he said.

It, therefore, came as a surprise to him when, in June 1975, two days after the declaration of the Emergency, police knocked at his door at midnight. He assumed they had come to search his premises, but he was instead tactfully whisked away to the police station. For the next three months, he languished in Tihar jail. He was one of the few journalists who refused to buckle under pressure.

India had fought hard for Independence in 1947 and paid the price of subservience. No government would trample on that freedom, Nayar thought. He was wrong, like many others. As the government suspended the fundamental rights of people, jailed its opponents, tortured civilians, and violated human rights in the guise of 'progressive measures', from mass sterilization to forcefully clearing slums, the media stood eerily silent all the while.

In theory, the press is often hailed as the fourth pillar of democracy, serving as a watchdog to keep the other three pillars—the executive, legislature, and judiciary—in check. However, in practice, its powers are often limited.

To understand how press freedom works in the country, one needs to know where the press derives its freedom from. Unlike in Western constitutions, the press in India exercises freedom not through constitutional guarantees but based on freedom of expression, ascribed in Article 19. But the Right to Freedom has its limitations, which have been conveniently used by the people in power—to silence it when required and control it when deemed fit.

No one particular event in India's history entirely serves as a lesson in media accountability and encompasses the evils of unfettered power other than the Emergency. It is a lesson on why India will need a robust and free press to realize its vision for 'Viksit Bharat'—a developed and prosperous nation.

When the Past Informs the Present

By the summer of 1975, Indira Gandhi was increasingly threatened by critics of her government. Gandhi had been elected to power in 1971 and was averse to criticism from the beginning. So, when upper echelons of power stared at a blank in the upcoming elections and power was fast slipping through her hands, she declared the Emergency on 25 June 1975.

Like other leaders before and after her, Indira Gandhi slowly but surely realized that a free press can significantly deplete its fortune, as it can propel you to power. A free press is expected to report fairly and accurately on matters of national significance without fear or favour. A free press is antagonistic to the ruling dispensation.

Among the arguments used to silence the press was that economic productivity and social justice are more important than civil liberties and freedom of expression. The media criticizing the government will work against the people's interests.

The press acts in a manner that seriously hampers government efforts to promote economic productivity and social justice. Freedom of the press does not mean going against the country's national policy, the then prime minister, Indira Gandhi, had declared in Parliament. It is, therefore, incumbent upon the government to silence it.

Control of press rights will help the government promote the cause of growth, prosperity, and nation-building.

But what is more lucrative than silence, the tool used to inform people? Using that very tool to effectuate control on mass media and use it for 'thought control'. Hence, curbs are necessary, but control is even better.

Gandhi is said to have used at least three methods to control the media.

Allocation of government advertising was only limited to those publications which were favourable to it. Financially draining out those that did not support it. Merger of the news agencies to control the flow and the narrative. A single-channel flow of information to the media from the government-controlled agencies. Finally, use fear-arousal techniques on publishers, journalists, and individual shareholders. Raids, threats, and run-ins with authority can be avoided by being pliable. At the end of it all, more than 250 journalists were arrested, and others were co-opted.

The obeisance to the ruling government at the end of it was dangerous. 'You were asked only to bend, but you crawled,' BJP veteran leader L.K. Advani famously said while assessing the aftermath of the Emergency.

Any connection to the present is real and imminent.

The Devil Is in the Freedom

The authors grew up watching and reading several Indian journalists, including Punya Prasun Bajpai, Ravish Kumar, and Karan Thapar. They were known for their astute and meticulous reporting and have had a strong voice in Indian mainstream journalism since the late 2000s. They commanded the respect of their peers and critics alike and were considered, by many standards, doyens of contemporary new media until they were not. However, one by one, they disappeared from the public eye.

In 2014, Indian prime minister Narendra Damodardas Modi was elected to power. Modi is known for his articulate leadership and shrewd political skills, which helped him unite the Indian electorate in a way his predecessors could not. His promise of 'development' and corruption-free governance resonated with the growing aspirational middle class. While Modi enjoyed immense popularity, his relationship with the media remains complicated.

Narendra Modi's handling of the Godhra riots has been a controversial topic since his chief ministerial days in Gujarat. When a BBC reporter asked him about his one regret regarding 2002, Modi responded that he could not 'handle the media'. A regret his critics say he tried to undo in subsequent years as the prime minister of India since 2014.

Since then, there have been concerns about the increasing government stronghold over the media, with foreign press and some Indian publications repeatedly highlighting this issue.

These authors have witnessed how access to power corridors has been limited, and official one-way channels have been put in place to deliver statements from government agencies to the press. No questions asked.

Media players who have been critical have experienced mid-air broadcast cuts and dwindling advertising revenues. There have been allegations of journalists being shunned, thrown out, made redundant, or worse, bought in. Managements have changed, and businesses close to the government have taken over media houses.

Journalists are afraid to question government policies due to intimidation, raids, and the threat of losing their jobs. Anyone who dares to criticize the government's policy framework is labelled as 'anti-national'.

All this while, India has dropped from 140 to 161 out of 180 positions in the annual World Press Freedom Index, ranking behind Laos, Pakistan, and Afghanistan.

The authors can attest that India's press ecosystem is not robust. However, it is hard to believe that India is behind a Taliban-governed Afghanistan. Upon further scrutiny and deeper learning of the international reportage, it becomes clear that the narrative is laden with traditional Western bias.

The India Story

India has emerged as a formidable force, boasting a robust media network that includes over 17,000 newspapers, a staggering 100,000 magazines, a multitude of 178 TV news channels, and a plethora of Facebook pages and websites claiming to be independent news platforms. With such diversity and its tentacles spread out, one would assume that the press will be immune to government pressure. However, some argue that history teaches us that it only takes one woman or a man with the power to challenge the free press. Yet, it is more complex as opposed to a linear story.

Two distinct perspectives have emerged in the last decade. Since 2014, there has been an emergence of a group of journalists and media organizations who believe that traditional Western media have ignored the India story for far too long and India must reclaim the narrative.

A country of 1.4 billion people often only finds itself in the news for its hunger, abject poverty, and rape cases, among others. It is still covered as a 'land of snake-charmers' and not for its prowess in human resources, IT services, engineers, and doctors. The Western media has been accused of being biased in its reportage of India, showing only stories that will evoke pity, contempt or horror, a classic eye-ball-grabbing tactic.

It is believed that the only way to challenge the status quo is by reporting on everything India and the Indian government are doing right. Every attempt to question or criticize the ruling dispensation is considered an assault on India, both from journalists outside and inside, even if it means keeping the very fundamentals of 'non-partisan' reporting at bay. The result is a pliable, self-serving media—one that is perhaps worse than its predecessors both in action and in integrity quotient.

And yet, you cannot paint all journalists with the same brush. Journalists with moral compunction like Kuldeep Nayar who stand up to power and question continue to exist, living under the constant fear of being silenced. Both by their peers and otherwise. Some of the tactics used against them are the classic ones discussed above: threat, fear, and intimidation. Then there is the question of sustainability. Without adequate channels of funding, they die a slow death.

The question is whether journalism or content creation, as we know it today, will evolve fast in the coming decades. The question is whether technological advancements and the rise of digital platforms reshape the nature of the challenges faced by the media industry.

Will Today's Journalism Exist Tomorrow?

If someone were to read this chapter in 2047, they might find it hard to believe that a human physically typed this content on a machine called a 'laptop' that had physical buttons and had been pressed in a sequence of alphabets that make up words to form sentences and so on.

Why would you believe that human beings would be subjected to such laborious tasks when machine learning-based artificial intelligence would have evolved to a point that what you think gets augmented on devices so seamlessly? It is quite believable that by 2047, the premium would only be on thinking. The 'best mind' will eventually win, no matter how other motor skills function.

By 2047, the world of content creation and journalism as we know it today will be almost vintage. First, the process of shooting and editing, as we know in 2024, would be almost history. Generative AI would have advanced to the point that a few instructions to a tool would make a film. It would be a distinct, copyright-free, original work of art. But for those who would prefer to do it the old way, life would be easier.

For one, the cameras would be smaller, packed with more megapixels and powerful sensors, and the iPhone 15 would seem like a bulky device to lug around. Raw footage would be edited on the go as the shoot progressed. The machine would know what music to add to the edit by understanding the content shot. Graphics would be created again by understanding the content captured on camera.

To sum up, all one would need to create audio-visual content would be an idea and AI. And then, you may not need real people facing the camera since avatars would suffice.

YouTubers-alike of 2047 would be single artists with powerful, portable, affordable machines and nothing else. Filmmakers would be smaller crews, delivering a lot more creative content with the time and technology available to them.

But news desks would continue to be labour intensive. News, unlike other content, would need sources. Sources will be human beings because machines do not leak, have incentives, challenge the status quo, or blow whistles. And machines would not lie either. So, one would still need actual human faces to do the job.

There are fundamental questions that emerge when you crystal-ball gaze at the future.

Will the world read newspapers in 2047? Will radio exist? The simple answer is no. Complex answer—there would be no need because the *metaverse* as we know it today would have developed to a level where information—news or otherwise—would be displayed on VR-like (albeit smaller and less cumbersome spectacles) devices on the go. The need to physically publish newspapers would be gone. The cost of material input, carbon emission, distribution, etc., would be prohibitive. Customizing content would also allow the news feed to be crunched to the length and style you appreciate.

Airwaves would be free of AM/FM. It would be satellite-based internet connectivity. Radio-like or podcast-like audio-only content would be available on demand, with automated playlists like today. The exception is that audio content will be automatically generated based on what genre you would like to listen to and what voice you like, and the length will be altered based on the time you have available. The listener would be in the driver's seat of AI-driven productions.

Who will watch linear streams of television? Only those who would be so tired of 'selection' and find it hard to constantly give input to machines that will keep asking them questions. In simple words, the ageing population of 2047, those who are 50+ in 2024, would like to stick to linear streams that offer diverse information or entertainment. This generation's ultimate death will spell the death knell for linear TV.

The Future of News

News, by any account, will be broken for the masses. Big stories will be broken by journalists. But journalism will not be bound by traditional formats of TV, text, or audio. It will be made available across platforms and formats simultaneously.

Editorial or opinion pieces will be independent of artificial intelligence. That is where human editorial judgment will continue to be at work. Machines will only look at past data and comment on a possible future based on patterns that emerge by looking at the rear-view mirror.

Policymaking, where authentic journalistic input will play a vital part, will have to continue looking ahead. Machines will not ever be smart enough to do that.

Advertising will undergo massive changes in the next twenty-five years. It would need to be super-sharply targeted. Big data as we know it today will know exactly what you are looking for or aspiring (or not yet) to buy, and brands will pop up ads with deep-fake avatars, voices, languages, and scripts tailormade for you.

Stars and endorsers will live forever in their deep-fake digital avatars. They will charge a perpetual royalty, and rights of usage will pass down generations. Actors will be even more timeless than Botox or plastic surgeries make them look today. Amitabh Bachchan's voice will live for centuries, as would Tom Cruise's stunts.

Startups would emerge that would legally and aesthetically protect the deep-fake usage of intellectual property associated with once-human stars. They would work at the cusp of advertisers, talent managers of once-human celebrities, and their willed beneficiaries.

Demand and supply of deep-fakes will determine the fee associated with these 'been-human, now-digital' brand endorsers.

Referencing and fact-checking will be the most complex job in 2047 and beyond. AI would be able to mask plagiarism just as easily as it would mask fiction. The sources that will feed machines to learn would be hard to authenticate.

It would be difficult to decipher whether the input came from an independent or a vested interest source. News organizations will continue to form public opinion, and misrepresented facts will be as dangerous for society in 2047 as they are in 2024 or have ever been in the past.

Fact-checking will be the very cog in the wheel that personifies trust in the publisher of content. But as emerging trends in fake news, bots, and vested interests surface even today—publishers will be happier with distribution numbers than with facts. Unfortunately, fact-checking will be expensive and will die a natural death. The reliance on technology tools will be even higher, and therein lies the ultimate risk of misinformation.

Who Will Decide News?

Comment is free, but facts are sacred. We know it in 2024. We have believed it since 1921 when C.P. Snow wrote an essay on journalism on the hundredth anniversary of *The Guardian* as its editor. That will change.

By 2047, facts will be free and comments will be the editorial distinction. That distinction will come at a premium that consumers of news will need to pay for. Why? Because that will be the only differentiator between what one publication publishes versus another.

True journalism will command a premium market price, but takers will be few. Richer countries with better education standards will lead to the demand for quality journalism. Countries like India, even as among the largest economies in the world, will still be grappling with low per-capita gross domestic product (GDP), and hence, the growth will not be equitable.

That will keep the demand for quality subscription-based news low until further development with a lower population and, hence, higher per-capita GDP will once again turn the ride in favour of quality journalism. Will it be too late? Perhaps yes. Will corporate ownership of media continue to be dictated by governments? Yes, until education levels improve. The editorial skew notwithstanding, society-wide education standards will determine the demand for authentic news. Until then, the news will remain free.

In the threads of media control, from the Emergency to the speculated future of journalism, India stands at a crossroads. The lessons of the past echo warnings, urging a delicate balance between progress and press freedom. As we navigate the shifting sands of power, the role of a free and robust press becomes indispensable for realizing India's vision of a developed nation. In this intricate dance between the past, present, and future, the torchbearers of journalism must remain vigilant.

12

Tradition as a Remedy to Religious Polarization: A Harmonious Bharat @ 2050

Yashowardhan Tiwari and Shivani Badgaiyan

Introduction

Religions and religiosity in India have been the subject of study, commentary, propagation, political rhetoric, and social churning for centuries, especially post-independence. The history of religious conflicts in India dates back to centuries. Religion is perceived to play a central role in both individual lives and the lives of communities. Religion features prominently in many aspects, whether in the public display of religious festivities, the dominance of public spaces through religious assertion, or communal conflicts and clashes over religious antagonism.

It is an incontrovertible fact that religion and religious beliefs influence both private and public life in India. Since gaining independence, India has celebrated the vibrancy of its cultural milieu, which is marked by the flourishing of a multitude of religions. However, the country has also been marred by recurring patches of communal conflicts and a charged atmosphere of religious polarization. Again, the undercurrents of religious polarization in Indian society and their supposed causes have been subjected to intense scrutiny, and tomes of academic literature have been produced. Yet, these studies have unfortunately failed to provide any redressal mechanisms or realistic solutions for ending communal conflicts. This essay attempts to address the dynamics of religion in India holistically and shall endeavour to carve out a manifesto for the future of religious harmony in India.

Communal Conflicts in India: A Brief Overview

Communal conflict has been a constant source of upheaval against peace and harmony in Indian society. With its history dating back several centuries, it has stayed in the subcontinent in some form, generating friction between various religious communities. An important point to be noted is that communal conflict has largely manifested itself through struggles between the indigenous peoples and their culture and the colonizers. Faced with waves of Islamic and Euro-Christian colonialisms, the indigenous Indian population has suffered subjugation and religious hatred throughout its history.

As the indigenous culture mobilized its resources to create a response on various occasions, it invariably resulted in clashes with the colonizers, thus sparking communal conflicts. With rampant conversions of the indigenous populace, whether forced or otherwise, across various geographies of the Indian subcontinent, the nature of communal conflict also metamorphosed itself from outright barbarism by colonizing groups to everyday communalism between the converted and unconverted people. While the medieval and early European colonial periods were marked by large-scale despotism targeted against the indigenous communities, the transition of colonial powers allowed space for the reassertion of indigenous cultures and traditions by the mid-nineteenth century. As noted by Dr Saumya Dey, a scholar of Indian cultural and intellectual history:

> Hindus were achieving trans-local solidarity as a society, or 'communitas', by conducting their public religious ceremonials with greater verve… There was, in other words, a proper cultural conflict underway in North India at this historical turn, with Hindus deploying and asserting their cultural symbols…The franchise and representative institutions, thus, were further imperilling the 'Islamicate' cultural paradigm which had once been hegemonic in the urban spaces of North India.[1]

With the transference of colonial power to the European colonial forces and the loss of hegemony over political power by the Islamic colonizers, the mid-nineteenth century began witnessing a transformation in the articulation of communal conflict. Under the shadow of British imperialism, communal conflict changed itself into a more permanent feature in everyday politics by rigidifying religious identities and openly advocating Islamic separatism on religious lines. Simultaneously, proselytization activities carried out by the Christian missionaries in every nook and corner of remote parts of India led to permanent communal tension between the indigenous groups and mass proselytizers on the prowl. Moreover, separate electorates for religious minorities and electoral campaigning along religious lines to capture representative institutions ensured that religious polarization would remain embedded in Indian polity.

Religion and Tradition: Discerning a Nuanced Differentiation

While scholars have provided varied interpretations of communal conflicts in India, most of them have emphasized their religious nature rather than examining the cultural aspects. Ignoring the struggle of cultural paradigms has led to a partial understanding of the roots of such conflicts and a failure to provide amicable resolutions. In this backdrop, a promising research project that provides a starting point to decode the nature of communalism in India is the 'Comparative Science of Cultures', curated by Prof. S.N. Balagangadhara (lovingly referred to as 'Balu') over a period of four decades at the University of Ghent, Belgium.

At the core of his research project lies a scientific hypothesis that challenges the very idea of 'religion' as it is understood today. Balagangadhara argued, 'The theoretical frameworks and the existing methodologies in the domain of religious studies are secularized variants of Christian theology.'[2] This essentially implies that the general understanding of religion as we know it today is rooted in a Christian theological framework. This also means that we approach our indigenous traditional practices from a similar framework. Balagangadhara's hypothesis points towards a huge gap in our knowledge of cultures and traditions and indicates a lack of accessibility to our own cultural frameworks. The exclusive claims to absolute truth made by Abrahamic religions push the existing cultural practices to the margins. It is due to a failure to comprehend cultural differences that we tend to identify resistance to issues such as proselytization and the 'universalization of religion'[3] by indigenous societies as the source of religious conflicts.

What we actually witness are not religious conflicts per se but conflicts between religions and traditions. This is a very important distinction that needs to be noted. Tradition may be described as 'a specific set of ancestral practices characterizing a human community'.[4] Traditions are practised, protected, and 'upheld not because they contain some exclusive truth binding the believer to God, but because they bind a community together'.[5] The interaction between religions, which are based on absolute truth claims, and traditions (inter-woven clusters of ancestral practices, such as those which we identify under the rubric of the Hindu pantheon) results in an inevitable clash due to the proselytizing nature of the former, as described by Balagangadhara:

> These aspects of the Semitic religions and pagan traditions - namely, proselytization and non-interference - are bound to collide in a society where the Semitic religions encounter pagan traditions *as a living force*. This is exactly what is happening in India today. Though a growing number of Hindus speak in such terms, the widespread discontent about conversion is not generally caused by the fear that the whole of India will become Christian or Muslim. Some groups may take this scenario seriously, but it does not explain the equally strong aversion towards conversion among those who do not. Many reasonable minds who do not see an imminent threat of India becoming an Islamic country still consider religious conversion to be a violation of the social fabric, for it goes straight against the traditional Hindu stance of non-interference.[6]

Religious conflicts, protests over proselytization and conversion, and religious polarization cannot be understood without reflecting upon the fundamental cultural differences within Indian society, as explained above. Any attempt to draw up practical solutions to ending such conflicts needs to take these into account and address the issues accordingly.

State Intervention and Religious Conflict: The Impossibility of State Neutrality

The post-independence discourse of secularism has been deeply influenced by its Western, a.k.a. Christian origins. The core problem faced by the secular ideal is a failure to clearly demarcate the secular and non-secular spheres. Blurred and porous boundaries separating the secular and the sacred often result in state intervention in the sacred sphere despite its mandate being legally restricted to the secular sphere only. State intervention in the sacred sphere creates an atmosphere of aversion towards state action. It generates the image of a state mostly eager to diminish the expanse of the sacred sphere free from any external intervention.

The modern state also claims a position of neutrality, a position that is inherently untenable due to the flawed conceptualization of the state's role in governance over religious societies. State neutrality is an impossibility precisely because it adopts a secular character. Although the secular character of the state implies that it does not associate itself with any religion, however the very assumption that societal activities can be divided into secular and non-secular shows that the state implicitly accepts the Christian theological framework.

The state deploys this framework in its assessment of indigenous cultural activities and traditional practices, which results in a biased approach and renders all claims of neutrality false and impossible to achieve. This impossibility of state neutrality is very well explained by Balagangadhara and his research colleagues.[7]

A definitive example of the impossibility of state neutrality is the Indian judiciary's use of essential religious practices doctrine. The doctrine has been propounded on the Christian theological assumption that the public sphere can be divided into the secular and the sacred and that the state can rightly identify and distinguish one from the other.

Over the decades, the essential religious practices doctrine has diminished Hindu cultural practices and legitimized state intervention even in the governance of Hindu sacred institutions such as mathas and temples. It also gives legal sanctity to the judiciary's power to judge the legitimacy of certain traditional practices in accordance with Hindu philosophy and scriptures.

Such a disposition of the modern Indian state towards the indigenous cultural milieu undoubtedly leads to the generation of antipathy towards the state. It creates openings for conflict in the society.

A Cultural Manifesto for Harmonious Bharat @ 2050

This write-up has attempted to identify the core issue at the roots of communal conflicts and a lack of understanding of the distinction between religion and tradition. The operation of the modern Indian state in a Western framework only exacerbates the conflicts without providing any proper remedy to avoid them.

Some recommendations are in order so that we may pave the way for a permanence of harmony in Bharat and realize a Bharat proud of its cultural roots and immersed in the practice of its living traditions while simultaneously making huge strides in consonance with the demands of contextual modernity.

Below are some bulletin pointers that should shape a definitive manifesto for the future of Bharat as a civilization:

Religion versus tradition: bridging the divide: An acknowledgement of the distinct nature of traditional practices and a nuanced perception of their difference from the structure of religions shall lay the foundations for any possibility of addressing communal divides and conflicts. A realization on the part of religious communities about their proselytizing tendencies shall lead to a push towards organically evolving constraints over such tendencies and attempts to fuse with the cultural milieu of indigenous communities.

The indigenous communities of Bharat, largely clubbed under the 'Hindu' rubric, shall also have to resist any attempts for their organization along Abrahamic lines, or else polarization will be a stark and permanent reality. The academic community will have to take the lead in the clear theorization of these differences and their smooth communication among the masses.

Moreover, the state and its various organs also need to incorporate the language of this distinction into their official discourse. This implies that organs such as the judiciary will have to rework their understanding of 'religion' and may have to bury the essential religious practices doctrine for better criteria of state regulation of religious activities.

Reinventing the secular state: The modern Indian state will have to do away with its tacit acceptance of the secular-sacred divide and problematize it so as to reinvent its secular foundations. Secularism has been accepted as an ideal for its promise of state neutrality and ensuring the flourishing of cultural pluralism, but the Indian secular state fails on both counts due to inherent contradictions in the nature of secularism.

The Indian state should devise a better political theory for its relation with culture and religion, a theory that advocates the equal celebration of cultural manifestations, provides a supportive ecosystem for plural cultures, and balances its interventions into traditional practices such that the need for interference should arise only to ensure cultural pluralism and against discrimination. Whether such a theory would have to stick to the label of some form of secularism may be rendered irrelevant.

Freedom of sacred institutions: Sacred spaces such as temples and other religious complexes have been the backbone of our cultural ecosystems for centuries. State governance and intervention in such spaces have only caused the corruption of such institutions and a decline in their sanctity and destruction of the social ecosystem around them. A harmonious Bharat in 2050, which shall also be the Indian republic completing its 100th year, cannot be achieved without freeing our sacred institutions from the clutches of state governance.

The temple freedom movement, which has made a space for itself in today's public discourse, must be taken to its logical conclusion in order to restore the resurgence of social, cultural, and aesthetic institutions and practices that thrive as a part of temple ecosystems. A rolling back of state machinery from our sacred institutions will once again restore our society and the people as active stakeholders of their own sacred spaces.

State patronage for the rejuvenation of sacred spaces: For a large part of its existence, the Indian state has been a rather reluctant player when it comes to state support for the rejuvenation of sacred spaces. Since 2014, this attitude has surely changed drastically and now the Indian state sees itself as an important agent in the rejuvenation of these institutions.

The state should actively oversee the task of providing patronage for rebuilding and uplifting such institutions and should also deeply involve various social segments. Thus, the agency and stakeholder-ship of upliftment of our sacred spaces is equally divided between the state and Bhartiya society. The rise of sacred spaces shall mean the rise of a strong, culturally anchored Bharat.

Decolonizing the Indian mind: Decolonizing the Indian mind is an ongoing project and will remain so in the near future. The Indian mind needs to be made aware of its colonial history and grasp the impact of colonialism on the Indian psyche. It also needs to break the compartmentalized categories of religious identities and root itself in the broader framework of identity shaped by its indigenous cultural framework.

This will require questioning neat religious identities and pushing the Indian mind towards redefining the Indian communities in line with the cultural markers associated with its traditional practices. A multitude of indigenous identities embedded in our civilizational framework shall be the promise of Bharat to itself in 2050.

Peace and Reconciliation Commission: A beautiful experiment in post-apartheid South Africa, carried out under the able supervision of Desmond Tutu, is a model for soothing communal conflict worth replication and implementation. Given the centuries-old, bloody colonial history of India, which ended with an equally painful partition, the establishment of a Peace and Reconciliation Commission could be a potential guarantee for providing a calming remedy to the ingrained communal flares and passions in Indian society.

Even post-Independence, issues such as the genocide of Kashmiri Hindus can only be persuasively addressed and provide the traumatized communities with a peaceful closure to their agony by the public acknowledgements and apologies for the hatred and atrocities perpetrated against them.

Civil society organizations as flag bearers of cultural harmony: The role of the state as a guarantor of cultural harmony should be replaced with civil society organizations, which can very well gel with the masses and directly connect with the grassroots. Such organizations shall take up the mantle of establishing cultural harmony in Bharat. In contemporary times, organizations such as the Rashtriya Swayamsevak Sangh, through their affiliated wings like the Muslim Rashtriya Manch, have already made deep inroads into our society and have been playing an instrumental role in soothing communal passions and bringing about cultural harmony.

Bharat should aim to completely delegate the task of defusing religious polarization to such organizations so that harmony may be brought about by those who constitute the Indian society.

Civilizational nationalism as the future of a viksit Bharat: Bharat is a living civilization, and it needs to embrace its civilizational ethos, which has been the strongest guarantee of peace and harmony for ages now. Bharat needs to articulate a fresh paradigm of civilizational nationalism for itself, which shall stand out as the biggest marker of communal harmony and a decisive message to the world about *Vasudhaiva Kutumbakam*.

Conclusion

Bharat has already begun its journey towards reclaiming its civilizational identity and has confidently embraced its quest for decolonization. A significant part of this process of decolonization is the distancing of our political discourse from the language of communalism and communal conflicts.

Cultural harmony, based on the primacy of traditional practices and the moulding of Bhartiya identity in consonance with our civilizational ethos, shall be the perfect antidote to religious polarization and a sure-shot guarantor of a harmonious Bharat @ 2050.

Part IV

Imagining the Enablers of a Superpower in the Making

13

Housing for All: Atmanirbhar Bharat @2047

Niranjan Hiranandani

India's vision for 2047 is to become a leading global superpower. This era belongs to us, and we are committed to achieving it through a range of initiatives. Our political stability provides a solid foundation for growth and development. Several structural reforms have also been implemented that have streamlined regulations and improved access to capital, creating a business-friendly environment.

Our infrastructure growth has also been impressive, with significant investments in transportation, energy, and telecommunications. It has brought opportunities to rural areas across the country. Similarly, our demographics are favourable, with young, dynamic people who strive for success. As a result, Indian entrepreneurship has surged, driving innovation across a variety of industries. Now, we are at the forefront of the technological revolution, developing cutting-edge solutions that drive growth. As a result of all of these factors, India is well-positioned to succeed on a global scale in the years to come.

Since independence, India has undergone multiple revolutions, all aimed at promoting economic growth and enhancing its citizens' standard of living. From the Green Revolution to the textile revolution, the time is now ripe for a housing revolution. India has a housing deficit, so it is imperative to transform the housing landscape throughout the country. To embark on this revolutionary journey, Prime Minister Narendra Modi has outlined an ambitious goal of providing housing for all. The programme aims to provide affordable housing for all citizens.

India has set its sights on holistic economic development. To this end, it has enacted active measures such as 'Make in India' and 'Digital India' programmes to encourage investments and promote sustainable growth. Additionally, multiple other key factors such as population growth, increased appetite for consumption, a rising middle class, robust real estate and capital market, a thriving start-up and entrepreneurship climate, and tax reforms will enable us to outpace other global economies.

The vision of *Atmanirbhar Bharat* has the potential to transform India's economic landscape. In addition to achieving a high gross domestic product growth rate, it also involves diversifying the economy, attracting foreign direct investment (FDI), increasing per capita income, and stimulating innovation and technological advancement in various sectors.

Further, India has the opportunity to become a global skill capital by leveraging its young and skilled demographic. India's young population gives it a competitive edge and a wide domestic market, which can be leveraged to stimulate its economy.

In India's rise as a global economic superpower, one sector stands out as a key driving force: real estate, construction, and infrastructure.

In 2047, Indian Real Estate Is Expected to Reach $5.8 Trillion

The real estate, construction, and infrastructure sector is exerting a profound influence on India's path to emerging as a global economic powerhouse. With the current momentum, it is poised to play a pivotal role in driving economic expansion, enticing foreign investments, and fostering extensive job creation.

These sectors presently account for a substantial 18 per cent of India's total economic output. The performance is intricately linked with the nation's gross domestic product (GDP) growth, making it a cornerstone of economic development. Furthermore, real estate amplifies its impact through diverse channels spanning residential, commercial, and industrial spaces. This dynamic mechanism has a snowball effect on the growth of 270 ancillary industries together, resulting in a larger economic footprint. This, in turn, leads to more jobs, higher wages, and improved quality of life for citizens.

Second, this sector is a key driver of job creation in India. The construction sector is known to provide substantial employment opportunities, both directly and indirectly. It is estimated that employment in the construction sector in the country will reach 100 million by 2030.

Third, the real estate and infrastructure sectors attract substantial investment from domestic and international sources. The development of infrastructure, such as roads, airports, ports, and power plants, requires significant capital investment. Simultaneously, the flourishing real estate sector, fuelled by the increasing demand for residential and commercial properties, becomes a magnet for significant investments. Together, these sectors create diverse investment opportunities and play a pivotal role in advancing overall economic development.

In addition to economic benefits, this sector also addresses the affordable housing deficit in India and contributes to social security. The real estate sector plays a crucial role in bridging this gap and providing housing options for the population. The government's initiatives, such as Pradhan Mantri Awas Yojana

(PMAY), aim to provide affordable housing for all by 2024. Adequate housing provides shelter and contributes to improved living conditions, social stability, and overall development of individuals and communities.

In conclusion, the real estate, construction, and infrastructure sectors in India play a multifaceted role in supporting economic growth, job creation, investment, social security, and overall development. They contribute significantly to GDP growth, generate employment, address the housing deficit, and attract investments, fostering the overall social and economic development of the country.

Real Estate Wireframe Redesigned

The real estate and construction sectors in India are significant contributors to the country's economy in terms of size, GDP contribution, and employment generation. The industry is expected to reach a market size of $1 trillion by 2030 and contribute 13 per cent to the country's GDP by 2025.

In terms of employment, the sector provides various opportunities across different roles, including developers, architects, engineers, project managers, and construction workers. The industry is estimated to generate substantial employment opportunities, both directly and indirectly.

The real estate sector in India has witnessed the emergence of new asset classes, which have opened up new opportunities for investment and growth. These asset classes include senior living, student housing, residential education campuses, co-living, fractional ownership, and multi-living. These new asset classes cater to the changing demands and preferences of the population and offer potential for future growth and development.

In addition, new business models have emerged in the real estate sector, such as development management, service consultancy, joint ventures, joint development agreements, and project management. These business models allow different stakeholders to collaborate, share risks, and optimize resources, contributing to the overall growth and development of the sector.

Strong credit borrowing from multiple funding avenues has been observed to support the growth of the real estate market. banks, FIIs (foreign institutional investors), NBFCs (non-banking financial companies), AIFs (alternative investment funds), IPOs (initial public offerings), PE (private equity), REITs (Real Estate Investment Trusts), and equity debt have been important sources of funding for real estate projects.

Looking ahead, the future scope of the real estate sector in India looks promising. The rise of new asset classes, along with the implementation of supportive government policies, technological advancements, and increasing urbanization, will continue to positively impact the industry. The demand for housing, infrastructure, commercial spaces, and other real estate developments is expected to drive growth in the sector further.

Indian Homebuyers: An Insightful Profile

Indian homebuyers are diverse, encompassing urban and rural mindsets, varying income levels, professions, entrepreneurship, and psychographic characteristics. This diversity translates into significantly different needs.

In urban metropolises, homebuyers often exhibit higher income levels and a preference for modern amenities, convenience, and proximity to workplaces and social infrastructure. Conversely, rural home buyers prioritize affordability, space, and a closer connection to nature and traditional values.

Delving into income levels, homebuyers in the mid and luxury segments exhibit changing or evolving preferences. Mid-segment homebuyers are increasingly looking for affordable and compact homes with well-designed layouts, good connectivity, and basic amenities. Luxury homebuyers, on the other hand, are seeking exclusivity, premium features, high-quality construction, and unique architectural designs. They prioritize spacious interiors, panoramic views, advanced home automation systems, and top-notch security.

High-net-worth Individuals (HNIs) are attracted to plush homes in metro cities for various reasons. Metro cities offer a cosmopolitan lifestyle, excellent infrastructure, renowned educational institutions, world-class healthcare facilities, and vibrant cultural and entertainment options. Moreover, these cities serve as major business and financial hubs, providing lucrative investment opportunities and facilitating networking and career growth.

Non-resident Indians (NRIs) are actively investing in Indian real estate, benefiting from several advantages. Investing in Indian real estate allows them to have a tangible asset in their home country, providing a sense of security, financial stability, and a connection to their roots. It is a long-term investment option that generates rental income and capital appreciation. Additionally, the Indian government has introduced reforms and regulatory policies to attract NRIs, such as simplified processes for property acquisition, repatriation of funds, and tax incentives for certain categories of NRIs.

Geopolitical turmoil often nudges NRIs to buy homes in their homeland for social safety. Uncertainty in global markets and political situations in foreign countries make NRIs re-evaluate their investment strategies, potentially leading them to consider investing in India.

In essence, investing in Indian real estate provides a sense of security during uncertain times and serves as an emotional and financial anchor. It allows NRIs to have a place to return to and potentially provides a backup plan in case they need to relocate to the country.

The combination of changing preferences, urbanization, rising income levels, and investment opportunities for HNIs and NRIs will likely drive the country's real estate demand. The government's focus on affordable housing, infrastructure development, and ease of doing business creates a conducive environment for home buyers and investors, contributing to a positive outlook for the real estate sector and the potential for sustained growth.

Millennial Homebuyers

The millennial generation is a significant demographic group reshaping the housing market. They prefer convenient and seamless homebuying processes and highly value customer services, buying experiences, and an integrated living ecosystem.

Home Buying Preferences

Location: Millennials value convenience and proximity to urban hubs, public transportation, and access to amenities, restaurants, and entertainment.

Smart home technology: Millennials embrace smart home automation technology. They actively seek homes with smart features such as programmable thermostats, security systems, motion sensors, and energy-efficient appliances.

Sustainable features: Millennials are actively seeking homes that are sustainable and environmentally conscious.

They prioritize features such as energy-efficient appliances, solar panels, and eco-friendly building materials.

Financing Mechanism

Millennials are utilizing various financing options to purchase their homes. Here are some common methods they use:

Home loans: Millennial homebuyers often rely on home loans from banks and financial institutions. These loans allow them to finance a significant portion of the property's cost and repay it in EMIs over a designated period of time.

Government schemes: Many millennials use government schemes, such as PMAY, which promote affordable housing and make homeownership more accessible.

Down payment assistance: To bridge the gap between the property cost and the loan amount, millennial homebuyers frequently explore down payment assistance programmes offered by banks. Notably, 50 per cent of the down payment burden is available as an interest-free loan. Some may opt to borrow funds from family members, while others choose to utilize their personal savings to meet the down payment requirement.

Rent-to-own: Some millennial homebuyers opt for rent-to-own models, where a portion of their monthly rent payments is deducted as a down payment towards purchasing the property in the future. This model allows them to build equity while renting the property gradually.

In fact, millennials are increasingly looking for homes that prioritize convenience, sustainability, and connectivity. Understanding these preferences and trends is essential for real estate professionals and developers to cater to millennial homebuyers' evolving needs.

Conducive Policy and Reforms Landscape

The Indian government has devised strategic policies and reforms to support the real estate sector's growth actively. The development of affordable housing, rental housing, and infrastructure drives the Indian real estate landscape. Implementing these measures will open new real estate markets and mitigate issues associated with population density and rapid urbanization.

The government's focus on infrastructure development plays a pivotal role in creating last-mile connectivity and opening new real estate markets. Initiatives like the Smart Cities Mission, Atal Mission for Rejuvenation and Urban Transformation (AMRUT), Bharat Mala, Sagar Mala, mass rapid transit system, multimodal corridors, and the metro rail projects contribute to enhanced connectivity, better urban planning, and the development of necessary socio-civic infrastructure. As a result of these initiatives, employment, investments, and economic activity are fostered.

Creating well-planned smart cities and urban centres with modern-tech amenities can generate ample employment opportunities with sustained GDP growth. As a result, talent is attracted, the strain on existing urban areas is alleviated, and balanced regional development is promoted. This decentralization eases the burden on mega cities, reduces overcrowding, and facilitates the growth of new real estate markets in emerging regions.

The government's commitments to affordable housing, rental housing schemes, and infrastructure development demonstrate its proactive approach to addressing housing needs, improving quality of life, and fostering inclusive growth. India can achieve sustainable and balanced growth by investing in infrastructure, creating jobs, and providing incentives for investors to stay invested in the country.

Real Estate Upswing Cycle

Rapid urbanization and population growth in India are currently creating significant demand for housing, commercial spaces, and infrastructure. India is actively investing in infrastructure to accommodate the increased demand. Moreover, the country is ensuring adequate resources to finance these projects. Finally, India is also creating incentives and policies to encourage the private sector to invest in these projects. Consequently, the following are the trend drivers:

Housing demand: Rapid urbanization is exacerbating housing demand in metros and rising tier 2 and 3 cities. Increasing home demand from the aspiring middle class is prompting a healthy mix of residential properties, including affordable, mid-range, and luxury apartments.

Commercial spaces: In response to increased urbanization, commercial spaces such as office buildings, retail streets, and business parks are in high demand. Cities' growth as centres of trade and industry requires adequate infrastructure to support their operations. Commercial space growth not only attracts investments but also stimulates the creation of jobs, fosters entrepreneurship, and stimulates the economy.

The combined demand for housing, commercial spaces, and infrastructure has a rippling effect on the economy. Besides stimulating the manufacturing and construction industries, it provides revenue to the government through taxes and fees. Further, robust real estate and infrastructure sectors contribute to a city or region's attractiveness. Businesses, investors, and tourists are attracted by this integrated growth, which results in a flourishing economy. Such multiplier developments improve private CAPEX, sustainable growth, living standards, and per capita income.

With a proactive approach and focused strategies, India is well-positioned to harness this sustained demand, foster inclusive growth, and build a resilient and prosperous nation.

Tech Transformation and Sustainable Development

Digitalization and immersive automation technologies are transforming the Indian real estate sector, providing unprecedented opportunities for growth and efficiency. A new generation of smart technologies, sustainable designs, and prefabricated construction methods are changing how the industry operates. Consequently, this will improve quality, reduce costs, speed up delivery, and prevent home delivery delays. Let us try to understand this in detail:

Digitalization: Integrating smart technologies like artificial intelligence (AI), machine learning (ML), and drone surveys brings a new era of innovation and intelligence to the real estate industry. With the internet of things (IoT)-enabled devices, homeowners can control their properties remotely. AI-powered bots streamline customer interactions, optimizing the buying and selling experience. In addition, ML enhances decision-making processes and risk management strategies.

Sustainable practices: The green real estate market is gaining prominence amid the climate crisis. To build environmentally friendly buildings, the government must incentivize using energy-efficient materials, renewable energy solutions, recycling of water and waste, and dust mitigation. Adoption of prefabricated construction methods can significantly contribute towards long-term cost efficiencies, mitigate perils of delays and ensure timely project delivery. Thus, by integrating sustainable green practices, the industry can commit to customer-centricity and climate adhesive social responsibility.

Foreign Investment and Collaboration

India's favourable economic and demographic factors are poised to attract significant institutional foreign investments and collaborations to put India on the global economic stage. We can understand the theme through the following points:

Growth potential: With a population of over 1.3 billion, India offers a vast consumer base and a growing market, ensuring sustained demand and profitability for investors.

Ease of doing business: The Indian government has implemented significant reforms such as RERA, GST, and Insolvency and Bankruptcy Code (IBC) that have improved transparency, streamlined processes, and enhanced investor protection. Additionally, India's improved ranking in the World Bank's Ease of Doing Business index reflects its commitment to creating a business-friendly environment, instilling confidence in foreign investors.

Collaborations and joint ventures: Foreign investors can benefit from strategic collaborations and joint ventures with Indian-rooted companies. By combining international expertise with local insights, investors can navigate the complex regulatory landscape, tap into regional networks, and unlock growth opportunities.

Institutional foreign investors can earn attractive returns on investment in Indian real estate. In addition to portfolio diversification, they can access skilled labour and technology. Strengthening bilateral ties can also promote economic development. Through the collaborative business approach, foreign investors can help India transform into a global economic powerhouse.

Challenges and Solution

The Indian real estate sector, while full of potential to grow, faces particular challenges that need to be addressed for optimal growth. The challenges are as follows:

Regulatory hurdles: Navigating complex regulatory frameworks can be daunting, leading to project delays and increased costs.

Sustainable environmental practices: Due to a lack of incentivization, awareness, and promotion, developers are reluctant to embrace sustainable technologies or materials, hindering the widespread adoption of environmentally conscious construction practices.

Certain solutions to the above challenges can be described as follows:

Government interventions: Creating single-window clearance mechanisms, standardizing approval timelines, and digitizing processes can significantly improve the ease of doing business in the sector.

Tax SOPS: Government incentives, such as tax benefits and grants, can encourage developers to adopt sustainable practices.

Additionally, inclusive development can ensure that real estate development benefits reach all sections of society. Affordable housing initiatives, mixed-use developments, and integrated urban planning can help address the housing needs of economically weaker sections and promote socio-economic inclusivity. Implementing such solutions will enable the real estate sector to unlock its full potential and create a multiplier effect on sustainable economic growth.

Slum-Free India

Achieving a slum-free India requires the active involvement of the real estate sector, which can play a significant role in providing adequate housing for the urban poor. Here are some strategies that can be employed:

Slum redevelopment projects: Transforming existing slums into affordable housing complexes with improved socio-civic infrastructure and better amenities will change the city's skyline. Real estate developers can create slum-free neighbourhoods by collaborating with the government and leveraging their expertise.

Affordable housing initiatives: The real estate sector can focus on constructing affordable housing units targeting the urban poor. Public-private partnerships can be formed to ensure funding and land availability for such initiatives.

Inclusive housing policies: It indicates that economically weaker sections and low-income groups of society are given priority in enabling affordable housing. A policy like this ensures decent housing options for the urban poor

Slum rehabilitation: Participating in a slum rehabilitation project involves relocating slum dwellers to better housing areas where their livelihood opportunities are not disrupted. The government and developers can collaborate to identify appropriate rehabilitation projects and revamp cityscapes.

Access to finance: To make homeownership more accessible for the urban poor, developers can explore innovative financing models. As a result, they will transition from informal settlements to formal housing.

Real estate can, therefore, play an active role in achieving the slum-free India goal if these strategies are implemented. To ensure the success of these initiatives, collaboration between the government, developers, and financial institutions is essential.

Impetus to Formal Education and Skilling

Formal education in the Indian real estate business can transform the industry by generating a skilled workforce. This would increase efficiency and productivity in the sector, leading to higher profitability. Formal education would also help address the industry's existing skill gap and enhance customer service, product innovation, efficient operations, and better competitiveness.

Let us explore how formal education, internships, and apprenticeships can contribute to this growth:

Skill development: Formal education programmes in the real estate stream will provide the workforce with comprehensive industry knowledge, including legal frameworks, financial analysis, and property valuation. This will equip students with the skills to make informed decisions.

Industry exposure: Internships and apprenticeships provide invaluable practical learning opportunities for aspiring professionals. This exposure fosters a deeper understanding of the industry landscape and prepares one to navigate real-world scenarios.

Policy comprehension: It helps the workforce to understand how policies are shaped and government schemes that influence them. Consequently, they can navigate complex regulations, contribute to policy discussions, and strategize real estate development in accordance with policy.

Job creation and entrepreneurship: Armed with a strong foundation, these professionals can initiate their own real estate ventures, fostering entrepreneurship and innovation in the sector.

Attracting the women workforce: Education in real estate promotes gender diversity so that relevant talent can be tapped. Women's participation in the real estate sector is a double-engine growth factor, enhancing innovation while driving economic growth.

Thus, formal education is crucial for driving the real estate sector forward and ensuring the country's economic resilience.

Real Estate: A Wealth-Generating Asset

Real estate is a formidable wealth-generating asset, showcasing its potential for long-term appreciation, consistent rental income, and advantageous tax benefits. Beyond its monetary value, real estate often carries deep emotional significance, making it a common choice for those looking to secure a lasting legacy.

The asset historically holds long-term value appreciation and higher rental yields. Rental income can be a source of cash flow and contribute to wealth building. Moreover, real estate investments come with various tax advantages tied to property ownership. These include deductions for mortgage interest, property taxes, and depreciation, allowing investors to optimize their taxable income. Leveraging these benefits not only mitigates the overall tax burden but also enhances the potential return on real estate investments.

Real estate is a robust component of portfolio diversification, presenting an effective strategy to minimize risk and maximize returns. It also serves as a social security asset after retirement. However, it is imperative to acknowledge that real estate investing involves risks and requires careful consideration of factors such as market conditions, property management, and financial obligations.

Therefore, research and professional advice are essential before investing. In the end, real estate is a powerful catalyst for wealth-generating assets and contributes to building a secure financial future. This will be an important consideration for India's future evolution.

Pivotal Confluence for Global Dominance

A powerful combination of the real estate, construction, and infrastructure sectors will propel India towards becoming a global economic powerhouse. Furthermore, as mentioned earlier, these sectors stimulate 270 allied industries, including cement, steel, logistics, finance, and retail, creating a virtuous cycle of economic progress. India's economic advancement hinges on the intertwining growth of these sectors.

Moreover, employment generation is a critical aspect of India's quest for prosperity and social well-being. Real estate, construction, and infrastructure sectors have the potential to create millions of jobs, spanning skilled workers to professionals and entrepreneurs. This surge in employment improves living standards, drives consumption, and fuels economic growth. By investing in these sectors, India can harness the power of job creation and unlock the full potential of its young and dynamic workforce.

Finally, continuous investment, innovation, and sustainable practices are essential to leverage real estate's transformative power truly. These sectors can enhance efficiency, adopt cutting-edge technologies, and modernize processes with substantial investment. A resilient and environmentally friendly urban landscape can be created with innovative approaches such as smart cities, green building practices, and sustainable infrastructure. India can mitigate environmental challenges and attract global investments by embracing sustainable practices.

In addition to elevating India's international standing, creating a business-friendly environment in these sectors will also help it flourish. Given these realities, one can be confident that India is on the right track to emerging as a global leader with the right vision, commitment, and collaboration.

14

The Psychology of Banking

Rajeev Pawar

The Origins of Banking

At every point in time, big and small pockets of money move around the world. A good banker channels this money, holds on to it for a little while, keeps a little bit, and sends it on in the right direction.

Banking is most likely the second oldest profession in the world. Its origins can be traced back to 2000 BC in India and Assyria (now Iraq), when merchants gave loans to farmers who took goods from one city to another.

Temples in ancient Greece and Rome took deposits and gave loans, possibly making them the first bank with assets and liabilities. Modern banking was, of course, popularized by the Medici family of Florence, who were bankers even to the Pope.

The initial banks in India were not too successful. The Bank of Hindustan started in 1770 but shut shop in sixty-odd years. The General Bank of India was founded in 1786 but went belly up in just five years. State Bank of India (SBI), an amalgamation of three banks, is now the country's oldest and largest bank. It is 218 years old.

Why Banking Works

On the face of it, banking is a pretty easy process—borrow low, lend high. Lending is not a difficult task. Stand with a chequebook, and people will take funds from you at your rate. More difficult is managing the credit and ensuring the money comes back. But the most difficult is raising deposits. Retail liabilities sit at the bottom of the banking food chain but are the most difficult of banking tasks.

After all, what do you get in exchange for a deposit? Just a receipt. A piece of paper. And in today's world, even that has gone digital.

So why do people place their savings with banks? In a word, trust. That is the core of banking. This is why deposits with public sector undertaking banks even today exceed those with private sector banks, even though services may differ. The primary objective of a bank depositor is safety. They are willing to earn less for the assurance that their money will come back to them on the promised date.

Thus, banks were the first ones to provide a credit-mitigating structure. They absorb the risk, for which they, of course, get a return and keep the depositor safe.

On the other hand, they are providing funding to a cash-starved client—someone willing to pay the interest cost and able to return the principal but not the creditworthiness to raise the capital. In this case, the bank provides the client with a credit enhancement structure.

The bank model works because it can provide safety to the depositor and liquidity to the borrower. This model has survived for years and will probably outlive most of us by 2050 and into the next century.

The Banking Process

While banks will always exist, the channels will keep evolving. Decades ago, you had to visit the bank premises to deposit, withdraw money, or take a loan. This then moved to ATMs, where you could deposit and withdraw cash.

We now have electronic transfers, and India is the leader in this field. Our UPI is probably the most successful fund transfer machine in the world. With the advent of the central bank digital currency (CBDC), this process will be further refined.

But a bank's core deposit-raising model is unlikely to die out any time soon. Very simply, it is the most cost-efficient way to raise liabilities. While Fintechs will develop sophisticated credit evaluation, lending, and collection models, it will be long before they reach the 'trust stature' of an SBI or an HDFC Bank.

Consider the numbers. As of 30 September 2023, SBI's balance sheet was approximately Rs 63 lakh crore. This is 20 per cent of India's gross domestic product (GDP)! The Reserve Bank of India's balance sheet, which, amongst other things, reflects the reserves of the banks of the country, is about 25 per cent of the country's GDP. In effect, between the central bank and the country's largest bank, we can fit in half the country!

It is quite amazing when you realize that the thousand rupees you left lying around in your savings account may be funding a small tea stall owner to grow his business or helping a petrochemical giant acquire a new refinery. Banks put your money to work. They also create a multiplier effect not just in interest income but also in their impact on the economy.

Consider the following: X deposits Rs 10,000 with a bank. Y takes a loan of Rs 10,000 from that bank and buys a mobile phone. The store owner who sells the mobile takes the Rs 10,000 and buys clothes for his family. The clothes store owner uses the same Rs 10,000 to pay rent for his store.

The landlord deposits Rs 10,000 from the rent in his bank account. And the process starts again. A very simplistic model, but that is how Rs 10,000 in a bank has a 5X impact on the economy.

Banks and Their Money

The importance of the banking sector can be gauged by the fact that every country has a central bank exclusively focused on the working of banks. The stated purpose of the Federal Reserve in the US or many other central banks may be inflation control and growth, but the execution is always done through banks.

Monetary and fiscal policies are primarily aimed at banks. Controlling liquidity and the cost of funds to banks has a direct impact on a country's economy. Growth can be increased or reduced, and prices controlled.

The early bankers funded the rulers. Nothing much has changed, even today. Banks still directly or indirectly fund the ruler, in this case, the elected government. The structure of banks is such that a substantial part of their deposits flow into government coffers.

Regulatory reserves, which are set up to make banks more secure and liquid, in effect, lead banks to invest in government bonds and deposits. The only difference is that now these funds are not used to fight wars but are supposedly used for the betterment of the populace at large.

In many countries, including India, government borrowing is so large that it crowds out private borrowers. The government bond curve is considered the sovereign or most secure curve, and all other borrowers are expected to pay a higher cost to borrow. Banks thus set a benchmark for corporate and retail borrowers. Thus, how a bank manages its money is very important.

Broadly, banks have three core areas in which they lend or invest. The first is retail, which includes all your individual loans; micro, small and medium enterprise loans; personal loans; vehicle loans; home loans, and credit cards, among others. The second is corporate. These are the big chaps—large corporations that take loans for working capital or capex.

The third is treasury or investments. This is the eclectic part with bonds, equities, forex, commodities, and derivatives. It involves investing in various asset classes and taking a call on the direction of the markets.

Being highly regulated entities, banks have a plethora of regulations that cover each of these asset products. There are norms to be followed, limits to be kept, returns to be filled, margins to be met, and stop losses to be avoided.

A banker needs to be a credit analyst, a cash manager, a bond trader, and an equity investor—all in one. This is not an easy task and one with many pitfalls. Wrong credit or investment decisions can cost the organization dearly. For the employee, it can even cost them their jobs.

There are many conflicting views on where a bank should lend. The government might believe that the lending should help build the country's infrastructure and help those who deserve it the most. Some believe they should lend only to large corporations as that will create jobs. Yet others feel bank funding should be directed towards the retail consumers who drive consumer demand.

For a bank, the only thing that drives lending is the ability of the borrower to pay back. Everything else is moot. Whether wholesale lending drives jobs and growth or retail lending stokes inflation is a matter for the central bank to ponder. For a commercial banker, the first concern is the safety of depositor funds. Trust must be maintained.

The Future

Artificial intelligence, machine learning, robotic processes—yes, all these are probably present in the future of banking. But even more importantly, what the future holds for banking is specialization.

The days of one-size-fits-all banks are slowly receding. Smart central banks like the Reserve Bank of India have already seen this. This is why, over the past few years, they have given specialized bank licenses. Small finance banks (SFBs) and payment banks are just two such examples.

SFBs, for example, focus on micro banking, lending to the unbanked and underbanked. The model has seen great success. In India, specialized banks will thrive.

There will be banks that focus only on long-term retail products like home loans and others that give short-tenor loans. There will also be investment banks that are market-risk-driven. The fintechs that we have seen so far are the front runners of this; they are the digital banks of the future.

However, one thing that is unlikely to change even in 2050 is the banks' deposit model. On the asset side, there are multiple product and delivery options, and the deposit model for liabilities is efficient and strong. As the Americans say, If it isn't broken, don't fix it! While the concept of taking deposits from individuals, slowly building up current and savings accounts and convincing senior citizens to keep their life savings in a bank account sounds outdated, it actually works.

This is why the RBI continuously asks banks to build up their retail deposit base, especially current account savings accounts. These are deposits that will not leave the bank overnight. They are the kind of liabilities that bankers love—sticky deposits.

Last year, the Silicon Valley Bank crisis in the US showed us what happens when 'hot deposits' take flight. For any bank to succeed today or in the future, it needs assurance that its deposit base will be there. India's high savings rate has enabled it to be well-positioned in this aspect.

Twenty-five years from today, this will work even more in our favour. Our current demographic is under thirty. They are more inclined to borrow and spend. But twenty-five years from now, they will be older and probably wealthier. At that point, they will again turn to banks for security.

The tricky part is connecting these two seemingly different banks: the safe, secure deposit-taking bank and the new-age online loan-dispensing bank. Fintechs and new-age banks pride themselves on disbursing loans super-fast time. One can get a loan in under 10 minutes with a minimum of documentation.

Sure, these organizations have well-tested processes and models that allow them to dish out fast credit. But as a depositor, you will shy away from placing your money with a bank that gives out money so fast. By the same token, one will not approach a staid, old-world bank for a loan, and for that very reason, they will not be able to process the loan fast enough!

This is the nub of the problem. The bank of the future has to be two things at the same time. No bank can survive without a strong deposit base, and there is no use in this base if you can lend that money out efficiently and safely. The future thus holds the exciting promise of many partnerships and a lot of consolidation. Neither the existing banks will vanish nor the fintech will collapse, but both will need to evolve.

Of all the businesses in the world, banking is the one that has accepted change and grown with it. The most outstanding example is the ATM. When it was first introduced, it was expected to put tellers out of jobs and shut down branches.

But even in 2023, some of the largest banks in India opened 1,000 branches each. Technology in banking has always been an enabler. It has created opportunities, products, and jobs.

India is on the cusp of a huge revolution in how it handles its money. Amongst the earliest roles that banks had was safeguarding and transferring cash. It is ironic that as we move to a near-cashless society, the banks are again at the forefront.

Today, a bank does not spend as much on physical security as it does on cyber security. Malware and ransomware are today's bank dacoits. Cyber policing is a 24/7 activity at banks. With information databases increasing, storage is a huge challenge. The Cloud provides many options but comes with a multitude of security issues. Banking is getting smarter every day, but so is your cybercriminal.

India's bank of the future will be a lot of things.

- It will be omnipresent: in your car, phone, office, home, store, and bank branch.
- It will function 24/7/365. The concept of bank holidays will become extinct.
- It will be a shapeshifter. Your local grocer, favourite bar, coffee shop, and *paanwalla* will all be banking outlets for you.

Everyone wants to be a banker, or more correctly, manage your payments and investments. In the very foreseeable future, this will happen. The likes of Apple, Google, Meta, and Jio will all be your bankers. They will call themselves by different names and offer various value propositions, but, in the end, it is your money that they are after. Any organization that has information access, especially in terms of behavioural data or social connections, will aspire to sell you products and direct your money flow. While this may worry us, it is not necessarily a bad thing.

For one, it will reduce transaction costs and increase efficiency, especially in terms of time. Be it a stock or a shoe, if a person can buy it at the lowest price and with the least effort and time, they will come back for more. Banking in the future will be a lifestyle concept. It will be woven into the tapestry of your needs and seamlessly satisfy your requirements—wherever, whenever, whatever.

15

Embracing Sustainability and ESG: A Pathway for India's Ascent to Great Power Status

Sankar Chakraborti

In recent years, India has significantly changed its approach to environmental sustainability and climate change. At the forefront of this change is the Indian prime minister Narendra Modi's commitment to achieving net-zero carbon emissions by 2070. This ambitious goal, articulated at major global forums, reflects the country's dedication to playing a pivotal role in addressing the global climate crisis.

Prime Minister Narendra Modi has outlined a comprehensive plan for India to achieve net zero in his addresses at international platforms like the COP26 summit. 'It is our sacred duty to leave a healthy planet for our future generations,' the prime minister stated, highlighting the urgency of climate action. His vision encompasses not just a reduction in carbon emissions but a holistic approach towards sustainable development, balancing economic growth with environmental stewardship.

In his speeches, the prime minister often emphasizes the concept of 'climate justice,' arguing that it is crucial to consider the needs and challenges of developing countries in the global climate agenda. He remarks, 'For a country like India, which is diligently working towards eradicating poverty and ensuring health, education, and dignity for billions, a just approach to climate change is essential.'

Strategies for Achieving Net Zero

Achieving net-zero emissions is a multifaceted challenge that requires a blend of policy, innovation, and societal change. The Indian government has laid out several strategies to reach this goal. These include significant investments in renewable energy, aiming to increase India's non-fossil fuel energy capacity to 500 GW by 2030. The government is also focusing on reducing the carbon intensity of its economy, promoting energy efficiency across various sectors, and enhancing green cover through extensive afforestation programmes.

The prime minister has highlighted the role of technology in achieving these objectives. In his words, 'Technology and innovation are key to our climate action strategy. We are focusing on new technologies to convert waste to wealth and exploring green hydrogen as a future energy source.'

The prime minister's commitment to net zero is not just a domestic agenda but also a call for international collaboration. Recognizing that climate change is a global challenge requiring a united response, he has urged developed nations to support developing countries through technology transfer and climate finance. 'We need to bring countries together to find collective solutions,' he asserts, emphasizing the importance of global solidarity in climate action.

India's leadership in international initiatives like the International Solar Alliance (ISA) and Coalition for Disaster Resilient Infrastructure (CDRI) is a testament to its commitment to proactive international engagement on climate issues. Through these platforms, India is not only sharing its experiences and knowledge but also learning from global best practices.

Challenges and the Road Ahead

While the commitment to net zero is a monumental step, it comes with its set of challenges. India faces the dual task of lifting millions out of poverty while transitioning to a low-carbon economy. Addressing these challenges will require innovative solutions, sustained policy efforts, and an inclusive approach that considers the socio-economic realities of India's diverse population.

The prime minister's vision for a net-zero India is a bold and necessary step towards a sustainable future. The journey to net zero is not just a policy goal but a reflection of India's ancient ethos of living in harmony with nature, now being reimagined in the context of modern challenges.

India's journey towards becoming a global power is uniquely defined by its rich cultural heritage, emphasizing sustainability and harmony with nature. In a world increasingly driven by Environmental, Social, and Governance (ESG) principles, India's ancient traditions offer vital lessons for sustainable development.

The Roots of Sustainability in Indian Culture

Sustainability has been a cornerstone of Indian culture, with ancient scriptures advocating for a balanced coexistence with nature. The *Arthashastra*, composed by Kautilya in the 4th century BCE, exemplifies this ethos. It not only deals with statecraft and economics but also emphasizes environmental conservation and judicious resource management. Kautilya's foresight in recognizing the interdependence between a kingdom's prosperity and its environmental health mirrors today's sustainability ethos, underscoring the timeless relevance of India's cultural legacy in the global ESG dialogue.

Ancient India's approach to sustainability extends beyond the *Arthashastra*. The concept of *rittha*, a sustainable agricultural practice mentioned in Vedic texts, highlights the importance of crop rotation and soil health, predating modern sustainable farming methods. Additionally, India's traditional rainwater harvesting systems, like the *johads* in Rajasthan, demonstrate an innate understanding of water conservation and management, which is crucial in today's context of water scarcity and climate change challenges.

Environmental Stewardship: A Pillar for Sustainable Growth

India's environmental landscape presents significant challenges, including air and water pollution, deforestation, and biodiversity loss. For instance, the *World Air Quality Report 2020* indicated that twenty-two of the world's thirty most polluted cities are in India, underscoring the urgent need for environmental action. Harnessing renewable energy is a vital step towards mitigating these challenges. India's commitment to expanding its renewable energy capacity to 450 GW by 2030, as per the Ministry of New and Renewable Energy, reflects a strategic shift towards sustainable energy sources. This transition is crucial not only for environmental health but also for economic resilience and energy security.

The success stories of regions like Ladakh, which is aiming to be carbon-neutral, and the solar-powered Cochin International Airport, the world's first of its kind, are testaments to India's potential for sustainable energy utilization. Inspired by traditional environmental stewardship and modern innovation, these initiatives pave the way for a greener and more sustainable future.

Social Equity and Inclusion: Building a Resilient Society

Diverse challenges, including poverty, gender inequality, and access to education and healthcare, characterize India's social fabric. Addressing these issues is imperative for building a resilient society. India's initiatives in social entrepreneurship and corporate social responsibility align with its cultural ethos of social welfare. Programmes like the midday meal scheme, which feeds over 120 million children daily, not only tackle hunger but also improve school attendance and education outcomes. This initiative resonates with ancient Indian traditions of community dining and sharing, showcasing how traditional concepts can be adapted to address contemporary social challenges.

Furthermore, India's efforts in financial inclusion, exemplified by the Pradhan Mantri Jan Dhan Yojana, which has opened over 400 million bank accounts for the unbanked population, demonstrate a commitment to social equity. Such initiatives, rooted in the principle of inclusive growth, are crucial for building a society where opportunities and resources are accessible to all.

Governance: Strengthening Institutions for Long-term Prosperity

Effective governance is at the heart of India's ESG journey. India's strides in enhancing transparency and accountability are evident in initiatives like the Digital India campaign, which aims to digitize government processes, and the goods and services tax (GST), which has simplified the tax structure and improved revenue collection. These reforms reflect ancient principles of efficient governance and are vital for attracting foreign investment, boosting economic growth, and ensuring policy stability.

The significance of robust governance is further highlighted in India's efforts to combat corruption and promote ethical practices, as seen in the implementation of the Real Estate (Regulation and Development) Act and the Insolvency and Bankruptcy Code. These reforms not only enhance investor confidence but also contribute to a more equitable and just society, in line with India's ancient ethos of dharmic governance.

Leveraging Sustainable Technology for Technological Advancement

The intersection of sustainable technology and innovation is where India's future potential lies. India is making significant strides in areas like green energy, smart cities, and eco-friendly transportation. The rise of start-ups focusing on sustainable technologies is transforming the country's technological landscape. For example, Bengaluru-based Sun Mobility's innovations in swappable battery technology for electric vehicles represent a breakthrough in sustainable transportation. Additionally, projects like Smart Cities Mission aim to develop 100 smart cities across the country and integrate technology with sustainability, focusing on areas like waste management, efficient energy usage, and sustainable urban planning.

The Indian government's support for policies like Faster Adoption and Manufacturing of (Hybrid and) Electric (FAME) vehicles underscores a commitment to fostering a sustainable tech ecosystem. These initiatives not only address environmental concerns but also position India at the forefront of the global sustainable technology movement.

The Road Ahead: Integrating ESG into India's Growth Strategy

India's ascent to great power status necessitates a deep integration of ESG principles into its growth strategy. The challenge lies in balancing rapid economic development with environmental sustainability and social inclusivity. The country's pledge to achieve net-zero carbon emissions by 2070, as announced at the COP26 summit, is a significant commitment towards this balance. Achieving this ambitious goal will require innovative solutions that blend ancient wisdom with modern technology and practices.

Policymakers must focus on creating frameworks that foster sustainable economic activities while protecting the environment and ensuring social welfare. The integration of ESG metrics in corporate and government functioning can guide this process, aligning India's growth trajectory with global sustainability standards. This approach not only secures economic prosperity but also ensures a sustainable future for its citizens, resonating with India's age-old principles of balance and harmony.

16

Reimagining Indian Railways: A Vision for 2050

L.C. Trivedi

My journey with Indian Railways (IR) began on 10 April 1983, when I boarded an express train to Howrah from Delhi en route to the Garden Reach headquarters of South Eastern Railway to assume my role as a probationary officer. Little did I know then that this rail journey would mark the beginning of a more than thirty-eight years-long commitment to Indian Railways, a commitment that would take me across geographies and roles in multiple verticals, with railways becoming my alter ego.

Indian Railways improved the rolling stock, expanded and electrified the network, and uni-gauged it to broad gauge with electronic signalling instead of mechanical one during this period.

Indian Railways, often hailed as the nation's lifeline, has been a key driver of India's socio-economic progress since its inception. As we cast our gaze towards 2050, envisioning the future of Indian Railways necessitates a holistic strategy that incorporates technological advancements, sustainability measures, and an elevated passenger experience. This essay presents a visionary roadmap for Indian Railways in 2050, with a focus on innovation, efficiency, and inclusivity, all of which are crucial for the continued success of this national institution.

Technological Advancements

By 2050, Indian Railways will have undergone a profound technological transformation, leveraging cutting-edge innovations to enhance its operational efficiency and safety standards. Implementing high-speed rail networks, magnetic levitation (Maglev) trains, and hyperloop technology will revolutionize long-distance travel, reducing travel times and enhancing connectivity between major cities. Additionally, the widespread adoption of artificial intelligence (AI), the internet of things (IoT), and blockchain technology will optimize railway operations, predictive maintenance, and passenger safety measures.

Sustainability Measures

In line with global efforts to combat climate change, Indian Railways in 2050 will prioritize sustainability measures to minimize its environmental footprint. Integrating renewable energy sources such as solar and wind power will reduce dependency on fossil fuels, significantly reducing carbon emissions. Furthermore, introducing eco-friendly train designs, including energy-efficient locomotives and lightweight materials, will contribute to a greener and more sustainable rail network. Moreover, initiatives to promote eco-friendly practices among passengers, such as waste recycling and water conservation, will further enhance the environmental sustainability of Indian Railways.

Enhanced Passenger Experience

By 2050, Indian Railways will offer an unparalleled passenger experience characterized by comfort, convenience, and seamless connectivity. State-of-the-art train interiors will prioritize passenger comfort, featuring ergonomic seating, entertainment systems, and onboard amenities. Advanced ticketing systems, including mobile apps and contactless payments, will streamline the booking process and ensure hassle-free travel. Moreover, integrating high-speed internet connectivity and digital entertainment platforms will improve the onboard experience, catering to the evolving needs of tech-savvy passengers. In addition, enhanced accessibility measures for differently-abled passengers, including wheelchair-friendly facilities and sensory-friendly accommodations, will promote inclusivity and ensure equitable access to rail travel for all.

Infrastructure Development

In 2050, Indian Railways will boast a modern and robust infrastructure network with state-of-the-art stations, rail terminals, and transit hubs. Exposing existing stations into multi-modal transit hubs will integrate rail, metro, and bus services, facilitating seamless intermodal connectivity for passengers. The expansion of high-speed rail corridors and dedicated freight corridors will optimize freight transportation, bolstering India's logistical capabilities and boosting economic growth. Investments in smart infrastructure, including digital signalling systems and autonomous train operations, will enhance safety standards and operational efficiency across the rail network.

Railways play and will continue to play a crucial role in building India on social, economic, and security fronts. In my dream of India@2050, railways will play a vital role in improving the productivity of the transportation system, providing an economy with an edge over global peers, strengthening social cohesion by promoting mass mobility and achieving environmental goals.

My vision of IR@2050 will be of a railway hauling 50 per cent of the country's cargo, up from the current level of around

27 per cent, helping to bring down logistics costs by 8 per cent from the current level of around 15 per cent.

I expect regular fast trains running at 200+ km per hour to connect major cities spaced 500–800 km apart in less than 4 hours, thus providing a better option for people to travel than airways. I would love to see the elimination of long waiting lists for express trains, industry getting railway rakes within a reasonable period after indenting for it, and suburban metro rail coverage in all cities with a metro population of over a million.

IR@2050 will be a carbon-neutral entity making a major contribution towards India's achieving environmental goals. The IR@2050 of my dream will be without railway-roadway crossings, with fencing along the tracks, airport-type railway stations, and modern signalling systems with modern safety features like anti-collision systems and the capability of normal operations under adverse weather conditions like fog.

Indian Railways of 2050 will leverage technology to provide a safe, secure, and efficient means of transportation for both cargo and passengers. Digitizing systems and making railways customer-friendly will also lead to greater transparency and boost the ease of doing business. Modern cargo and passenger terminals will address issues related to first- and last-mile connectivities, reducing the lead time from doorstep to doorstep.

Action Plan

For this vision-cum-dream to translate into reality, while many steps have been initiated, many more will need to be taken.

Indian Railways is a unique system with a track gauge of 1676 mm called broad gauge. Why the British chose this unique gauge for the Indian subcontinent while keeping their railway gauge at 1,435 mm, which is the standard gauge for the European railroad system, is a mystery to me, defying logic and whose answer I am seeking till today and am not sure to find in future.

This 1,676 gauge resulted in the denial of state-of-the-art European rail technology to India and benefited China as they could almost lift from the shelf a design of their choice as they had the same standard gauge of 1,435 mm. This was the reason that, back in 2018, when we started working on India's first semi-high-speed train Vande Bharat, we had to design it from scratch. The same thing happened with an anti-collision device called Kavach, which we had to design indigenously after we found adopting European technology ETCS exorbitantly costly.

In a good beginning for the past few years, the government has been liberal with the fund provisioning for the railways, with \$30–40 billion being spent annually on capex. The annual rail network expansion has increased to around 5,000 km, with 100 per cent electrification of railway tracks; mechanical signalling has given way to an electric/electronic signalling system and coverage of Kavach, which is the indigenous anti-collision system, across the network is underway.

Major contracts have been awarded for freight wagons, high-speed railway coaches, and high-horsepower electric locomotives. Hopefully, production will commence soon, supplying an adequate quantity of vehicles required for transporting men and cargo, essential to liquidating the waiting list of passengers and pending indents at goods terminals.

Modernizing freight and coaching terminals to reduce first- and last-mile detentions is also important. The government has proposed setting up modern coaching terminals under the station redevelopment schemes. Similarly, a plan is to set up 100 Gati Shakti Terminals (multi-modal cargo terminals).

National Rail Plan

The aim is to build capacity by 2030 ahead of forecasted demand for 2050. Towards this, the action plan is as follows:

- Dedicated freight corridor commissioning (existing and proposed) 8,657 km by 2050.
- 160 kmph speed on selected corridors and 130 kmph on other routes.
- Development of passenger stations and freight terminals.
- Construction of high-speed rail corridor (HSR) (3,485 km).
- Multi-tracking of trunk routes.
- Signalling system for higher speeds, including TCAS (Train Collision Avoidance System).
- 100 per cent electrification.
- Planning of rolling stock (freight, passenger, locomotives).
- Options, evaluation, and prioritization of projects
- Mapping of the entire Indian Railways network done on the geographic information system platform.

The concern that rail traffic's 300 km+ lead share has come down from 52 per cent to 32 per cent remains a challenge. Nevertheless, the National Railway Plan (NRP) proposes to arrest and reverse this trend and increase the railway share from 26 per cent to 45 per cent by 2050. The railway's cost must decrease by 30 per cent for this to happen. NRP also forecasts that the total freight traffic will increase from 4,700 MT to 15,583 MT, and with a 45 per cent share, the railways need to build infrastructure to handle 7,012 MT by 2050, up from the present level of 1,250 MT.

The Indian Railways aims to encourage private ownership of rolling stock with innovative designs alongside private freight and passenger trains. Wagon holding is expected to increase from 3 lakh to 11 lakh, locomotives from 12,000 to 47,000, and coaches to 150,000 by 2051.

Passenger traffic is estimated to grow from 8,080 million per year to 19,469 million per year. Also, to eliminate detentions, the Indian railways proposes constructing fifty-two bypasses and forty-eight flyovers along freight and high-speed corridors. To further achieve these goals, the following policy initiatives include the following:

- PFTs (private freight terminals)/ICDS (inland container depots)/private sidings (plan envisages lease for connectivity, reduced staff costs, and development charges).
- Upgradation of existing goods sheds/terminals (plan envisages private investment in existing facilities and open access for all types of traffic).
- In the new standard user model, all public land will be used for common user facilities, with Indian Railways supporting land acquisition/land as equity.

Key Issues for National Rail Plan: 2030

- Indian Railways@2030: Future Perspective
- Promotion of Digital Systems & Smart Technologies for Indian Railways
- Make in India: Manufacturing for Indian Railways
- Capacity Enhancement and Congestion reduction
- Enhanced Customer Services
- Introducing New technologies in Railways
- Land & Railway Infrastructure Modernisation
- Enabling Ecosystem of Material Procurement
- Track Modernisation & Renewal of Tracks
- Innovative and Advance Energy Technologies
- Decarbonisation & Energy Efficiency of Indian Railways
- PPP for Container Freight Terminals
- Signalling & Electrification
- Innovative Financing Solutions
- Investment Opportunities for New Projects
- Station Redevelopment
- High Speed Network
- Security & Safety Measures
- Tools and Trends in use of Data Analytics for Enhancing Safety
- Big Data & Cybersecurity Challenges

Various incentives for reducing the cost of transportation have also been enunciated. The funding requirements for implementing NRP are estimated to be Rs 38 lakh or around $500 billion.

Additionally, multiple steps are proposed to attract private investment into the rail sector. The government has shown its commitment to implementing the NRP by ensuring funding, including unprecedented budgetary support and asset monetization, and providing credit at concessional terms.

Bilateral international funding arrangements, like the one with the Japan International Cooperation Agency for the Ahmedabad–Mumbai Bullet Train project, are one such move.

International Railway Routes

In a world of geopolitical uncertainties, international railway lines can play a major role in developing alternate trade routes, mainly dependent on international sea shipping lanes. China has demonstrated the potential of railways in international trade through its Belt and Road initiative.

My vision for India@2050 will be to have a Trans Asian Railway connecting Hanoi in Vietnam to Istanbul in Turkey via ASEAN countries. South Asian continent (Bangladesh, India and Pakistan), Iran, Iraq and Turkey and rail lines connecting northeastern states of India, such as Mizoram, South Assam, Manipur, and Tripura, with Kolkata via Bangladesh. Similarly, I visualize rail connecting Kathmandu, Nepal's capital, with the Indian railway network. Manipur and Nagaland are landlocked states that share an international border with Myanmar. The Indian Railways is currently providing connectivity to these states with its pan India Rail network. If this connectivity can be extended across the international border with Myanmar to connect with the Myanmar rail network, the landlocked Northeast region of India will get access to major Myanmar sea port at Yangon.

Conclusion

The vision for Indian Railways in 2050 encompasses a bold and transformative agenda that embraces technological innovation, sustainability, and passenger-centricity. By leveraging cutting-edge technologies, prioritizing sustainability measures, and enhancing the passenger experience, Indian Railways will emerge as a global leader in the transportation sector, driving economic growth, fostering inclusivity, and connecting communities across the nation. Through concerted efforts and strategic investments, we can realize this visionary road map and unlock the full potential of Indian Railways as a catalyst for progress and development in the twenty-first century.

17

Visions for India in a Fragmented World Trade Order

Sankalp Mathur

In his 1920 book *Economic Consequences of Peace*, John Maynard Keynes asserted,

> Any man of capacity or character at all exceeding the average, into the middle and upper classes, for whom life offered, at a low cost and with the least trouble, conveniences, comforts, and amenities beyond the compass of the richest and most powerful monarchs of other ages.... He regarded this state of affairs as normal, certain, and permanent, except in the direction of further improvement, and any deviation from it as aberrant, scandalous, and avoidable.... The projects and politics of militarism and imperialism, of racial and cultural rivalries, of monopolies, restrictions, and exclusion, which were to play the serpent to this paradise, littlee more than the amusements of his daily newspaper.

As much as we hoped, the serpents of this paradise have made a resurgence into the average man's life, haunting him from the capitalist comforts of a life of free markets to that of conflicts and a potential decline in international social cohesion. Protectionism, wars, populism, polarization, pandemics, climate catastrophe, and geopolitical fragmentation have marked the last few years. How will the world evolve through this structural transformation? How do we navigate a potentially fragmented global trade order? What challenges and opportunities exist for India? Where does our comparative advantage lie?

Globalization has been a potent force in changing the economic landscapes of countries, communities, and the world. It has gone through cycles of busts and booms since the eighteenth century. However, since the late 1980s and 1990s, many developing countries have followed the path of liberalization and trade openness, which has flooded the gates of 'hyper-globalization'. Hyper-globalization led to millions of people being lifted out of poverty while advanced economies enjoyed lower prices and increased varieties of goods. All of this led to an astounding and impressive convergence in the income per capita across countries, which had never been seen in the last century.

However, the global financial crisis in 2008 and the recent compound global shocks have laid bare the vulnerabilities of the international trade order. Countries are now reassessing the benefits of neoliberal openness and financial liberalization. This chapter details the significance of the global trade project, why and if we are straying from an open trade world, and most importantly, what lies for India in a potentially new international trade structure.

The benefits of open trade have been documented in theoretical economics since time immemorial. The differences in capital, labour, geography, natural resources, culture, etc., across countries give us an absolute and comparative advantage in producing certain goods against other countries and a potential disadvantage against others. This explains why India has a comparative advantage in capability centres, the US in technology, Brazil in agricultural commodities, Saudi Arabia in fossil fuels, etc.

Trading these goods with other countries enables us to source goods that are otherwise expensive to produce domestically while reaping profits by selling the abundant goods in the foreign market. It is a win-win situation. As countries experimented with open trade in the decades after the Second World War, the system enabled middle-income countries to scale up production for selling in foreign markets, boosting employment and income opportunities, and lowering poverty. Moreover, lower trade barriers fostered competition as foreign firms competed for market share with domestic firms.

Consequently, Western consumers and firms revelled in reduced prices and an increased array of product choices. Open trade enhances consumer welfare and facilitates capital flows from the abundant North to the starved South. These flows embark on numerous investment projects in the developing world. Open trade also expedites technological transfer, which enables concurrent progress in science, medicine, policy, education, research, etc. Moreover, economic interdependence reduces the likelihood of countries going into conflicts, fostering an environment of peace, cooperation, and international coordination. Though it is not entirely unlikely, trade dependence reduces the war friction among countries. The world realized these trade benefits under policy and regulatory changes in the world institutions post–Second World War. The setting up of the World Trade Organisation, IMF, World Bank, United Nations, etc., facilitated an international forum of trade, justice, and peace.

In addition, technological innovation in containerization, computers, satellites, information and communication technology, the Internet, etc., reduced the cost of shipping goods from one country to another. The geopolitical and institutional changes in many countries in the late 1980s and 1990s further facilitated the growth of the global trade project. The fall of the

Iron Curtain paved the way for neoliberal ideas and the rejection of communism as a way to govern societies. This was followed by the two most populous countries—China and India—passing a slew of liberalization policies and opening up their economies.

One of the most striking consequences of open trade is the convergence in the international distribution of income per capita. While advanced economies benefitted from lower prices and increased varieties, hyper-globalization coincided with median and per-capita income increases and poverty reduction in many developing countries.

However, this period of hyper-globalization entailed a few episodes of economic crises, including the global financial crises, which cast doubts about the effectiveness of free market capitalism. There are several reasons why open trade might have a detrimental effect. As trade barriers lower, many firms offshore the production of critical inputs to other countries for lower costs. Consequently, it led to the establishment of global value chains where stages of production are spread across national borders that manipulate the stringency in regulatory standards.

The subtle exploitation of cheap labour through harsh working conditions in developing countries massed criticism of the global value chains. Companies offshore carbon-intensive production to countries with relaxed environmental policies, adversely impacting local pollution and health. Firms set headquarters in tax havens to avoid tax payments to certain jurisdictions to extract maximum profits. Apart from the exploitative impact on the developing world, the US monetary policy caused several episodes of capital outflows and sudden stops as investors pulled back money from developing countries in search of higher returns in the US. The era of hyper-globalization, marked by economic crises and doubts about free market capitalism, revealed negative consequences such as the exploitation of cheap labour, environmental concerns, and capital outflows from developing countries.

In the Western economies, free trade has, most importantly, generated structural reallocation, which has concurred with rising inequality. The US manufacturing employment decline coincided with increased imports from China. Along with automation and technology, trade caused damaging effects on those US countries that relied on manufacturing jobs. Some evidence shows these countries shifted right on the political scale and voted for populist political candidates.

As the political threats from open trade became evident, many Western economies retreated from their position of free trade and neoliberal progressivism. This is noticeable in the US protectionism trade policy under President Donald Trump, which the Biden government has continued.

Many countries, including the EU, China, Canada, and Mexico, responded with retaliatory tariffs. The United Kingdom quit the European Union. India increased tariffs on goods from China due to border skirmishes and national security concerns. Most importantly, the pandemic and the Russian invasion made the West exceptionally vulnerable to foreign shocks, realizing their unusual dependence on other countries for critical inputs.

These supply shocks have caused domestic inflationary pressures not seen in the last few decades. Generally, most major countries have turned inwards, retreating from decades of open trade and free-market liberalization. Economic interdependence, sought to be a beacon of global peace and unity, is now, ironically, being used as an economic weapon to choke countries of critical inputs for geopolitical gains.

We are currently at an inflexion point where compound shocks and geopolitical tensions have fostered a novel yet familiar economic nationalism. This has led to a modern rise of government interventions and the use of industrial policy. Consequently, the US enacted the Chips Act and the Inflation Reduction Act (IRA), providing colossal subsidies to direct investments into setting semiconductors and upcoming green industries (renewable energy, electric vehicles, etc.) on the US soil. Though the IRA is regarded as one of the most influential pieces of environmental legislation, it has garnered criticism as a protectionist measure to quell China's growing domination in chip manufacturing and green industries. The European Union has accused the US of flouting the World Trade Organization rules by using the deep pockets of the US government to reallocate production to the US, which other countries cannot afford to do.

Some critics have gone so far as to say that the proxy economic war with China will delay the green transition as it will take time and money for the US to match China's capacity. As countries trade off globalization with national security, what will be the distributional consequences across and within countries? Is a fragmented world trade order sustainable in the long run?

While some of the concerns regarding free trade are justified, we must remember that free trade has enabled economic convergence across countries. While the pandemic made countries vulnerable to foreign shocks, free trade provided the necessary buffer in delivering shortages of emergency equipment. Mutual collaboration on science, technology, and medicine among the countries led to the invention of vaccines in record time.

In any case, onshoring and friendshoring will not eliminate the spillover effects of shocks. Increasing bilateral trade barriers will potentially reallocate production to a third country, increasing time taken and cumulative import costs, indirectly exposing countries to third-order shocks. Furthermore, onshoring production only guarantees a partial proof solution as countries lose the ability to import in case of a severe domestic shock.

Nevertheless, the great trade reallocation seems pervasive in the current geopolitical environment. The critical question is, what opportunities lie for India in this new trade order? What must be India's economic and social policy to realize its full potential?

One obvious pathway is to take advantage of the reallocation out of China and attract manufacturing in India. As the West becomes wary of China, India has this rare opportunity to attract those investments and shore critical industries at home. This could be achieved by partially imitating the economic policies implemented in China and other East Asian countries in the last few decades.

This will involve making it easier for firms to conduct their business, providing them tax cuts and subsidies, eliminating red tape, facilitating public infrastructure, providing seamless environmental clearances, and creating a docile labour force by enforcing a homogenous culture.

Some aspects of this manufacturing push have been integral to the government's economic policy in the last few years, particularly with the 'Make in India' campaign. Like many countries, India has been attracting international firms to set up manufacturing plants to generate employment opportunities for the youth. This is done by providing subsidies and tax breaks financed by the government budget.

However, we must realize that these manufacturing plants will only generate a minuscule percentage of the total jobs required to sustain long-term growth for India. We must recognize that the excessive resource allocation towards manufacturing will not only be costly but also impossible without the requisite workforce upskilling. The following paragraphs will provide a brief explanation of why a misplaced manufacturing push may not be the optimal policy for India to realize the objective of being an advanced economy in the coming decades.

First, even after decades of a push towards enabling manufacturing in India, it remains less than 20 per cent of the total GDP. Usually, the country transitions through three phases in the stages of development: from agriculture to manufacturing and then to services. However, in the case of India, services have almost entirely captured the pie out of agriculture.

It hints at how India's historical, cultural, and institutional environment might not be conducive to being a global manufacturing hub. Second, even if we push for future opportunities in manufacturing, we will be competing with other Asian economies such as Taiwan, Vietnam, and Indonesia, which have an established infrastructure for quick and cheap manufacturing and potentially will have a comparative advantage over us.

Third, the assembly of the final good, a stage in the manufacturing process where India has gained some market share, captures only a minuscule percentage of the value added to the product. The intermediate stage of the production process, which involves manufacturing and assembly of products, has relentless international competition, bringing down the value it generates in the production process. Almost 60–70 per cent of the product value lies in the initial and end phases of the production process.

The initial stages broadly involve design, conceptualization, financing, and generating ideas for a product, and the last stages essentially involve customer services, business consulting, marketing, accounting, etc. Thus, the programmers, designers, lawyers, engineers, consultants, business executives, or, more generally, the flagbearers of ideas, concepts, and creativity extract the maximum value of a product.

Should we not redirect our economic policy towards targeting the first and last steps in the production process? Lastly, the recent data shows that while manufacturing trade has seen a reversal owing to geopolitical concerns, services trade, particularly trade in digital services, continues to grow across countries, offsetting some extent of the deglobalization trend.

India's challenge in becoming a global manufacturing hub stems from institutional factors and intense competition from established Asian economies. Redirecting economic policy towards the initial and final stages of the production process, where value is maximized, may offer a more promising avenue for growth, especially as services trade continues to expand amidst geopolitical uncertainties. The government's efforts in facilitating ease of doing business, attracting manufacturing jobs, and building the necessary physical infrastructure to support it are commendable.

The critical point is that we should put only some of our eggs in one basket. We will need a more vigorous push in the direction where the maximum value is. The positive news is that we have the demographic advantage in our favour. We already export the best engineers, scientists, and doctors worldwide.

The challenge is, how do we create the institutional capacity to retain the talent that India produces? How do we devise an environment that enables discussions and debates on compelling ideas? How do we forge a situation where this and the future generations are healthy? How do we become the idea-generating factory of the world?

To be able to do so, our priorities have to pivot towards facilitating world-class education and health infrastructure. India still ranks poorly on the human development index.

None of our universities rank in the top 200 in the world. Many parts of India still face acute malnutrition, stunting, and sub-optimal learning rates. Our female labour force participation is incredibly low.

Only when we fix these core structural issues will it be easier to envisage India becoming an advanced economy. We must ensure that our schools, colleges, and universities have a vibrant, liberal environment to exchange diverse ideas. It must be a gateway for upskilling our future generations with technical and vocational skills that open up the roads for innovation.

As the world grapples with novel compound challenges, the power lies with those with the intelligence, skills, and expertise to find solutions. This is only possible when we provide the appropriate institutional environment that retains talent in the country.

This can be done by allocating more funds towards tertiary education, providing research support in emerging fields, and incentivizing private firms to do in-house research and development. The positive news is that we do not have to look elsewhere to find the policy environment that works for us.

Even within India, we have pockets in the states of Kerela and city centres in Bengaluru, Gurugram, Mumbai, etc., which have comparable world-class living standards. The objective is to learn from these development models and apply them to other backward pockets of the country for holistic growth.

We currently have many forces in our favour. We have the demographic dividend with the largest employable population in the world. We have the government that has incessantly focussed on building the public infrastructure with ports, roads, highways, tunnels, and railways, which until a decade back was marred with corruption.

We have become the leaders in digital payment infrastructure, which seemed unrealistic until a few years back. Our youth is dedicated, hard-working, passionate, and eager to learn. We have a vibrant culture from which the world has much to learn.

We are a unique experiment in history where diverse races, languages, castes, and religions are bound with foundations of democracy and unity. There are campaigns to change the narrative of what our country is, but our strength lies in these liberal foundations. Inspired by Rabindra Nath Tagore, if we have to sail the ship from the treacherous currents in a potentially fragmented world, we must be a country where the mind is without fear and knowledge is free.

To capture the maximum value from the industries of tomorrow and the services, we will have to push towards a unique growth model that grounds itself in holistic human development and discovering innovation to the current and future challenges.

Achieving India's transition to an advanced economy necessitates a strategic focus on elevating education and health infrastructure, addressing shortcomings in human development, and fostering innovation through vibrant educational environments. By investing in these core areas and drawing inspiration from successful pockets within the country, India can aspire to holistic growth and global competitiveness.

The potential multi-polar world of the future will bring its unique threats, particularly when challenges such as climate change, artificial intelligence, and cyber security know no sovereign borders and are universal. We defeated the serpents of our global past by enforcing new institutions and created an imperfect yet idyllic 'paradise'.

The flaws of yesterday's orders have spawned new serpents powered by modern technology, warfare, and industrial might. In this fragmented world, India must pursue a leadership role in the ideals of global cooperation for these global challenges.

We must optimize our demographic dividend and channel our comparative advantage where the maximum value is. Today, we have a unique opportunity to set rules and orders for global institutions that will dictate our future. We must ground the vision in our democratic foundations, which celebrate diversity and the exchange of ideas to invent solutions for the coming age. May the world of tomorrow be holistic, sustainable, just, and, most importantly, powerful enough to overcome future projects and politics that will play serpents of the new paradise.

18

Brand India to Brand Bharat

Amim Ahmed

Long years ago, we made a tryst with destiny. Now, the time has come when we shall redeem our pledge—not wholly or in full measure—but very substantially. 'At the stock of midnight hour, when the world sleeps, India will awake to life and freedom.' Jawaharlal Nehru's first speech post-independence in 1947 clearly announced India's new journey. Today, seventy-six years later, it seems the world is still waiting for India.

India has always played a significant role in the world's socio-economic development and has assumed a pivotal role in shaping global society. From the ancient Indus Valley Civilization to the modern era, India has been called '*sone ki chidiya*', representing a top-tier brand for the world to comprehend, study, and admire. This exemplifies the power of Brand India.

Made in India, Made for the World!

India has a rich history of invention or creation, dating back to the Ashoka era and continuing through to the present day with leaders like Narendra Modi. Throughout history, India has introduced many ground-breaking inventions, such as the concept of zero, yoga, Ayurveda, cataract surgery,[1] the value of pi,[2] and important contributions to artificial intelligence.[3] These inventions have had a profound impact on the world. How about a world without zero?

Moving Forward with the Right Mindset

Changing the attitude towards creating something new is essential for growing Indian brands. In the words of J.R.D. Tata, 'Never start with diffidence, always start with confidence.' Success stories are made only when someone decides to change the course of their life. This is precisely how independent India was shaped under the Nehru regime. Under his leadership, India got '*nau ratan*' (nine jewels): IITs, IIMs, and AIIMS.

As we advance, we have had some well-established brands and some that we have created. Each year, we have witnessed new growth in the manufacturing sector. Despite starting anew as a nation-state after the British Raj, we have never had a dearth of home-grown brands. While Unilever, Fiat, Seiko, Citizen, Panasonic, and P&G ruled the world, we had Tata, Godrej, Nirma, HMT, HM, Voltas, Parle Agro, Amul, and Allwyn.

The 1970s and 1980s were milestone years for India. During this period, India experienced a paradigm shift in consumer demand, leading to the launch of many home-grown brands to cater to this demand. Throughout the 1980s, companies such as Titan, Liberty, Bajaj, Usha, Sonodyne, Texla, Bush TV, Videocon, Onida, Action Shoes, Kismi Bar, and the iconic Indian soft drinks such as Torino, Gold Spot, Thumps Up, Limca, and Citra, became household names.

The growth of India's consumer market reached new heights when a Japanese car maker partnered with the Indian government to launch the iconic Maruti 800. The 1980s marked a new era of joint ventures in India. Companies such as Maruti

Suzuki, Kawasaki Bajaj, Lehar Pepsi, Hero Honda, National Panasonic, and many more emerged, as the Indian government did not allow standalone foreign brands to enter the market without local joint venture partnerships.

Additionally, to compete with rivals like Marvel and DC Comics, Amar Chitra Katha became India's answer.

Generic and Monopoly

Indian consumers are known for their loyalty among major countries despite the country being a very price-sensitive market. Due to limited brand options in the 1980s, terms like 'generic' were coined, for example, Maggi, Hawai, Bata, Surf, Rasna, Amul, and Bisleri. A few of these are still market leaders and enjoy a monopoly despite globalization. Some that stand out include but are not limited to Amul butter, ITC cigarettes, Bajaj autos, Hero bikes, etc.

India Becomes Global

In 1991, India experienced a significant turning point that ushered in a new growth story. The Government of India implemented three major economic reforms: liberalization, privatization, and globalization.

This phase not only helped the country to recover from the recession that ravaged the Indian industry but also provided a significant boost to the manufacturing and IT sectors. Before these economic reforms, Narayana Murthy, Azim Premji, Shiv Nadar, and Ramalinga Raju were the pioneers of IT brands. However, following the reforms, we witnessed companies such as TCS, HCL, and others enter the market. Consequently, India transformed into a hub for IT brands, many of which now dominate the global market in IT services.

Leader, Follower, Challenger

The economic reforms of India helped many foreign brands to successfully launch themselves in the country, leveraging newfound money and consumer aspirations. Companies such as Coke, McDonald's, Pizza Hut, Nokia, Samsung, LG, Pepsi, Honda, Hyundai, Mercedes, UCB, BMW, Audi, P&G, and Philips, among others, entered the Indian market in the years that followed. We appreciated this change as we no longer depended on a few brands. The access to global products elevated consumer sentiments, which in turn fuelled India's domestic demand-driven economic growth.

Taking advantage of these changes occurring in the Indian market and the evolution of demand, China also entered the market despite geopolitical issues. This led to the rise of local Chinese brands such as Haier, Oppo, Redmi, and TCL, which aggressively targeted the Indian consumer market.

China also became a manufacturing hub, motivating many new-age and rising entrepreneurs from India to launch their own brands with manufacturing bases in China. Nevertheless, these entrepreneurs either challenged or just followed the global giants. Nokia versus Micromax, Amazon versus Flipkart, Videocon versus LG, Kent RO versus Aqua Guard, Syska versus Philips—the list is long. While some of the home-grown brands managed to survive, most were either acquired or could not withstand the fierce competition.

Now, as India is relaunched as Bharat, it has aspirations to become the third-largest economy in the world. The country aims to achieve a $5 trillion economy by 2026 and a $30 trillion economy by 2047 (India's 100th-year after independence).

But for a country that aspires to be one of the world's superpowers, having recognizable brands will be important not only for business generation but also for national association. Nevertheless, what is worrying about India's evolving brand story is that despite a demonstrated capability, we have become acquirers rather than creators of brands in recent history.

Although Tata owns Jaguar Land Rover, and Reliance has been acquiring more than 100 top international brands, we are still some distance away from actually experiencing a stand-alone derivative of such brands that are globally recognizable and can be considered a truly Indian brand.

The point is that we are still short of visionary leadership to create global consumer brands despite the capacity to sustain them. Our homegrown brands, such as Tata, Mahindra, Hero, Ashok Leyland, Haldiram, and the like, have great potential, but they lag way behind the world's most valuable or iconic brands.

While India will undoubtedly become a superpower in terms of economy, we have not yet reached a point where the world proudly associates with Indian phones, cars, dishes, and laptops! We must get our acts together as soon as possible to reach our full potential.

But in the meantime, our brand ambassadors Shahrukh Khan, Amitabh Bachchan, A.R. Rahman, and Virat Kohli will continue to compete fiercely with people from all walks of life, and our technocrats will lead Fortune 500 companies with assurances showcasing to the world that brand Bharat has arrived, and there is more to come.

Part V
Safeguarding the Republic
(Two Arguments)

19

Argument I: Reimagining the Political Economy with Twenty-three Dreams for a Better Republic@2047

Benn Kochuveedan

As we tread through the *Amritkaal* towards the *Satakaal*, every ordinary citizen has the right to ponder over the current contours of our socio-political economy and dream of what our Republic should be when she hits a century. For someone like me—one of those nearly extinct species of lesser mortals who are petrified of thinking straight—it is more imperative to think aloud now. Such stocktaking is crucial as the history of our young nation, of late, has been marked with sheer administrative incompetence and over-centralization of executive power, reckless disregard for constitutional morality and due processes, the capture of all statutory organs of the Republic, and an arrogant and petty vilification of critics.

I do not consider this era to be *Amritkaal* or the golden era, as it is being brashly branded by the faithful of the regime of the past decade as it considers itself to be more infallible than the pope when it comes to constitutional and administrative impunity. Sadly, after a decades-long churning, the elixir is missing in the fractured, divisive, muted, and bruised land that is a pale shadow of what the founding fathers envisioned for our democracy, socio-political morality, and federalism. Power corrupts us mortals, and the signs are still very vivid. As many as 146 Opposition members were shunted out of Parliament on flimsy grounds during the 2023 winter session, history is being rewritten with brazen blindness, the very identity of the nation got changed from India to Bharat one fine morning, Hindi is being imposed on a populace as diverse as the typical Babel of the Biblical yore who speaks in over 1,600 tongues, constitutional organs are captured without turning a hair leaving them as mutilated as a mangled heap of iron wires, over 60 per cent of the soon-to-be $5-trillion economy is owned by just 7 per cent of the population, while the remaining 93 per cent struggle to make both ends meet, and crony capitalism is the order of the day that a few groups have become default sovereigns as if the way forward for political economy is a one-nation-one-company model. The list of the imploding perils is growing longer and longer with each passing day. Signs of the times clearly tell that Amrit is being enjoyed by just a handful.

Standing at the crossroads and looking from a political-economy perspective, I dare to list my twenty-three dreams for the nation, which as a Republic is a pale shadow of even what it was at her birth. So, we have twenty-three years to the 2047 tryst with destiny and I believe my twenty-three dreams can help restore the constitutional, parliamentary, and democratic morality and sanctity, regain institutional credibility and morality, reform our political discourse, reinvent our diverse and multicultural ethos, and repose the trust of our teeming but hapless and hopeless youth who account for 66 per cent of the population.

Redeem, Restore the Constitution

Let us accept that we are a dying democracy. While the ills of our democracy have been growing over the years, the last decade has seen them imploding on our faces. To put it pithily, we are in an undeclared emergency. Each nakedly illegitimate executive decision is becoming acceptable to the wider public to such an extent that the institutional capture of Parliament—the higher judiciary, key federal agencies such as the Election Commission (EC), Enforcement Directorate (ED), Central Bureau of Investigation (CBI), and Income Tax Department—looks so kosher and legitimate.

Federal law enforcement agencies are thinking with their feet while taking orders from their political masters. I wish these agencies followed the rule book in letter and spirit, and not according to the whims and fancies of their political bosses. I wish they ensured justice the way they are constitutionally mandated to administer and deliver. I wish they regained the constitutional stature and morality and showed the teeth without biases as the late T.N. Seshan showed us in the not-so-distant past. All the four pillars, including the media, of our democracy need to be revived and sanctified in the manner as enshrined in the Constitution.

Reinstate the Supremacy of Parliament

Barring the only declared emergency (June 1975 to March 1977) when Parliament was suspended, the temple of our democracy has never been so dysfunctional, effeminate, and decimated. If we are to continue with the parliamentary model, we must return to the Constitution and re-read what is laid down there for us to be a parliamentary democracy.

How can a government bar the House from debating a key bill or an issue of national importance—be it the disastrous demonetization, China snatching away vast stretches of our land, or the tens of thousands of unfortunate deaths due to the unplanned and brutal COVID-19 lockdowns just to pander to the ego of the regime, or the abrogation of Article 370, or the violence in Manipur, or the canister attack inside Parliament by a few disgruntled jobless youths? Is it too non-consequential for the government to make a statement in the House? We need to transform it again as the temple of power.

Restore Rule of Law

The bedrock of any democracy is respect for the rule of law—by the executive, by the political leaders, and by the public at large. Sadly, we have been competitively scampering in the opposite direction for a long time as federal law-enforcement agencies are directed to target those opposing the regime while sparing the regime's supporters. The law should take its own course, irrespective of party or religion.

Let's Go the Presidential Way

Given the near demise of the parliamentary system, a presidential form of government can be better because it can at least make our government and national politics more explicit and direct. It can also usher in better accountability right from the grassroots and all the way up to the top. Coalition political compulsions, eroding federalism, a multi-party structure, political parties without principles or agenda, rampant horse-trading and politics of convenience have defeated the very concept of our parliamentary democracy. Sadly, for our politicians, there is no permanent enemy at all. Why do we not try the presidential form? Of course, the challenge is to have a balanced and impartial president.

Nurture Federalism, Stop the Widening North-South Divide

The past decade has seen the peaking of jingoism, hyper-nationalism with a deep majoritarian hue, and political and executive bigotry where every opposing voice was silenced and branded as traitors—which sadly has become the most-used word in the political lexicon of late. Sadly, a government that came to power offering more governance and less government has ended up being exactly the opposite. The binary of the minority-us-vs-the-majority-you is seeped so deep into the public consciousness now.

The north–south or Hindi–non-Hindi divide is getting shriller every day. Hardline Hindutva has become an overarching idea of Indianness now. The net result is the loss of the federal structure and cultural, political, and linguistic diversity which this nation has been known for since her birthing.

So, if we are to remain a federal state, north Indian politicians should stop pushing Hindi down the throat of the Southern masses. The much overdue delimitation exercise will have the South and other better-performing states like Maharashtra heavily losing their Parliamentary representation. Kerala and Tamil Nadu—the two most successful states in population control, poverty eradication, education, etc.—will be the biggest losers, while the underperforming northern bunch led by the nearly fully dysfunctional Uttar Pradesh and Bihar will gain the most despite being the worst laggards on every developmental metric.

Along with Maharashtra, the five Southern states contribute more taxes but get much less from Central devolution. For every Re 1 that Uttar Pradesh contributes in taxes, it gets back Rs 1.79 from the Centre; but for every Re 1 that Karnataka contributes, it receives just Re 0.47, and the worst is when it comes to

Maharashtra, the biggest contributor to the national tax kitty, it gets a paltry Re 0.32. Where is the reward for development?

Hindi, which is one of the youngest languages with only around 120 years of history and is a just mixture of much older Urdu, Hindustani, and many other northern regional languages, just cannot be the official language of a diverse nation that speaks in more than 1,600 tongues! Moreover, Hindi in all its derivatives is not even spoken by 40 per cent of the 1.44-billion people!! The simple point is, what does a South Indian get from a professional or educational perspective by learning Hindi? Zilch. Why does a language have to be proof of patriotism and national identity? The simple fact is that Hindi is as foreign as Hebrew or Greek to a South Indian, and she is more at home with English. So, stop using Hindi as a political tool and official medium of communication.

Reform the Electoral Process

If we choose not to have a presidential government, at least we must abolish the first-past-the-post system and make 51 per cent of valid votes mandatory for an electoral win. In 2014, the BJP got a mere 33 per cent of the vote cast, and in the 2019 hustings, it inched up to just about 39 per cent despite the number of seats increasing disproportionately. If we consider the voter turnout of 67 per cent in 2019, of the 912 million eligible voters, around 611 million voted, and BJP got 238 million votes. It means the current majority matrix is meaningless.

We must also end the universal voting rights and cap the voting age, say, at 80, and also make some basic education, say an SSC pass, a must for exercising the franchise. This will foster education, too. Also, cap the age for candidates, maybe at 70. For any job except running the government and law-making, an academic qualification is a must, and age limits are binding in this country!

Though electronic voting machines have their benefits, with rampant corruption and manipulation taking place in one poll and another, let us ensure all voters get to check their own voting results by introducing the voter-verified paper trail at all booths and counting all of them. An equally effective way to address fake voting and manipulation is to link the voter card to the ubiquitous Aadhaar. Also, why do not we introduce online voting in a foolproof manner so that more people can vote? Excuses for security in online voting are lame, as we do promote digital currency and digital transactions.

We also must revisit the anti-defection law. Currently, an elected member can mock the voter by switching sides at will, and a paranoid speaker or an effeminate court can rule that to be legit. Make it impossible to switch sides after the election or during the life of the house by making party-hoppers lose membership instantly and banning them from contesting the next poll. Party-hoppers have no business being in the electoral fray time and again, donning different hues.

Clean the Judiciary's Augean Stables, Set Hearing Timelines

The biggest bane of our judicial system is the inordinate delays in delivering justice. As of 2023, there were over 50 million pending cases, of which around 69,000 were in the Supreme Court alone. One reason for this is the poor infrastructure, both physical and personnel, including that of judges. The other is the greed of lawyers, as Mahatma Gandhi talked about in *My Experiments with Truth* and also of litigants.

Let us bring in some sanity. A beginning can be made by filling the massive numbers of vacant posts of judges, especially in the higher judiciary and other key supporting staff. Another step can be setting a timeline for disposing of cases, at least serious cases involving fundamental rights and constitutional issues. Also, let us have adjudication mechanisms for petty civil cases and curb a litigant's rights to approach higher courts.

Another crucial reform is ending the game of musical chairs in the Supreme Court when it comes to the appointment of the Chief Justice of India (CJI) under the collegium system. Why should a CJI be installed only for a fortnight? Can we bring back a better version of the National Judicial Appointments Commission, set clear benchmarks on the CJI's appointment, and end this musical chair in the higher judiciary? Can we have a law mandating a CJI candidate-judge should have at least two years of service left in order to be eligible for the post? Also, ban retired judges of the apex court and high courts from taking up government jobs so that they can deliver judgements without keeping in mind a post-retirement appointment. A better way is to remove the retirement age for apex court judges, especially the CJI.

End Freebies, Pensions for Politicians, and Government Employees

One of the biggest fiscal pains will come from the pension burden for government employees and politicians. How can you justify the massive benefits even a one-time MP/MLA gets after her/his term ends even mid-way? Increase their wages for sure, but stop all freebies like bungalows, unlimited travel, phone calls, etc.; give them all these for sure, but at market rates, please. If at all we raised the salaries of MPs, MLAs, and ministers ten-fold after ending all the freebies and pensions, the cumulative cost would be far lower than the huge financial burden accruing from these doles they enjoy all their lives.

Similarly, the steel frame, I mean the civil service–led government's administrative machinery right from the top to the lowest rungs, has been enjoying too much of a cushy life at the expense of the citizens. Why should the taxpayers feed them and their spouses with pensions, gratuities, free healthcare, and travel, among others, till death? Of course, barring the top ladder, government employees are low-paid, but combined with their freebies, they are paid well above market rates. If those in the private sector are asked to fend for themselves after retirement, what makes government employees so special? Why are they the responsibility of the taxpayers even after retirement? In a country of over 1.44 billion, why should a few million enjoy all the benefits and comfort at the cost of the public? So, let us stop all these so that they do not become a fiscal time-bomb for future generations, and India will not join the league of Cyprus and Greece.

Maybe the only ones requiring a pension are defence personnel, but that, too, should be capped and should not be extended to their spouses. A better way is increasing their wages.

As of fiscal 2023, the number of Central government employees was 5 million, plus over 1.4 million with the railways, 1 million across central public sector units and over 0.8 million across state-run banks—totalling 8.4 million, and the corresponding numbers for the states were 13.2 million. According to the Union budget for 2023, salaries and pensions were 44 per cent of the revenue expenditure. Stated differently, 29 paise from every rupee the centre earned that year was spent on salaries and an additional 9 paise on pensions.

The number of pensioners is more worrisome at 7 million as of March 2022, with an annual fiscal burden of Rs 2.54 trillion for the Centre. And when it comes to the states, the pain is much bigger. At Rs 4.67 trillion in FY23, this was 9 per cent of their combined expenditure budget and a third of their non-development expenditure. The states combined spend on average

27 per cent of their revenue receipts on salaries and pensions alone, and in the case of Uttar Pradesh (with a 2.7 million workforce), Maharashtra (1.7 million), Tamil Nadu (1.6 million), and the tiny Kerala (0.5 million), this is a whopping 40 per cent.

Once we end these freebies, we should divert some of the savings to launch a social security net or a universal basic income scheme for everyone, beginning with the poorest, the farmers, and others.

Scrap all Farm Subsidies

We have to do away with all subsidies, be it for food, fertilizers, power, water, and minimum support prices (MSPs), too as they distort markets. Farm subsidies, in fact, do no good to the farmer; instead, they do more harm to the land and public health. Instead, give the farmers direct income support according to their landholdings. The PM Kissan scheme, under which every landowning farmer gets Rs 6,000 annually, is a good beginning. Extend this to the landless farmers, too, and in the second phase, increase the amount on a real income basis so that it becomes a real positive income. If Andhra Pradesh can give Rs 12,000 in cash to each farmer per acre annually under its Rythu Bandhu scheme, why cannot other states and the Centre do this?

Abolish the inefficient agricultural produce market committees (APMCs) and let the farmer sell his produce wherever he wants or to whoever pays him a better price than the corrupt and politically manipulated APMCs do. Minimum support prices have been helping only middlemen and increasing the waste amount at warehouses of the food corporation.

The fertilizer subsidy in fiscal year 2023–24 was Rs 1.75 trillion. If this was distributed to the targeted 87.5 million or so farmers, it could be Rs 20,000 to each farmer! So, there is no dearth of money but only a clear lack of political will as politicians love considering themselves *anna daatas*.

We must also scrap the joke called the public distribution system (PDS). In 1985, the then prime minister Rajiv Gandhi famously said only Re 0.15 from every rupee disbursed reached the intended PDS beneficiary. Neither the system nor the quality of food distributed through ration shops has improved much since then. The direct benefit transfer scheme looks better as people can make their own choices in buying.

End Abject Poverty; Offer Universal Basic Income

The question is how we can take care of the poor and the needy after scrapping all subsidies, including the food rationing shops. The best way is to start a universal basic income (UBI) programme. With the near-perfect delivery we have achieved through the direct benefit transfer scheme, I do not think rolling this out will be a challenge at all, either in terms of implementation or delivery or in finding the money for it.

With 10 per cent of the bottom of the pyramid earning less than Rs 6,000 a month, the 7 per cent upper crust cornering over 60 per cent of wealth and earning 57 per cent of national income (a recent Goldman Sachs report), 16 per cent of the nearly 230 million of the 1,440 million officially under the poverty line (latest the United Nations Development Programme multi-dimensional poverty index), and 160 million of them are in extreme poverty, that we are a $3.94-trillion economy is a sad joke. If the idea of becoming a developed nation by 2047 is to be realized in any meaningful manner, we must, on a war footing, take this 16 per cent of people out of poverty and the way forward is ensuring that our villagers and those in the city slums are out of income poverty, and enjoy real positive wages and earn enough to have some savings, too. To achieve all these, the

Centre must first stop changing the methodologies of income or poverty calculation and goalposts.

Curb Religious Freedom, Especially of Minorities

Why should a secular democracy allow unbridled freedom to practise one's religion? My problem is more with the way minorities are misusing these provisions. Going by their sheer numbers, considering Muslims a minority is nothing but solecism, to say the least. Christians, on the other hand, have been misusing constitutional protection to further their commercial interests. In fact, all religious structures are nothing lucrative but real estate business!

As a first step, remove all the tax exemptions that all religious bodies enjoy now and begin by imposing a tax on the offerings coming to temples, churches, mosques, and gurudwaras at both ends. If done, most of the man/woman gods and one-person-run places of worship will vanish.

Also, regulate the construction of any new places of worship and charge property tax in accordance with the prevalent circle rate. Secularism should mean no favour or punishment to any particular religion.

Reform Education

Our education system is so dysfunctional that we have the dubious distinction of producing the largest number of unemployable graduates, including engineers, in the world because over two-thirds of the tens of millions of our college graduates are not just employable! Let us revamp our education curriculum to focus on skill development. A good beginning can be made by not asking our hallowed IITs, IIMs, and other institutes of higher education to teach yoga and mythologies.

When it comes to school education, it is nothing but alarmingly pathetic. A January 2024 Union education ministry report said close to 57 per cent of the 14–18-year-old rural schoolchildren cannot do Class III maths and 25 per cent of them cannot even read! What an achievement in *Amritkaal*.

Our schoolchildren must also be taught basic respect for others, especially women, and also civic sense. It must focus on public hygiene and social responsibility. Our boys must be taught that women are not just sex objects. Also ensure a child leaving her school knows driving and swimming.

End Tax Terrorism

The tax regime has become a tool to settle political scores and terrorize the public and businessmen who seem to be on the opposition side. To begin with, increase the income tax rate to, say, a flat 30 per cent but massively slash the indirect tax rates. Probably, we are the only ones who pay 28 per cent goods and services tax on biscuits and 3 per cent on gold, despite it being a single tax structure; and then pay multiple levels of taxes on anything and everything, including an 18 per cent GST on bank penalty. What a penal service it is? An equity investor pays securities transaction tax while buying and selling and also dividend tax along with GST on those, but has to pay income tax on the profit earned from an already doubly taxed income.

Tax the super-rich and wealthy farmers, as well as temples, churches, mosques, and gurudwaras, along with donations to places of worship. Why should a temple/mosque/ church not pay property tax? Why do the Ambanis and the Adanis pay the same rate of income tax as their mid-level employees? Let us have a super-rich tax and bring back wealth tax and inheritance tax.

Bring ED, CBI, EC under Apex Court Watch

We've seen the decimation of many a businessman who seemed to be siding with Opposition parties, while a few groups have become default sovereigns in recent years. The normal course of making a seemingly unfriendly businessman toe the government line has been to serve an income tax notice first, if not fell in line, then send ED and CBI sleuths. Anybody who wishes to lead a simple life will just fall in line. The same sinister method has been employed to tame Opposition members and the number of such men and women who got purified in recent years runs into hundreds.

So, let's have the 'lawless' law enforcement trinity—the income tax, ED, and CBI—report directly to the Supreme Court to prevent naked government misuse for their petty political gains.

Scrap the Office of Governor

Since 1950, the office of the governor has never justified the cost it incurs on the taxpayer, maybe with a few good exceptions in the long past. But by and large, they are just the resting palaces for corrupt retired judges, seeped in graft but the favourite civil servants and failed politicians who all toe the line of the government of the day. And the perks and pelf that come with this constitutional post and the attendant cost to taxpayers cannot be justified at all.

The idea of federalism and each state will be better served by not having more of them from now onwards. And the way forward is amending Article 155 to make it mandatory for the Centre to consult chief ministers on gubernatorial appointments, something the Sarkaria Commission report suggested way back in 1988. If we cannot find a decent alternative, include the CJI in the governors' selection process. Till we find a meaningful replacement, let chief ministers report/consult their high court chief justice on key matters.

Abolish Rajya Sabha and Legislative Councils

One wonders what the contributions of the Rajya Sabha and the State Legislative Councils have been except being guzzlers of public money. When was the last time we heard a sensible debate in the House of these so-called elders? Or when was the last time we saw some sensible persons elected/nominated to this 'august house' or did these worthies justify their salaries and perks? Has not the Rajya Sabha become a retirement home for the most astute political and corporate cronies?

Let us start by not allowing a person who lost in a Lok Sabha election to be nominated/elected to the Rajya Sabha. And when it comes to the nominated ones, can we set some terms of service? The point is if most states can function normally or even better without a bicameral system, why not Parliament?

Similarly, abolish the legislative councils. Only Andhra Pradesh, Bihar, Karnataka, Maharashtra, Telangana, and Uttar Pradesh have legislative councils. So, abolish these white elephants too. After all, states with only legislative assemblies have not done badly when it comes to better law-making. So end them and save taxpayers' money.

Right-size Governments

Let us have a constitutional provision to rationalize and right-size governments by limiting the number of ministries. Why should the prime minister and chief ministers have a free hand in creating more ministries—with the latest joke being a cow ministry in many BJP-ruled states? The cruel joke is that the innocent cow is wandering on streets for food and water, but the cow minister is enjoying all the pelf and leading a cushy life; or a ministry for cleaning up the Ganges, when everyone knows how clean the mighty river is and how the minister behaved when thousands of COVID-19 victims found their final journey in the very river and the fate of the newspaper that carried some pictures of the fish-eaten blown-up souls floating around awaiting their entry into the other world.

Contain the Steel Frame; Go for Lateral Hiring

Along with rationalizing ministries, we should also contain the rising power of the steel frame—that is, the civil service. Just because civil servants have to be employed does not mean all departments should be headed by them. Why cannot we get outside experts to lead key departments at least? Why should an Indian Administrative Service officer handling animal or child welfare department in his/her previous posting be heading the finance, law, or department later?

Divest, Divest, Divest

Government after government wasted hundreds of trillions of taxpayers' money to manufacture condoms, tea, coffee, bread, steel, copper, aluminium, and everything else under the sun, or in operating absolutely inefficient telecom and public transport networks like airlines and bus services, or in making non-flyable planes, no-sailable ships, non-drivable scooters, and what not. History has well documented the gains from all these. For the sake of our future generations, let us end this monumental waste. This is also one of the easiest ways to end the pain of budget-funded pensions and salaries. After all, a government has no business to run businesses.

Begin Contractual Hiring; Ban Trade Unions

Let us make a beginning by stopping regular government employees and moving on to contractual hiring. Of course, an exception has to be made for civil service personnel to a certain extent.

This also calls for an outright ban on trade unions in government and the private sector. In my over thirty years of service across multiple organizations, I have not come across a single instance of members benefiting from their union memberships, but leaders do immensely. Top management and union leaders are in cahoots and serve their own interests. It is as simple as that. Also, contract hiring can automatically end the fiscal pains coming out of pensions and other retirement benefits.

Let's End Petty Corruption

The what's-in-it-for-me approach of politicians and public servants, including cops, is the main reason for poor service deliveries and, thus, corruption. Corruption in top echelons has gone up drastically over the years. But the graft that affects the common man directly is petty corruption at the lower rung. The best and possibly the only way to end this is to increase the salaries of cops and clerical staff of the steel frame because there is no more effective way to contain greed than feeding the elements that spawn the malice.

The police structure is geared towards corruption. Those in the Indian Police Service get fat salaries and all other freebies, while the bottom-rung is paid peanuts. Let us pay our cops decent wages so that they can discharge their duties without having to extort money from people to pay their bills.

The Singaporean model, which has the cleanest and most efficient government and politicians with the highest salaries, can be our model for having a clean, efficient government and public service machinery.

Incentivize and Formalize Political Funding

Let us formalize political funding by making donations by companies and individuals transparent and even incentivizing them with tax exemption.

A first positive step came in when the Supreme Court, though after sitting on the petition seeking to scrap the electoral bonds system for so many years, finally thrashed its legality in February 2024, which otherwise would have been the biggest legalized corruption not just in our country but in the entire world. Ironically, the petition challenging its constitutionality and legality was pending for seven years in the apex court. Had it not been annulled, the nation and the whole world would have always remembered the current government for this enduring gift.

Stop the Brain Drain

Misusing federal law enforcement agencies and taxmen has been so bad that millions have abandoned their citizenship or are fleeing this country. Just look at these numbers: between 2011 and 2022, as many as 1.66 million abandoned their Indian citizenship and adopted foreign nationalities. During 2014–18 alone, when the *Amritkaal* began, a whopping 23,000 desi millionaires took foreign citizenship, according to a 2018 Morgan Stanley report.[1] The same period also saw close to 1 million fewer mortals doing the same.

These claims are borne out by figures from the Wall Street investment bank Morgan Stanley. A 2018 bank report found that 23,000 Indian millionaires had left the country since 2014. A more recent report by the Global Wealth Migration Review reveals that close to 5,000 Indian millionaires, or 2 per cent of the total number of high-net-worth individuals, left the country in 2020 alone.

Indians top a list prepared by the London-based global citizenship and residence advisory Henley & Partners of those seeking citizenship or permanent residency in other countries in return for investment. And the report blames tax terrorism as the main reason for this. Tax raids on businessmen have more than trebled in the past five years alone.

On average, annually, another 2 million migrate for a better living or maybe just to eat what they want, marry the love of their hearts, dress what they prefer, or pursue the education of their choice. Plus, there are over 30 million toiling in foreign lands. Only in 2022, 0.22 million Indians renounced their citizenship, according to the government's own data as of July 2023.[2, 3] This was over 85,000 in 2020 and 87,000 in the first half of 2023.

And the official version for this is that these are still our own brain banks!!

Summing Up

I started the wish list by saying we are a dying democracy because most of our constitutional organs are on ventilators, and our personal freedom and fundamental rights are under the regular shameless onslaught. My worries are less about the supine nature of our political parties on the Opposition benches or their callous approach to upholding constitutional rights, morality, values, and freedom. I am more worried about the civil society that has become so kosher with all the muck around. Because the biggest enemy of our democracy is not a charging ruling party or an enervated Opposition but the public who have fallen for the call for a majoritarian nation with all the attendant jingoism, xenophobia, and minority phobia or are forced into utter silence.

This essay may sound like a critique of the current regime. To a certain extent, yes, it is. But I have written so because a decade is too long in the life of a 77-year-old nation, and a crucial national election is around us while it is being written. The past decade has wrecked our sociopolitical, institutional, cultural, and intellectual fabrics so badly that it will take at least another decade to repair and recover from the abyss.

While elections are a mechanism to form a government, democracy is a much larger, wider idea in our constitutional scheme to achieve the bigger objectives of social, economic, and political transformation. So, what is urgently needed is finding a new meaning to our national political discourse by moving away from the secular-communal binary and beginning a dialogue on the contested meanings of democracy and social justice that will eventually shape or reshape the future of our democracy as envisaged in the Constitution.

I am sure by implementing my dreams, we will be a better nation and our children and grandchildren will have a brighter future on our own soil. I also hope the January 2024 consecration of the Ram Temple in Ayodhya, done in utter disregard for the basic religious, constitutional, and legal principles and morality, but as a sheer political project with all the might of the State in all spectacles to assert political Hinduism and communal triumphalism, is the beginning of the end of politically correcting the many historical wrongs that we are besotted with. I also ardently wish we become more accommodating and understanding and respect our past, present, and future while also stopping making more contesting claims from a cultural and religious prism.

20

Argument II: Protecting the Indian Republic: Threat Identification and Action

Debdeep Sengupta

Introduction

Since its birth on 15 August 1947, the Indian Republic has seen four wars with Pakistan, one large war and one small war with China, daily large-scale exchange of heavy fire with Pakistan even under ceasefire conditions, and from 2020 onwards, regularized confrontation and occasional hand-to-hand combat with the People's Liberation Army (PLA) (both sides had agreed not to use firearms in a 1988 treaty). India also fights daily counter-terrorism battles with Pakistan-trained-and-armed 'irregulars', trained under Pakistan's 'bleed India with a 1,000 cuts' philosophy. We are possibly the only major democracy and major economy in the world who are engaged in everyday warfare with our neighbours and their proxies, a warfare we cannot avoid as it has been thrust on us. Just like any sovereign nation, our military is an extension of our statecraft, in one small corner of the vast spectrum of engagement we share with other nations. Yet, India existed much, much before 1947, and the nature of aggression it faced has continuously changed with time. For a mathematically inclined nation, it is thus time to adopt a data-driven approach to what actually threatens us and will threaten us and to understand how we can respond to such developments by learning our history lessons.

Nature of Threats

Territorial: This aims at appropriating portions of Indian territory and then effecting demographic change either through genocides, indigenous displacement, or forced religious conversions.

This can be achieved through:

Illegal occupation of Indian territories through military conflict, just like Pakistan has done with Gilgit-Baltistan and China has done with Aksai Chin, and ensuring the legitimacy of those occupations via the Organization of Islamic Cooperation and Western nations. These allies of Pakistan also encourage further military adventurism on Indian territory under the goal of Ghazwa-i-Hind, a 1,000-year-old Islamist fantasy of converting the land of Hindus, i.e., Dar-ul-Harb to Dar-ul-Islam. Pakistan, Turkey, Qatar, and Saudi Arabia have been direct advocates of this 'conquer-and-convert' ideology.

Illegal occupation of Indian territories without direct conflict, just like China has done with 60 sq km of Indian territory from 1999 to 2013, taking advantage of cartographic ambiguity.[1]

Secessionism on religion/ethnicity: India gave in to religious secessionist blackmail on 14 August 1947, making the one-year '*Ladke lenge* Pakistan' movement successful and laying a template for how it is done. Following that template,

- In the 1980s, Khalistanis tried unsuccessfully to split Punjab from India, an attempt they have resurrected under direct support from the Biden administration. In the 1980s, this was attempted with large-scale genocides of the Punjabi Hindu population by Khalistani Sikhs. From 2020 onwards, similar attempts have been made, under the protection of the opposition party ruling the state, on law enforcement infrastructure, with military-grade weapons.

- From 19 January 1990, Islamists have tried unsuccessfully to split Jammu and Kashmir from India, aided by men and weapons from successive Pakistan governments and funding and diplomatic cover from successive Western governments, with China also providing direct support.
- From the 1990s, All Bodo Students Union, All-Assam Students Union, Gorkha, Asom, Bodo, United Liberation Front of Assam, and related terrorist movements in the Northeast of India resurrected their 'independence movement' from India, with direct military help from China, Pakistan, and Western governments. The objectives of NATO countries in arming the rebels were different from those of China and Pakistan, but the effect was the same on us. The armed mobilization against India has been done on fertile grounds of a long-running resentment against New Delhi running through the Northeast, which stemmed from Indira Gandhi's 1966 air strike on Aizawl to daily 'Chinki' comments and racial violence Indians from Northeast faced in other parts of the country.
- There have been long-running intra-tribe/inter-tribe conflicts exemplified by the Naga-Kuki clashes in the first decade of this century, and the current Meitei-Kuki conflict in Manipur. In all these instances, weapons have been supplied from Myanmar-Bangladesh borders, and the supply line of both money and weapons either leads to China or to Christian rebels in Myanmar fighting the military junta
- Ethnic separatism and sub-nationalism of the type we see in Tamil separatism, Bengali sub-nationalism, Kannadiga

and Maratha sub-nationalism, and religious separatism, evidenced in the frequent demands from Islamists of a 'separate country' for them, on the lines of Pakistan. These separatism movements are designed from the west or north of the Himalayas, using religion and 'identity' strawmen, and then executed by Indian regional political parties governing these states to justify their cash flows from their sponsors while securing their own captive constituencies against the idea of Hindi-speaking Hindu India. Most of these separatist movements are also encouraged directly by the Indian National Congress, historically, as a political tool to undermine their opponents, without considering the long-term implications of encouraging secessionism.

Displacement of the indigenous population by illegal migrants: This has happened with increasing frequency and severity under local political patronage [CPI(M), TMC, INC in West Bengal, INC in Assam, AIMIM in Andhra Pradesh, and INC in Meghalaya].

Politically approved cross-border illegal migration is often done by undermining the Border Security Force by the political party ruling the border state(s) has caused demographic changes in districts bordering Bangladesh in West Bengal, Assam, and Tripura, among the majorly affected states, and has created 'mini-Pakistans' that forcibly displace indigenous Hindus under the threat of religious violence or religious conversion, or target females of the Hindu families with targeted sexual violence till they accept religious conversion or their families are forced to migrate.

This proliferation of 'Muslim areas' within different parts of India following the same strategy of demographic displacement after achieving demographic superiority is a military action without formal weapons and soldiers.

Regime change and/or colonization: As former colonialists stare at their impending irreversible economic downfalls, aided by their mismanagement of finances and global trade, they will increasingly rely on the tried-and-tested-method history has given them to economic prosperity, leveraging their technological advantage over other nations.

That tried-and-tested method is regime change and colonization, sometimes with direct, time-framed occupation as the experiences of Iraq and Afghanistan show, or sometimes by installing a puppet regime that would denude the national resources to benefit the colonialists, as our experience shows from 1947 to 2014.

Post-1989, the regime changes are usually staged through skilled 'agent provocateurs' who can mobilize the masses and carry out targeted attacks/assassinations, as the fall of the Soviet-bloc East European countries such as Romania, Albania, and Hungary show in the last two weeks of 1989, a trend carried through Arab Spring and the 'Colour Revolutions' in Ukraine and elsewhere.

In countries like Iraq, Libya, and, currently, Iran, where 'agent provocateurs' could not secure beachheads, direct military intervention has been carried out. In other countries like ours, political parties have been created and funded by quasi-intelligence forums guided to undermine Indian sovereignty and deny Indian governance to the areas/states they control by subverting democracy.

As the West increasingly shows its Nazi roots and support for Islamofascism expansionism, knowing well that Saudi Arabia may relapse to Islamist fundamentalism and that China is actively investing in Islamist organizations like Hamas and expansionist fantasists like Turkey, we see an 'alignment of global evil' against us leveraging the worst aspects of Abrahamic fundamentalism to secure political victory.

It is worthwhile to mention that the NATO member countries have practised an evolved form of colonialism since the 1940s rather than the primitive 'territory-capturing' practised by Pakistan and China. These countries do 'regime changes' and install a remote-controlled administration that rules the local population with an iron fist and creates an underclass of political minions and business elites who directly benefit from that rule so that they, in turn, can create vote banks and constituencies fractured enough to keep the 'installed head' in power during the general elections in the country, using a combination of political coalitions.

This scenario sounds so familiar because this is what the Indian National Congress (INC) has been doing to India largely since the 1990s, funded by the same colonialists. This cash flow is effectively routed not only to the INC but also to multiple smaller regional political parties in the south and the east of the country.

The results of the cash flow evidence themselves in a phenomenon we are seeing more and more as 'denial of Government of India governance', in specific opposition-ruled states, where elected representatives deny central government investigative agencies space to pursue corruption investigations, use the state police as 'private militia' to harass central government investigators, and of late, as evidenced in West Bengal and Tamil Nadu, mobilize political cadres to directly attack central government officials physically using numerical superiority over CRPF. Evidence of these have been seen in Sandeshkhali in West Bengal,[2] where Enforcement Directorate officers were attacked in the course of their duties, and in Tamil Nadu.[3]

The result, when viewed together, is essentially achieving 'pockets of remote-controlled governance' within the state of

India using the federalism of the Indian Constitution as a shield, which takes their orders from transatlantic or trans-Himalayan nations, no different from having foreign colonies inside India.

Economic disruption: This is the usage of composite military methods to disrupt India's trade and food supply lines, and industrial/utility infrastructure. This can be achieved as follows:

- Freezing of the H1B supply line and friendshoring of strategic IT outsourcing to Poland, whatever is left of Ukraine, with large outsourcing businesses such as banking, consulting, insurance, and IT mandated to absorb higher costs of the transition. We have seen glimpses of this move from October to November 2021, when all US-Hqed investment banks and consulting giants started working on Russian sanctions at the behest of their political bosses.

  With the Biden administration cutting down the H1B applications from 1 million to 850,000, there is a designed, calculated squeeze on Indian IT labour immigration to the US to put curbs on Indian IT as part of indirect sanctions and relocation of global delivery centres of big tech, big banking, and consulting giants from India to Five Eyes nations, or even to China, with businesses mandated to absorb the higher costs of the move.

  The whole purpose of such 'blockades' is no different from sanctions, i.e., wage economic warfare against the Indian-educated middle-class segment that usually forms the bulk of the employees of Indian IT and US multinational corporations, so that they, and their employers, are provoked into taking a visible stance against the Government of India, and facilitate 'regime change' through elections.
- Targeted attacks on and hijacking of Indian cargo ships in key geopolitical chokepoints, targeted disruption of

India's energy supply route, as we have seen in the latest drone attacks on Indian ships coming from the Red Sea, and increasing attempts to hijack Indian ships near Somali coastal waters or near the horn of Zanzibar.

- The sabotage of Nordstream pipeline has opened possibilities of similar nameless military attacks on India's communication infrastructure, which may include severing of its internet cables undersea, disabling/hijacking/shoot-down of India's satellite network, targeted disruption of India's key imports like crude oil through targeting of Indian containers, an act encouraged by NATO when Western countries denied Indian oil shippers insurance cover for transporting Russian oil.
- Targeted cyberattacks on India's digital financial infrastructure, systematic, and progressive cyberattacks on India's utility network and air traffic network of the kind that reached a crescendo in 2020–21 during the Galwan confrontation with China, with cyberattacks on our Parliament, defence ministry, energy infrastructure, all of which necessitated our hasty move to the indigenous Maya OS in August 2023, and giving marching orders to Microsoft Windows OS.

  But the Kundakulam sabotage[4] experience in 2019 also reminds us to check 'human intervention' in the form of 'neutral-country' saboteurs who might inject malware into our key infrastructure control systems, just like a Dutch engineer, perceived as neutral by Iran, introduced the Stuxnet virus into the computer systems governing Iran's nuclear power plants.
- Deniable physical attacks on India's energy infrastructure near enemy borders, i.e., Gujarat, offshore oil rigs, and nuclear power plants along the coastline.

- We have seen a surge in information warfare attacks on India since 2021 January after DNC entered the White House designed to undermine public trust in governance and fertilize the ground for popular uprisings of the Arab Spring type, of the kind we have seen carried out by Western headquartered media during the second COVID-19 wave of 2021, or by spreading of continuous fake news and fake narratives by the Islamist domestic press and their supporting 'liberal-Leftist' media outlets funded by 'private actors' in west or overtly state actors like Qatar, or China.

  There are varieties of fake narratives—the most prominent being of the ruling party planning genocides against Indian minorities circulated time and again[5] to direct whitewashing of Islamist attacks or directing Islamist attacks on dissenting individuals[6] to outright fake news during the COVID-19 crisis about Modi taking a foreign vaccine[7] and about psy-ops on Indian soldiers being defeated by Chinese in 2020 using microwave weapons.[8] Quite recently, there has been an active massive commission of weaponized disinformation to influence the outcome of Indian elections.[9]

  This handicap can be explained by our historical approach of dealing with misinformation via our judiciary, who are ill-trained and ill-equipped to deal with the multiple dimensions of information warfare, and (in)famously countered once that 'misinformation should be fought with misinformation'. There are also information warfare attacks designed to drain Indians' wealth along the lines of Hindenburg's and the Organized Crime and Corruption Reporting Project's misinformation campaign targeting the Securities and Exchange Board and Indian financial governance institutions, using Adani as a front.

The objective of these attacks, similar to 'opinion shaping misinformation' by key 'business' publications, is to affect the qualitative aspect of India's sovereign rating as determined by international rating organizations with a view to making the country look like a 'risky bet', and limit flow of Western investments to India due to the perceived higher cost of capital. By the same yardstick, the Indian government would also find it extremely difficult to borrow money from the same Western asset managers, and thus India would be starved of any additional capital it may need to raise for its industry or infrastructure.

- Western nations have embarked on 'cognitive warfare' initiatives against India, using multiple electronic media, mainstream media, and targeted disinformation campaigns aimed at our largest religion and, thus, the largest segment of our population. This is deliberately designed for their citizens to develop cognitive biases against Indian citizens, to create a larger 'Us v/s Them' polarization that leads to increasing marginalization and exclusion of Indians and their Hindu citizens in their societies, in the MNCs that are headquartered in their country.

  This is also designed to affect the attitudes and behaviour of Indians working in MNCs or studying in their universities by influencing, protecting, or disrupting individual and group cognition to gain the advantage of these population segments. This is not a post-2014 phenomenon, but something they have been indulging in right from the 1960s, using mainstream media first.

Threat of life and limb to Indian citizens, particularly its majority community, is usually manifested through the following themes:

- There has been a calculated escalation in attacks on Hindu religious processions by Islamists since 2019[10] as the aggressors have figured out the near-perfect method of switching the victim-perpetrator narrative aided by 'liberal' and Leftist domestic English-language media, and globally, the labour-DNC backed section of the international English language media.

  These attacks are part of the same trend we have noticed in Pakistan and increasingly in Bangladesh against their Hindu minorities till their numbers reach extinction. Further away from India, we have seen these attacks against Yezidis in Turkey and against Christians in Armenia by Muslim Azerbaijan and Turkey, and also against Christians and pagans in Nigeria. The Qatar-funded media, expectedly, does not recognize such attacks. These attacks start with defining 'Muslim areas' in a country that does not recognize religious segregation and then directing attacks against Hindus or Hindu religious festivals for intruding in those 'Muslim areas'.
- While there has been a 77 per cent reduction in terrorism directed at Hindus from 2014 till 2024, the UPA era of 2004–14 is a stark reminder of the modus operandi at play—carry out serial, massive bomb attacks or 'commando-style' machine-gun attacks against a largely Hindu population, provoke the segment into retaliation, and then cry 'Hindu terror' to blame and persecute the victim till it accepts annihilation.

  The presence of Islamic State (IS) training camps in the jungles of Kerala and Karnataka, the repeated arrests of IS personnel in Kerala and West Bengal, and the periodic haul of explosives in trucks from West Bengal trying to enter Bihar are symptoms that the infrastructure and support system that protects Hindu-focused terrorism is alive and abetted in opposition-ruled states.[11] This is no different from a military situation where an enemy infiltrates a country with periodic killing sprees to cower its leadership into submission.[12]

Data weaponization via agriculture and health analytics: Such data is willingly shared by the Government of India with private transnational bodies. This is where we talk about 'avoidable traps' and resisting the lure of advantages offered as 'sandpits' of new technology in exchange for our genetic data. The Government of India has made two significant self-goals in this aspect in the last twelve years.

- Indian Data Protection Bill, 2023, allows the transfer of Indian personal data outside India, except to countries notified by the Government of India. This assumption of a 'friendly nation to trust data with', by default, is a Trojan horse. We have no friends in the West or East, and this cross-border transfer of Indian personal data was the biggest bone of contention between Western headquartered big tech and the Government of India for the last six years before the Indian government capitulated. With this agreement, we have provided the West with the personal data of Indians, which they can study and analyse to kill us.
- Indian states, such as Uttar Pradesh and Bihar, have been openly collaborating with international organizations on sharing their residents' health data in exchange for help and expertise on maternal and child health, family planning, immunization programmes, and control of infectious diseases, sanitation and agricultural systems. This collaboration provides our strategic enemies with the means to design specific biological weapons aimed at taking out the highest numbers of our citizens. As of 18

December 2023, the ICMR data 'leak' has compromised the health data of 81 million Indians in the dark web; all of this data, at the hands of big tech and big pharma, makes us their guineapigs.[13]

Key themes that emerge from these threats

Threat	Key cause
Illegal occupation of our land	• Powerful political blocs inside the country have a political and financial stake in the survival and progress of our declared enemy. • Not militarily ready to face a peer or 'greater-than-peer' aided by superpowers. • Lack of clarity over what to engage against with what results to achieve long term. Our ministers keep talking of getting Pakistan-Occupied-Kashmir back without admitting the myopia that such an action is no guarantee against further misadventures by Pakistan-China-Western actors against Indian soil. • Critical dependency on foreign original equipment manufacturers for key parts of the military supply chain, which can be choked at will by countries supporting our enemies.
Secessionism	• Lack of clarity over the 'scope of engagement' and tendency to view political solutions. • Hamstrung by the Constitution that does not understand hybrid warfare.
Economic disruption and cognitive warfare	• Lack of clarity over 'scope of engagement'. • Limited means of engagement. Our reaction, such as sending Indian Navy warships to guard the Red Sea route and Somali coastal waters against piracy or 'hostile intervention', has been historically reactive and ineffective. • Limited/lack of ability to counter information/cyber/electronic warfare.

Threat	Key cause
Threat to Hindus	• Lack of clarity over 'scope of engagement.' • 'Constitutional' and institutional blindness to hybrid warfare that is designed to trigger demographic and subsequent political and military change from the inside, just like what has happened in the land that became East Pakistan and, subsequently, Bangladesh.
Data weaponization	• Lack of clarity over 'scope of engagement.' • IAS babus in the Ministry of Defence and in the Ministry of Electronics and Telecoms do not really understand data and its implications due to their backgrounds.

Our Long-term Military Strategy

Our long-term military strategy should recognize from Indian history and elsewhere that a good defence, of merely repelling the invader and letting it live, only delays our defeat till the time the same invader(s) achieve massive numerical and technological superiority over us. So, I would propose updating our military strategy to this two-step approach:

1. Discourage and repel external invaders at our borders or much before they are anywhere near our borders—land, sea and air, or even in space.
2. Strike crippling blows in the countries of the invaders as a counterattack, from which they can never recover or take centuries to recover, and, thus, internalize the lesson of their misadventures culturally.

To achieve the same, I propose the following five guiding principles, which will also address the key themes/causes that keep recurring in the nature of threats we face:

Understand the numbers: A country with a landmass of 3.287 million sq km, a land border length of 15,200 km, and a coastline of 7,515 km, with a population of 1.435 billion, cannot be served by a military with

- an active personnel count of 1.455 million.
- a reserve personnel count of 1.155 million.
- covered by a budget of Rs 5.94 trillion.

This is exactly eighteen military personnel across all three services for every 10,000 Indians. As both Ukraine and Gaza and earlier, Vietnam and Korea, have demonstrated, huge numbers of even low-trained, low-armed military make a massive difference against a high-tech advanced enemy that has low numbers. And if that enemy combines massive numerical superiority with technological superiority, it nullifies the military experience of the smaller force—a key lesson of both the Gulf wars, 1991 and 2003. Numbers bring their own quality.

Yet, defence is not about defending alone. It is also about having the decisive ability to counterstrike so that the enemy learns a lesson for posterity if it survives or ceases to exist.

This element has been missing from our doctrine because the enemy was heavily defended by three permanent members of the United Nations Security Council. That is why we have only 632 fighters in an air force with 1,645 aircraft, incapable of facing an Iraq-type coalition or even a Pakistan–China two-front air war. Moreover, our 70–150 nukes do not denote an impressive number to deter an enemy.

So, we need to ramp up our numbers, both humans and platforms. The easiest way to do that would be to understand the demand for numbers in different theatres of military engagement and then carry out tailored recruitment.

The defence ministry needs to work with the Central Statistics Office to understand and design this demand for different theatres and future tail-risk military threats.

Ownership: Primary – defence ministry; Secondary – tri-services chief

No more cancer cells: The biggest lesson of the Ukraine–Russia war from February 2022 is that you cannot let a cancer cell grow to a point where it threatens your very existence, either by hosting biological labs and developing drone programmes to deliver those, or fostering a supremacist ideology that threatens your ethnicity, or asking for nuclear capability and membership in a hostile military consortium.

Pakistan has been our Ukraine since 1947. Just like Ukraine, it is birthed and run out of a fascist ideology that has dehumanized its non-Islamic population and actively conducts periodic systematic genocide against them. This habit is mirrored by Bangladesh to our east.

It (Pakistan) is also a security state and a special purpose vehicle for the West, which uses, and has used, Pakistan's 'irregular warfare' boots-on-the-ground in theatres such as Bosnia, Chechnya, Dagestan, Syria, and potentially Ukraine. Thus, like Ukraine, Pakistan is a major non-NATO ally, and unlike Ukraine, Pakistan has nuclear weapons developed with direct help from the West and China. Pakistan is also, and will be, a top recipient of key bleeding-edge military hardware, either from China or from the West, to keep us engaged in an arms race, if not direct warfare.

As long as Pakistan exists, it will be a galvanizing rod to all Islamists across India that the Government of India can be blackmailed by large-scale, directed violence backed by political intervention to achieve 'political and geographic' space.

So, we need to act so that Pakistan ceases to exist in its current state. We should annex the Indus basin from Kashmir to Sindh via Punjab and start massive land reforms and direct democracy reforms in the annexed territories to get local buy-in to the 'India model' of good governance and defang the 'two-nation' theory forever.

This move will be resisted militarily by those who have created Pakistan as a special-purpose vehicle, and, therefore, we should militarily be in a position to actively discourage Western military support by denying/destroying their supply lines to Pakistan.

Ownership: Primary – defence ministry; secondary – political executive (prime minister, president, and tri-services chief)

Understanding the scope of defence: Our military responds to terrorist strikes and encroachment by foreign militaries, mercenaries on Indian land, or properties on the high seas. It does not respond to information warfare attacks, economic warfare, or electronic warfare attacks on our electrical grid infrastructure and nuclear power stations designed to cripple our utilities and power infrastructure and destabilize 'established society'.

This lack of response can be attributed partly to the inadequate scope definition in its doctrine of what kind of threats to respond against and partly due to the civilian control of the military exercise through the defence ministry. Militarily ill-trained, potentially compromised with children working/settled/studying in the West and having a post-retirement ambition of settling in the West, and with a non-STEM/technocratic background and thus incompetent to understand the evolution of threats and the long-standing threats, our IAS babus in the defence ministry see Pakistan and, after much US prodding, China in isolation, as our single biggest threat.

This myopic approach ignores the puppet masters behind Pakistan and, to a limited extent, China, and also the growing symbiosis between a newly resurgent Nazism in the West and Islamofascism in the Turkey–Pakistan–Malaysia–Qatar axis. There is no recognition by the highest levels of our defence ministry that this symbiosis is midwifed by the DNC occupying the White House since 2021, though the natural progression of events suggests that this symbiosis might have been birthed much earlier with the Obama era from 2008. This 'collaboration' is, and will remain, the single biggest threat to India, coming from earlier colonialists beyond Pakistan and China.

Countering this threat requires defining the scope of our defence and taking a whole-of-government approach, with active collaboration and intelligence, the finance and defence ministries, and the three arms of our military. This also involves cultivating a security mindset at the country level, the responsibility of which has to be on the defence ministry with active help from the information and broadcasting ministry.

Once the scope of our defence is defined, the defence ministry and the Indian military can have an easier time defining the scopes of air defence, naval defence, electronic defence, information warfare defence, etc., and the right response to each.

The scope of defence here means:

- What kind of threats the Indian government should respond to militarily?
- What kind of actions would define a 'military response'?
- What kind of actors and threats should the Indian government prepare to defend against in the short and long run, using what means?
- What should be defended? That is point defence of key metros or area defence of population centres, or area defence of population centres and industrial belts, or large industrial infrastructure against military-grade industrial espionage, electronically or using humans, or sectarian local populations claiming 'independence' on religious grounds for the land they have lived on, or largely 'demographic equilibrium' to prevent us going the way of Zoroastrian Persia, Christian Syria, and Sun-worshipping Egypt.

The Indian Constitution, under Article 14 of equality to everyone does *not* recognize this implicit threat of demographic change via population explosion of specific religions (and conversion activities) and the ensuant political change and security challenges it presents.

Ownership: Primary – defence ministry; secondary – political executive (prime minister, president and tri-services chief)

Responsive supply line to the military and defence ministry: The Ministry of Defence became the largest employer in the world in 2022, employing 2.99 million people, surpassing the US Department of Defense and the People's Liberation Army (PLA). But what kind of people are being employed? What is the extent of interactions between the different arms of the Government of India's scientific establishment, the defence ministry, the three wings of our military, intelligence wings, the executive, and civil defence, including state police units?

The hybrid nature of warfare today and in the future requires that the defence ministry's decision-making be dominated by technocrats, scientists, computer scientists, data architects, and engineers who envision how we should shape our military and human/talent supply lines to protect the country and our interests. At least three areas of major evolution are visible from the latest hybrid wars.

Robotics and Drones

Much, much before Ukraine and the drone wars in Libya, Obama's war on terror involving drone strikes on Pakistan, Afghanistan, and Iraq showed exactly how the US military developed parallel, redundant supply lines of drone operators. The Smithsonian reported that till 2010, the USAF used manned aircraft pilots to fly drones but separated an RPA 'pilot career field' soon after and looked at enlisted reserved personnel, or even civilians, to fly drones actively from 2017. Hamas' terror strikes on Israel, Pakistan's drug and weapons delivery to Indian Punjab, and Ukraine's drone attacks on the Russian military and infrastructure using private service providers point out the need to raise a separate, part-time yet flexible army of drone and robotics operators who can do the following:

- Configure drones and flight paths for missions and retrieve and repair the same post-mission.
- Fly drones/guide robots and counter-drone/robot solutions according to configured missions.
- Envision a robotics strategy and implementation runway with the Indian military and train the three different wings of the Indian military to work together with semi-automated-remotely-controlled or automated sentient machines and be the constant operators.

Clearly, the educational and societal background of this 'army' of robotics operators will differ significantly from the usual recruitment profile the Indian army gets from the agri-belt of the Gangetic north India or from the traditional military families.

These recruits would be well-versed in computer gaming and drone handling from childhood and would have a stronger STEM academic background. The only problem in retaining this profile would be the pay the defence ministry can offer them based on their skill sets. So, the defence ministry should be open to these recruits having 'day jobs' outside the defence ministry, fully cognizant of the risk that multi-national companies can leverage their sovereign intelligence networks to use them to siphon confidential information.

Special Forces

Pakistan has been waging irregular warfare on India under the garb of terrorism since 19 January 1990, leveraging NATO's special forces doctrine its sponsors regularly train its military in, be it in West Point or Sandhurst. The Ukraine-Russia war underscored this aspect all the more when the severest parts of the conflict, around the occupation of Bakhmut, were fought between NATO mercenaries led by Western special forces on the ground and the special forces mercenaries from the Wagner group, without formal involvement of Russian land forces, but with plenty of direct involvement from Russian special forces.

The increased frequency of urban warfare and the relative ease with which our enemies can train in it using a combination of real-world and simulation games like call-of-duty derivatives means that the defence ministry must focus on increasing the cohort of Indian special forces. Now, the special forces come with a much higher physical and mental entry bar than normal armed forces, so the defence ministry has to work with the sports ministry to identify the right pool of recruits and to leverage the growing fitness consciousness among younger Indians.

The recent media coverage of 'unknown men' handling out rough justice to Pakistan-based terrorists operating against India shows the Indian government has started baby steps in the right direction. This thrust of 'more special forces' would be particularly relevant in urban warfare settings of the kind we should participate in when we deal with Pakistan.

Military-Industrial Complex

The Ukraine war brought about the demise of our defence ministry's fallacy of 'short, sharp, limited war' with warfighting stockpiles of twenty-two days or maybe a month more.

It has also shown that our enemies, when backed by NATO and the Chinese industrial complex, will have 'ammunition on tap'. Our geographical position means that a naval blockade by any coalition supporting Pakistan, along with a Pakistan–China two-front war in the north, east, and west enabled by a fractured Myanmar ruled by a China-friendly military junta, will completely choke our access to external emergency weapons supplies.

The experience of Russia in the Ukraine war also shows that our enemies will try every means to choke the supply of microelectronics—essential for radar, avionics, and missile guidance—to us while having high-tech weapons themselves. This requires establishing a resilient and well-protected military-industrial complex network with domestic suppliers and domestic raw materials to produce from.

The last is difficult to achieve given that the world's supply of rare earths—inputs in the manufacturing of microelectronics—is largely concentrated in China, with Congo a distant second. The world's largest producer of semiconductors also includes China but can be bypassed by an adequate inventory of the same in anticipation of future multi-front coalition conflicts.

Our private industry has shown great appetite for participating in the military-industrial complex so far, but its supply chains are completely reliant on external OEMs, which makes its *Atmanirbhar* state a suspect.

Ownership: Primary – defence ministry; secondary – political executive (prime minister, president, and tri-services chief)

Unconventional weapons and strategy: We depend on countries like Russia and the US largely to provide us with key conventional military platforms, such as jet engines, avionics, tanks, transport aircraft, surveillance aircraft, and, more importantly, rifles. Let us acknowledge that the fifty-year gap between us and them will remain in these conventional platforms due to their technological head start; history cannot be wished away.

No matter how *Atmanirbhar* we would like to become, critical dependencies in the military manufacturing supply chain and protected technologies for key components will always remain. So, we need to focus on homegrown unconventional technologies. Some of these may be, but are not restricted to:

Operationalization of directed energy and electromagnetic propulsion: We have heard far too many fanboy myths over DURGA and KALI. We should seriously operationalize both lasers and electromagnetic-propelled weapons, i.e., railguns, as well as a spectrum of microwave platforms on the battlefield to achieve redundant layers of air defence at all layers of space over us, even including ground-based lasers to blind/destroy enemy satellites/space weapons in orbit.

Parallel progress in energy storage, i.e., battery technology, and resilient energy generation can enable such a development, which should provide growing areas of employment for India's engineering graduates.

Miniaturization of directed energy weapons into handheld weapons: The idea would be to complement the gun, a 1,000-year-old invention firing gunpowder-propelled metal projectiles that cannot pierce Kevlar, metal or concrete, obsolete, with handheld railguns (for beyond line-of-sight) and handheld lasers—mediums which can be effective against both skin of humans, concretes of bunkers, and metal of robots/drones.

Just like the popularization of the gun, over the pike, sword, and bow and arrow considerably reduced the training time needed for civilians to be converted into military recruits, with significantly more lethality, the 'portability' of directed energy and electromagnetic-propelled-weapons will leverage on India's population size to create massive anti-tank, anti-drone, anti-ship and even anti-aircraft 'people's defences' against invading platforms.

Ukraine has shown that a relatively less-trained, more-civilian-less-military force armed with sufficient numbers of anti-tank missiles can take a heavy toll on the tank regiments of an invading army. We need to replicate the same model leveraging railguns at the hands of masses against invading helicopters and tanks, fully working side by side without their own platforms, which are more finite in number and thus risk being destroyed faster by larger enemies' guided firepower.

The widespread use of handheld lasers and railguns will provide insurance even if our tanks and anti-aircraft platforms are knocked out by a stronger, larger enemy. These will also double up as artillery that can destroy tanks and bunkers.

More satellites: Satellites are our 'eyes in the sky', which will be knocked out by an advanced enemy at the start of any serious hostilities to render our air force, navy, and missile guidance blind. So, we need to increase beyond the fifty-three operational satellites we have in space and create their defences against anti-satellite missiles.

The US has 830 satellites, China has 280, and Russia has 147. This tells us that we need to spread our risks out so that any hostile can take them out, arm them with orbital weapons that can act faster than any missile, and create an aerospace force to defend them against hostile. We also need a redundant, resilient layer of air-borne and ground-based LIDAR (light detection and ranging) networks to 'talk' to the satellites to understand how those are operating.

Electronic warfare dominance: The Ukraine wars of 2013 and 2022–24 have shown the central roles played by electronic warfare in weapons guidance, drones or projectiles, and anti-drone defence. Our enemies will always have the best-in-class, best-of-both-US-and-Russian legacies in electronic warfare principles and tools to use against us.

Our focus should always be to identify our enemies' strategic weapons sites and prevent those from being used against us. We should also develop our cyber warfare capabilities and doctrine to defend ourselves against state-sponsored cyberattacks and counterattacks to teach a lesson. We also need to expand the scope of our cyber counterattacks against State-sponsored wilful misinformation purveyed through a network of 'private' or state-run media channels or through non-state actors with a previous 'business credibility' working at the behest of sovereign intelligence.

As I have discussed earlier, much of this willingness to respond and the development of the capability to respond is a doctrinal question to be defined in the 'scope of defence'.

More nukes and longer-range missiles: The consistent lesson from Iraq, Libya, North Korea, Pakistan, and currently the Ukraine–Russia war is that if you have a large number of nuclear warheads mounted on a large number of long-range missiles, you can avoid full-scale military aggression by your enemies.

Our 75–150 nukes and our Agni-series of missiles, created ostensibly from a 'deter Pakistan and China' strategy, are not sufficient or long-ranged enough to deter our enemies. The Ukraine war also has shown that the enemy will have a supply chain spread across the world, involving private enterprises working on behalf of their sovereign governments. We do not have Russia's luxury of keeping that supply line active.

More Indian jets: This is the aspect most vulnerable to external sanctions/blockades on avionics/microelectronics and engine components, so this is where we should build multi-year-capacity for inventory to support huge numbers of 'heavy combat' and 'medium combat' double-engine desi jets, armed with miniaturized directed energy, or electromagnetic-propulsion weapons alongside India-made long-range air-to-air missiles, to ensure complete air supremacy over the Indian subcontinent and our sea boundaries.

The 'line-of-sight' limitation for directed-energy weapons would change to a massive advantage when deployed in the air at higher altitudes. Like Russia, which used MiG-31s initially with the sole purpose of tracking and shooting down cruise missiles and high-altitude, high-speed bombers, we should also evolve our operational doctrine to dedicate different kinds of Indian jets for defence of different altitude belts all the way up to the stratosphere: high numbers of counter-drone unmanned combat aerial vehicles and everyman-handheld-lasers, or tank-mounted lasers for lower airspace, high numbers of light combat aircraft and medium combat aircraft for defence, and air supremacy of airspace up to 50,000 ft.

The whole thrust should be safeguarding land, air, space and sea, and the fastest way to do that would be to dominate air and space.

Ownership: Primary – Defence ministry.

Conclusion

A sovereign military strategy is only successful after it achieves buy-in from every citizen it is designed to protect and every citizen understands sovereign security as a matter of personal ownership. While this ownership is culturally more common in Central Europe and the Nordics, Indian history shows that as citizens, we have an insularity towards personal ownership of security, either due to 1,000 years of colonial rule or due to the failure of our rulers to make security everyone's responsibility.

Our failure to successfully defend our independence against colonial rule is a direct function of this absence of a security mindset and our collective buy-in in the security of our country. We must learn from our mistakes to never repeat them. The security awareness of our country is essentially an educational process, just like any health/vaccination awareness programme conducted nationwide at the scale of our COVID-19 vaccination response from 2021 to 2022.

The defence ministry and the information and broadcasting ministry have the responsibility of sensitizing Indian citizens to the small, progressive steps they need to take to defend the nation.

us. *Roti, kapda, kaam, aur makaan* continues to remain at the forefront of what young India wants.

Roopak Gupta, a technologist and a Columbia MBA graduate, recounts his personal journey from Agra to New York. As an Indian kid growing up in the 1990s, Roopak narrates a tale of resilience, [illegible] and grit. Roopak is a man on a mission [illegible] the story of India's digitization itself and whe[illegible] dreams. In 2050, India would stand [illegible] not an echo but a [illegible] not an afterthought but the [illegible] technology serves all. Much [illegible] revolution must move [illegible] empowerment to truly [illegible]

[illegible] based Indian lawyer [illegible] small town of Ratnagiri, [illegible] scholar in law and constitutional [illegible] ledger technology (DLT) in [illegible] he writes, 'Looking ahead to the [illegible] India propelled by innovation, [illegible] growth. A nation where technological [illegible] social equity, where educational [illegible] and where governance reflects the [illegible] of a burgeoning populace. It is a vision of India as a [illegible] leader, not just in economic terms but also in fostering a harmonious society grounded in democratic principles and cultural pluralism.'

Part VII: Sector Spotlights: Sectors Pivotal for a Self-Confident India of 2050

This section is dedicated to certain sectors, which are often ignored but remain pivotal to economic prosperity. Planning for

Part VI

Imagining the Future of the Republic through Indian Aspirations and Dreams

21

Crystal-ball Gazing for India's Future

Pallavi Nahata

Skyscrapers, skywalks and flyovers, concrete forests and digital homes, automation and artificial intelligence, medical advancements, and maybe holidays to the moon—will marriage or religion as institutions still be held in reverence, and will as many Indians still want a child? India in 2050—what is it going to look like?

While we do not quite know what the years to come have in store, the year gone by has been a good one.

'Just looking like a wow!' The most viral line of 2023 appears to sum up sentiments around the Indian economy, too. Every day seemed to have brought with it a new headline about precisely when India will either become a developed economy or just how many trillion dollars the size of the Indian economy will be by 2030, 2047 or 2050. You get the drift.

While 'rizz' might have been the Oxford word of the year, for India, it was 'Viksit Bharat'.

2023 was also when Prime Minister Narendra Modi set an ambitious goal for India to become a developed economy by its centenary Independence Day in 2047. Of all the views and counterviews to this, one was of India's central bank. According to an article by the Reserve Bank of India (RBI), India's real gross domestic product (GDP) will need to grow at 7.6 per cent annually over the next twenty-five years to achieve the per capita income level to become a developed economy. That is higher than what potential growth is currently being pegged at. In the ongoing fiscal too, India's GDP is forecasted to grow by 7.3 per cent, according to advance estimates by the Central Statistics Office.

While it remains to be seen when India will become a developed economy, there is no denying that it is not rhetoric alone. India's GDP growth remains resilient, and the economy continues to perform better than expected.

Over the next few years, one of the key factors that the India story appears to hinge on is its young workforce driving productivity. Favourable demographics and whether India can reap its benefits. India has entered the next stage of demographic transition, with population growth set to slow markedly in the next two decades, along with a significant increase in the share of the working-age population—the 'demographic dividend' phase.

But what does this demographic want?

Whether India can reap the benefits of the demographic dividend, what about the other way around? What does it feel like to grow up in the world's fastest-growing economy? Does it mean much at all?

The pace of change around is palpable. Even for me, born the year the economy liberalized, today, life is already quite different from a decade ago. For instance, it still never fails to amaze me that there are start-ups that can deliver food from iconic restaurants around the country or a printout from the next-door store quicker than if you did it yourself.

But for millennials and Gen Z alike, work opportunities remain at the forefront of our concerns.

My salary hike after my last appraisal was 4 per cent. For perspective, that is lower than the average inflation for the fiscal year. That is also lower than how much my rent is contracted to increase every year. Maybe it is that industry, maybe that is the cost of not having followed the engineering/MBA route, or maybe it is the economy. To be sure, if I am still in a position to author a chapter in a soon-to-be-published book, with a steady paying job at a digital and TV news channel. I am probably among the better offs. Maybe among the best offs?

What Data Suggests

Macroeconomic data on employment is looking up. According to the last available PLFS by the Ministry of Statistics and Programme Implementation, between July 2022 and June 2023, the unemployment rate for all ages stood at a record low of 3.2 per cent in the survey's short history, accompanied by a rise in the labour force participation rate to 42.4 per cent.

While government data suggests a decline in unemployment and a rise in the labour force participation ratio, that is also because of the rise in self-employment and a rise in the share of unpaid workers. On aggregate, 57.3 per cent of all workers were self-employed in 2022–23. Of those self-employed, own-account workers comprised 39 per cent of all workers.

However, the Centre for Monitoring the Indian Economy (CMIE), a private business information company, pegs the unemployment rate higher. For instance, for December 2023, it pegs the unemployment rate at 8.7 per cent.

According to development and labour economist Santosh Mehrotra, the difference between the CMIE and PLFS data is that the CMIE data is internationally compliant and, by definition, does not count unpaid family labour as employment. He added that the government data on unemployment is misleading. Own account workers and those in unpaid self-employment have unstable jobs and earnings, said Mehrotra. Often, these jobs are accompanied by lower wages or earnings.

If you scratch beneath the surface, the challenges of productive employment and underemployment have risen further post-COVID-19, along with a rise in self-employment and a rise in unpaid family work, said Radhicka Kapoor, a labour economist. These are the key challenges going forward, along with a lack of productive employment opportunities for women, she added.

While he was dropping me off at my destination, I happened to ask auto driver Rakesh Mishra how he envisioned life in 2047. Mishra was shocked by the question. 'I am barely able to think beyond how my family and I will get through the next day,' he said. His son's school fees were due soon. Including past arrears, it had come up to about Rs 30,000. '*Mere pass jeb main abhi mushkil se tees rupay hai*,' he quipped. While he was able to save some money earlier, he now makes enough to make ends meet, he says. As things get costlier, earnings have barely inched up, added Mishra.

For him, 2047 is too far in the future. '*Kya maloom hum tab zinda bhi ho ya nahi*,' he said, as I was getting off.

While the macroeconomy appears to be a shining spot, is the correlation between economic growth and employment strong enough? On the one hand, while economic growth has drawn workers out of agriculture and from villages, manufacturing has failed to absorb them significantly. Instead, construction and informal services have been the main job creators.

While there is a rising impetus to manufacturing from the production linked incentives, it is yet to show up in employment. There is a need for a structural transformation. India must rebalance its economic structure by strengthening its industrial sector so that its share in GDP rises, states the article by the RBI.

India needs to follow a multipronged approach to absorbing the large pool of labour force productively and harnessing growth opportunities in knowledge-oriented sectors through sustained policy focus on structural reforms, infrastructure, logistics, digitalization of the economy, and upskilling the labour force.

A report, *State of Working India 2021*, by Azim Premji University proposes a framework for a National Employment Policy, which includes the promotion of public investment in social infrastructure as well as the facilitation of private investment. These, together with a comprehensive social security infrastructure that includes rights-based entitlements, portable benefits, and empowered worker welfare boards, can tackle the persistent problems of low earnings, low productivity, and precarity, it said.

For most Indians, the vision for 2050 is still the same. *Roti, Kapda, Kaam, aur Makaan.*

Can education and skilling become India's Achilles heel in the years to come?

It is hard to overlook the inability of the Indian economy to create non-farm jobs in the context of the current education system. In basic skills in reading and arithmetic for youth in the age group of 14–18, about 25 per cent of this age group still cannot read a Standard II text fluently in their regional language, according to the findings of the Annual Survey of Education Report. More than half struggle with simple division problems, the report finds. A little over half can read sentences in English. Of those who can read sentences in English, almost three-quarters cannot tell their meanings.

According to Goldman Sachs research, which projects the Indian economy to be the world's second-largest by 2075, the main downside risk would be if the labour force participation rate does not increase. 'If you have more opportunities—especially for women because the women's labour force participation rate is significantly lower than men's—you can shore up your labour force participation rate, which can further increase your potential growth,' it states.

Thoda Hai, Thode ki Zaroorat Hai

Beyond employment, crystal gazing into 2050, I envision not having to choose between passion and pay, affordable housing and healthcare, clean air and ease of commute.

I envision not having to wake up in the 500-sq-ft apartment that I currently spend half my disposable income on because it happens to be close to my workplace. Or still spend about an hour every day searching for a vehicle on the way back, because I refuse to have to pay for surge pricing.

Of course, some of these problems are exclusive to Mumbai. Bangalore, too, appears to be showing early symptoms. But are these really cities where employers can afford to expect employees to turn up to work every single day despite the gaping holes in civic amenities, infrastructure, and urban planning?

Should it really take the construction of a temple for the local administration to build a planned city?

The mandate given to the local authorities in Ayodhya was simple—to make the city the global spiritual capital. The juggernaut of infrastructure projects, along with planned layouts, civic amenities, restoration, and rejuvenation of blue and green infrastructure and their integration with grey infrastructure, taking into account climate and environmental sustainability, means Ayodhya might very well be India's best-planned city.

Apart from a plethora of religious sites, Uttar Pradesh also boasts 140 other heritage sites that are centrally protected. That is the tip of the iceberg. According to a working group report by the NITI Aayog on improving heritage management in India, an initial survey indicates the total quantum of India's built heritage and archaeological remains may roughly amount to a total of 400,000 plus heritage structures across the country, including the centrally protected monuments, state protected monuments, heritage buildings under various religious trusts, historic cities, and archaeological sites.

All remain in varying stages of restoration and repair. Bhimbetka, near Bhopal, boasts about one lakh-year-old art gallery cupules made in one of the rock shelters that are thought to have been among humans' earliest manifestations of creativity. Prehistoric art and the depiction of early life in cave paintings date back about 30,000 years, according to plaques by the Archaeological Survey of India at the site. Yet, one must be lucky to snag up the lone registered tourist guide at the site.

Currently, India's heritage is underfinanced. It not only constitutes the important markers of the country's past but also presents an opportunity for generating employment and income through heritage tourism and local development, more so given the recent surge in domestic tourism seen post-COVID-19.

The wish list can go on. But, at its core, a wish list is not too different from those before us. *Roti, kapda, kaam, aur makaan* continue to remain at the forefront of what young India wants.

To conclude, the Indian story of economic growth remains a coin with two sides—rising per capita incomes on the one side and continuing challenges on the other side. The way forward might be no different.

After all, as John Maynard Keynes helps sum up, 'But this long run is a misleading guide to current affairs. In the long run we are all dead. Economists set themselves too easy, too useless a task if in tempestuous seasons they can only tell us that when the storm is long past, the ocean is flat again.'

22

India's Digitization Journey: Towards a Future of Endless Possibility

Roopak Gupta

As the sun rose over the vibrant streets of Agra in the 1980s, the rhythm of radio music filled the air, carrying with it the spirit of an era. Growing up in this decade had its unique charm, marked by simple joys and the collective wisdom of a closely-knit community. In those days, seeking knowledge beyond schoolbooks often meant turning to an elder's tale or the quiet aisles of a library. Ambitions were modest, and securing a job was seen as the pinnacle of success, with few daring to tread the uncertain path of innovation.

It was a time when even a 20-km journey seemed an expedition, and the social fabric of India was such that the loss of my parents in early childhood did not leave me solitary. The community's embrace was a testament to a society where connections were not digital but heartfelt.

1994 marked a personal technological awakening as computers began to whisper promises of the future into the classrooms. With the curiosity of a young mind, I dreamt of a wooden box that could dance to the commands from my computer – a vision not too different from the robots that inhabit today's imagination. However, in Agra, my aspirations were met with well-intentioned advice to focus on my studies and not 'waste time' on dreams that would not secure employment. Yet, with my grandparents' secret support, I could spend a summer vacation in the libraries of Delhi, taking notes and fuelling my passion for creating the 'wooden box'.

By 1998, that passion had evolved into a prototype of a movable platform capable of carrying a vacuum cleaner that promised to revolutionize household cleaning. It brought me national recognition and even a 'Good Morning India' feature. But despite the accolades, the journey was stunted by the era's lack of structure for innovators seeking financial support.

This was the India of yesteryears, where the quest for information was arduous. But today, the nation stands transformed. Information is now at our fingertips, internet penetration is deep, and the shift from an agriculture-based economy to a digital one is unmistakable. India, where 200 km was a vast distance, now sees such journeys as routine, and a trip from Delhi to Kanyakumari is a matter of hours, not days.

Today, India's digital landscape is a testament to rapid growth and boundless potential, starkly contrasting bygone decades' limited access and resources. This essay embarks on a journey to explore how India's digital revolution is not merely an expansion of technology but a gateway to inclusive growth, poised to bridge societal divides by 2050.

Expansion of Digital Infrastructure

As the foundational framework of the digital revolution, the National Optical Fibre Network (NOFN), under initiatives like Bharat Broadband Network Limited (BharatNet), has begun stitching together a nation once fragmented by geographical and digital divides. This ambitious project is a leap towards connecting rural areas, exemplified by the transformation in remote villages where high-speed internet turns erstwhile unreachable dreams into tangible realities. However, the path is fraught with challenges, from geographical hurdles to the digital literacy chasm. Solutions lie in innovative models of public-private partnerships, community involvement, and adaptive technologies, ensuring that the fibre optic web spun today holds strong for the generations of tomorrow.

Advancements in AI and Machine Learning

The current state of artificial intelligence (AI) in India mirrors the audacious aspirations of my youth, as AI's tendrils weave through agriculture, healthcare, and education. This technology is not a mere tool but a harbinger of social good, nurturing crops through precision farming, safeguarding health with predictive diagnostics, and customizing education to the needs of every child. The ethical deployment of AI, guided by a robust policy framework, is imperative to prevent the misalignment of AI's potential with the nation's ethos. As AI continues to evolve, it must remain a beacon of equitable advancement, illuminating the path for the underprivileged and the underrepresented.

Digital Literacy Programmes

My quest for knowledge in the libraries of Delhi was a solitary pursuit, but today's India is etching a different story through initiatives like Digital India. These programmes are not just skilling citizens but are igniting a collective consciousness towards a digital-first mindset. Success stories abound, yet the digital literacy narrative is still dotted with challenges, from accessibility to the quality of content. Overcoming these hurdles requires relentless pursuit and unwavering commitment to ensuring that every Indian can navigate the digital world with confidence and competence.

Digitalization in Healthcare, Education, and Financial Inclusion

Digitalization has revolutionized healthcare through telemedicine, democratized education via e-learning platforms, and broadened financial inclusion with mobile wallets. These advancements echo my journey from ideation to realization, where once inaccessible services are now ubiquitous, redefining accessibility. However, the accurate measure of success will be how these services reach the last mile, integrating the unbanked, the unconnected, and the uninformed into the mainstream.

From Dreams to Digital Dominance: The Current State of AI in India

AI was a distant, almost mythical concept when I first envisioned a computer commanding a wooden box. Today, it is a vivid reality, transforming every facet of Indian society. Through initiatives like Digital India and AI4Bharat, the government's push has been pivotal in transitioning from a service-based IT ethos to becoming a frontrunner in AI innovation, focusing on solutions catering to our unique diversity and challenges.

My Own Tryst with AI: The Entrepreneurial Boom

The entrepreneurial landscape that once seemed barren now thrives with start-ups, particularly in AI. It is a boom reminiscent of my early tinkering days but on an astoundingly amplified scale. Startups in India now harness AI for social good, from Kashmir to the backwaters of Kerala, reflecting a nation's collective ambition. This is a testament to a cultural paradigm shift, one that values and nurtures the maverick minds that once struggled for recognition and support.

A Support System I Once Dreamed Of: Funding and Supporting Startups

The 'wooden box' of my childhood needed more financial backing to become more than a prototype. Today's young innovators, however, find themselves in a nurturing ecosystem where funding is increasingly accessible. Government programmes like Startup India have laid a fertile ground, while international investors eagerly seek the next big idea sprouting from Indian soil. By 2050, I envisage a nation with a well-established framework that provides every budding entrepreneur with the resources to realize their vision, much like the one I yearned for in my youth.

The Role I Hoped to Play: Impact on Employment and Economic Growth

The impact of start-ups on employment and economic growth is palpable. The start-up culture is crafting a new narrative for employment that values creativity, innovation, and resilience. As a boy who was told to concentrate on his studies and not 'waste time', it fills me with pride to see today's youth encouraged to innovate. By 2050, the employment landscape will be characterized by AI-driven roles, many of which are yet to be imagined, contributing to a robust, diverse, and inclusive Indian economy.

Conclusion

Reflecting on the digital evolution from my childhood to today, the strides made are undeniably impressive. The collective efforts to expand digital infrastructure, leverage AI for social good, bolster digital literacy, and digitalize key sectors lay the cornerstone for inclusive growth. By 2050, India stands on the precipice of a future where innovation is not an echo but a clarion call, and inclusive policies are not an afterthought but the blueprint of a society where technology serves all. Much like my youth's wooden box, the digital revolution must move to the commands of equity, ethics, and empowerment to truly bridge the divide.

23

Echoes of Progress: A Journey

Sharmin Nisar Chougule

Hailing from the picturesque town of Ratnagiri in India, I have traversed through an incredible journey marked by educational pursuits and societal observations that encapsulate the evolving tapestry of our nation.

My journey has been shaped by both personal resilience and societal change. Belonging to a conservative Muslim extended family, I was raised amidst a culture steeped in tradition and values. Despite the constraints of tradition, my parents, with their progressive outlook, provided unwavering support to my educational aspirations. This familial backdrop instilled in me a deep appreciation for the importance of education as a catalyst for personal growth and societal progress.

I grew up in Ratnagiri in a developing India. After completing my schooling, I ventured to Mumbai at the age of 17 for further studies. I obtained degrees in commerce, economics, corporate compliance, and law, and my academic pursuits were intertwined with the dynamic metamorphosis of urban landscapes and educational paradigms.

Growing up in Ratnagiri, I witnessed the gradual transformation of our nation from a developing country to one on the cusp of global prominence. Despite the challenges posed by limited resources and infrastructure, my upbringing was characterized by a modest yet comfortable lifestyle, courtesy of my father's employment in the Middle East. Therefore, while growing up, I was fortunate to experience a standard of living that was slightly higher than my peers. This afforded me luxuries like video games, personal computing, and internet access, which were considered blessings during my growing-up years. However, I also observed that inflation and high prices somehow made the purchasing power of my family go down because of no simultaneous real increase in income.

During my school days, I witnessed my town's transition from rudimentary infrastructure to the introduction of traffic signals and cable television, alongside the gradual introduction of sex education in schools, underscoring the nation's progressive strides. Later in the bustling streets of Mumbai, I found myself immersed in a whirlwind of transformation, symbolized by monumental infrastructure projects like the Mumbai Metro, which ushered in a new era of connectivity and accessibility. However, amidst these advancements, the issue of overpopulation loomed large, often causing logistical hurdles in the transportation, education, and employment sectors. Mumbai, perpetually under construction, epitomized the relentless pursuit of progress, albeit at the cost of congestion and scalability challenges.

Reflecting on the state of education in India, while critiques abound regarding rote learning entrenched in our educational system, it is imperative not to overlook the quality and rigour that underpins Indian academia. Indeed, the global success of Indian tech CEOs stands as a testament to the calibre of education imparted in our institutions. Personally, having experienced the corridors of Indian academia before embarking on a journey to Italy for my PhD in civil law and constitutional legality, I have witnessed first-hand the intellectual vibrancy that defines our educational landscape.

As a legal practitioner in India, I have been privy to the nuanced changes in policies and laws orchestrated by the government. While not devoid of criticism, these legislative endeavours, rooted in the principles of the Indian Constitution, have heralded significant reforms such as the triple talaq ban law, the Jammu and Kashmir reorganization by abrogation of Article 370 of the Constitution, the GST law, farm laws, the Citizenship Amendment Act, the Unlawful Activities (Prevention) Amendment Bill, 2019, the Constitution (124th Amendment) Bill, 2019, amongst others. While acknowledging the imperfections inherent in any system, I remain optimistic about India's trajectory, guided by the enduring principles of democracy, justice, and progress enshrined in our constitution.

Of course, in the annals of history, the defence of a nation stands as a bulwark against the tides of adversity and should be strong enough. Bolstering our national defence apparatus has emerged as a cornerstone of strategic imperatives, fostering a robust and multi-equipped defence infrastructure during the last ten years.

Looking ahead to 2050, one envisions an India propelled by innovation, inclusivity, and sustainable growth. A nation where technological prowess converges with social equity, where educational excellence transcends barriers, and where governance reflects the aspirations of a burgeoning populace.

It envisions India as a global leader, not only in economic terms but also in fostering a harmonious society grounded in democratic principles and cultural pluralism. In this India of the future, challenges will undoubtedly persist, but they will be met with the resilience and ingenuity ingrained in the fabric of our nation's ethos.

Part VII
Sector Spotlights: Sectors Pivotal for a Self-Confident India of 2050

24

Healthcare in India of 2050

Vinay Singhal

There has been much discussion about India's *Amritkal* period from 2024 to 2047 due to the advantages offered by its large working-age population. Indians are currently striving to become the third-largest economy within the next three years and a developed nation well before 2047, which marks the 100th year of India's Independence. However, to achieve this goal, we need to take action to ensure that all young people are healthy, as they will be needed not only in India but all throughout the world. This is because the population of most high- and middle-income countries, including China, is declining.

India's Demographic Advantage

As of 2023, adults aged 65 and older make up only 7 per cent of India's population. In comparison, the same age groups make up 14 per cent of China's population and 18 per cent of the population in the United States. India has a high percentage of young people, with more than 50 per cent of its population below the age of 25 and more than 65 per cent below the age of 35. In 2020, the average age of an Indian was 29, compared to 37 for China and 48 for Japan. By 2030, India's dependency ratio[1] is expected to be just over 0.4.

India has made great strides in terms of life expectancy. In 1947, it was just 35 years, but it increased to 72 in 2023. Furthermore, India's population growth rate has started to stabilize, with an increase of only 0.75 per cent in 2023.

India's Standing in Terms of Health Parameters

It is concerning that India's government health expenditure is only 2.1 per cent of the gross domestic product (GDP) while countries like China, Brazil, and Bangladesh spend 3.4 per cent, 4 per cent, and 2.5 per cent, respectively. India's out-of-pocket health spends is also high at 60 per cent compared to 30 per cent and 25 per cent for China and Brazil, respectively. In the US, the figure is 56 per cent, but insurance penetration reduces the burden on households.

Looking at the infant mortality rates, India compares poorly with Sri Lanka and Bangladesh, which have rates of 6 and 25, respectively, while India's rate is 30. This suggests that India's economic growth has not translated into health gains, and there is much to be done to catch up.

However, if one looks at India's life expectancy, between 1990 and 2020, there was a ten-year gain, which is significant. In terms of our other indicators, whether it is in terms of under-five mortality, which in turn is about 35.7 per thousand live births, infant mortality ratio of about 30 per thousand live births or maternal mortality ratio rate of 103 per hundred thousand live births—we are almost on par with other countries at the same income level.

India's Physical Health Infrastructure

India needs to significantly improve its infrastructure facilities as they are lower than the World Health Organization (WHO)-prescribed standards. Achieving this goal will require substantial investments in new hospital facilities, teaching hospitals, diagnostics labs, manufacturing units for medical equipment, etc. For all this, the government needs to come up with schemes so that the above facilities are installed at a higher pace both in the private sector and in the public domain (administered by both state and central governments).

Human Resources in Indian Healthcare

As of 2021, the Indian health sector is the largest employer, providing jobs to 4.7 million people. It is estimated that it generated 2.7 million jobs in 2017–22 in spite of COVID-19 and is expected to add 5 lakh new jobs every year. With the opening of new colleges and the expansion of healthcare services in rural India, it is expected that the number of job opportunities in this sector will continue to grow at an even faster rate.

Physical Infrastructure

India currently has around 70,000 hospitals, with 26,000 of them being run by the public sector and the remaining 44,000 being privately owned. As of 2019, there are more than 714,000 beds in government hospitals and an estimated 1,185,000 in the private sector. This infrastructure gives India 1.3 beds per 1,000 people, much below the WHO standard of 3 beds per 1,000 people.

Nevertheless, today, there are 706 medical colleges, 350 of which are government colleges. In 2014, there were only 387 colleges, which means that the number of MBBS seats has doubled in just nine years. The government has approved 157 new medical colleges, out of which 108 have already been established. Nursing institutes have also seen similar growth. The turnout of nurses from 1958 has increased dramatically to 99,000, and fresh nurse's school start-ups are announced every year.

Despite this growth, nursing is still considered a lower-level job in India, and about 33,000 nurses are working in foreign countries where they earn better salaries and social status. To address this problem, the Supreme Court has mandated a minimum salary of Rs 20,000 per month (in smaller towns, they get only Rs 5,000 per month). This will provide strong support for more nursing colleges to be set up and for nurses' output to increase substantially.

New Government of India Initiatives

Though Indian healthcare is among the largest in the world, it lags behind in providing adequate healthcare to poor people, especially in rural India, due to size and population.

Therefore, the government has devised multiple initiatives and policies to promote India's medical service sector.

National Health Mission: Separate bodies have been formed to serve the populations in urban and rural settings, as the requirements in the two areas are different.

Ayushman Bharat: The government is offering a health insurance plan that provides coverage of up to Rs 5 lakh per year for each family. This will cover 50 crore people, i.e., 10 crore family units, and is available in most Indian hospitals. Its main goal is to provide health coverage to lower economic strata to avoid out-of-pocket expenses. Currently, the upper-income group is covered by either employer group insurance or private insurance at reasonable rates. This means that only 36 per cent of the population is covered by such insurance, which needs to be increased to cover everyone.

Other healthcare-realed schemes: There are several healthcare-related schemes such as Pradhan Mantri Jan Arogya Yojana, Rashtriya Bal Swasthya Yojana, National Medical Commission, PM National Dialysis Programme, Janani

Shishu Suraksha Karyakaram, and Rashtriya Bal Swasthya Karyakaram. These schemes have been designed to provide healthcare to individuals in lower-income groups and require additional funding from the government. Therefore, it is crucial to stress the need for higher healthcare allocations in government budgets, both at the centre and state levels.

Use of New Technology in Providing Healthcare to All

We also need to focus on the introduction of newer equipment that can provide quick and accurate diagnosis of diseases with the help of high-tech solutions such as digitization of medical records, artificial intelligence (AI), the internet of things (IoTs), Gen IT, ChatGPT, etc. This approach will save a significant amount of capital investment and expedite health delivery, reducing the need for medical personnel. An example of this is the direct introduction of smartphones, as this obviates the use of laying of underground wiring for connecting billions of old dialling phones. India has successfully provided more than 1 billion affordable smartphones which are faster and involve only a fraction of the capital costs involved.

India has a robust network of Accredited Social Health Activist (ASHA) workers in rural areas who provide primary healthcare services. With the advancements in technology, most of these services can now be provided through them, reducing the dependency on primary health centres. The COVID-19 pandemic has taught us the importance of self-testing. Wearables and point-of-care diagnostics are rapidly advancing. These technologies can monitor a larger number of body parameters. India's digital health mission is aimed at enhancing the adoption of electronic health records, which will create a huge amount of digital data that can also be useful for developing faster, smaller digitized equipment for all purposes. The combination of teleconsultations and these technological changes will also revolutionize the diagnostic and medical device industry.

Given below are some such examples for saving costs and improving delivery:

- Using hand-held equipment for an AI-assisted ultrasound of pregnant women to enable advanced steps in case any complication in delivery is expected. It is estimated that 50 per cent of mother and child deaths can be saved through this method, saving both cost and manpower.
- Attaching private sector hospitals with medical colleges, just like it is done in public hospitals and private hospitals in the US (e.g., Harvard Medical School is associated with Partners and other private hospitals). Thus, the existing capacity for educating future doctors would considerably increase at a fast pace (60 per cent of hospital beds are in the private sector). Besides, these students would be trained in better facilities.
- Wider use of hand-held devices (also operatable by ASHA workers) for noting down vital parameters of villagers to identify cases of serious diseases right in the beginning. Another example is the use of nanotech-based instruments to check HIV, hepatitis, and other non-communicable diseases more accurately and at a lesser cost.
- Experts predict that Gen IT can be used very productively in healthcare, thus improving productivity and accuracy. One can expect several such instruments based on Gen IT in the market soon. Leading hospitals such as Apollo, Fortis, Medanta, and others are using ChatGPT for floor operations in their large hospitals, and this trend is likely to increase very fast once more people understand the advantages of using this new technology. It is felt that AI and IoT-assisted techniques will come into India almost at par with the USA.

- Using scan machines available in large centres that scan the whole body in one go while standing and get quick and accurate results. One can hope that the cost of such equipment will reduce considerably if produced in India as tech talent is available at a lesser cost here.
- Improving mental health services. Compared to developed countries, little attention has been paid to mental health treatment in India. There is a need to increase funds and produce a greater number of psychiatrists from medical colleges.
- Indian hospitals lack SOPs for different activities carried out by doctors and nurses. Considering peculiar Indian conditions, there is an urgent need to devise these. With the advent of AI and IoT, it will be easier to use them effectively and improve patient experience, fuelling industry-wide competition.

Pharmaceutical Industry

As evident, a strong pharmaceutical, active reagents, and vaccines industry is necessary, as shown by India's experience in handling COVID-19.

The pharmaceutical industry had a turnover of $42 billion in 2022 and is estimated to reach $130 billion by 2030. India is the world's largest provider of generic_medicines by volume, with a 20 per cent share ($25 billion) of total global pharmaceutical exports at about one-seventh of the price in the US and other countries. It is also the largest vaccine supplier in the world by volume, accounting for more than 60 per cent of all vaccines manufactured in the world. The Indian pharmaceutical products are exported to almost all countries of the world. India played a very laudatory role in supplying vaccines to most of the countries, especially the developing countries, and thus helped considerably in the avoidance of deaths caused by COVID-19.

Medical Devices and Equipment Industry

India's healthcare delivery system is quite extensive, but the country has struggled with developing a complementary medical device industry. This is due to international sellers insisting on importing equipment from their home bases to avoid capital investments. However, the Indian government's Atma Nirbhar Bharat campaign and demands from the Indian hospital industry have convinced prominent companies to set up manufacturing facilities in India. The expected result is that once these devices are manufactured in the country, their selling prices will decrease.

In the last decade, the healthcare equipment and medical device sector in India has grown significantly, with a wide range of medical devices produced from consumables to implantable medical devices. The majority of medical devices manufactured in India are disposables like catheters, perfusion sets, extension lines, cannulas, feeding tubes, needles, and syringes as well as implants like cardiac stents, drug-eluting stents, intraocular lenses, and orthopaedic implants.

The medical devices sector is highly capital intensive and requires continuous training of the healthcare system providers to adapt to new technologies. Better and smarter radiographic equipment is coming into the market, facilitating diagnosis and avoiding non-invasive treatment. These machines are becoming costlier day by day. India will be able to produce them cheaper in-house and export from here.

Despite the growth in the medical devices sector, there is still a significant gap between the current demand and supply of medical devices in the country. India has an overall 70–80 per cent import dependency on medical devices, which is why many medical device manufacturers (domestic and international) see this under-penetration of medical devices in India as a significant growth opportunity.

The size of the Indian medical devices market is estimated to be $11 billion in 2022 and is expected to grow to $50 billion by 2030 with a CAGR of 16.4 per cent. India's medical device market share in the global market is estimated to be 1.65 per cent. Currently, it is the fourth largest Asian medical devices market after Japan, China, and South Korea and is among the top twenty medical device markets globally. Furthermore, India's export of medical devices stood at $2.4 billion in FY22 and is expected to rise to $10 billion by 2025.

Medical Tourism

India's large healthcare infrastructure and medical staff, led by highly experienced doctors, have been able to attract a large number of foreign patients. It is estimated that in 2022 alone, 2 million patients from 78 countries visited India and spent about $6 billion on various treatments. This figure is expected to increase to $13 billion by 2026. Most of these travellers come from Southeast Asia, Africa, the Middle East, Russia, etc. Moreover, a significant number also came from Australia, Canada, the UK, and the USA.

Additionally, Ayush visitors have also been increasing in large numbers. They primarily visit Ayurvedic hospitals in Kerala and Tamil Nadu, attracted by substantially lower costs (one-eighth of the US costs), English-speaking personnel, doctors trained in the US/UK, a large number of Joint Commission International (JCI)-accredited hospitals, and beautiful tourist places. Most visitors go to Chennai, Delhi NCR, Bengaluru, Mumbai, Kerala, Jaipur, etc. This trend is expected to continue attracting medical tourists from many more countries in the years to come.

Steps that must be taken by India to achieve global standards:

- The first and most important step is to increase health expenditure from 2.1 per cent to 3 per cent of GDP as soon as possible and then to 5 per cent by 2030 with gradual increases.
- The government should aim to cover the entire population through some type of insurance system so that medical treatment does not result in the family becoming terribly indebted to future generations.
- Currently, no insurance system in India covers OPD and medicines expenditures. A suitable method to cover this needs to be devised.
- India should move to a larger 'wellness focus' from the current illness-centric approach. Advances in nutrition and enhanced societal focus on remaining fit will enable an enhanced focus on eating right, exercising right, meditating, and living a longer life. Science has made a lifespan of 100 possible for most populations.
- The use of technology-supported diagnostic tools will enable the detection of diseases in earlier stages and their fast treatment, enabling longer lives.
- There is a need to move towards the use of better medicines, better equipment, and digital support. This will allow India to lead the world in this field, as it has done by adopting digital systems in financial dealings, communications, and research.
- We should also utilize large private hospitals to train the new MBBS doctors by allowing them to attend medical colleges that train more doctors.

With the help of the above, India will emerge as a world leader in individual health and happiness by 2050.

Note: Figures mentioned in the chapter are from WHO, FICCI, CII, *Economic Times*, and the Big Four consulting firms.

25

The Role of Reinsurance in the Economic Growth of India till 2050

Pratap Tambe and Rahul Ugile

The Indian insurance market is poorly developed, and many Indians struggle with the concept of insurance itself. This essay is about reinsurance, the insurance of insurance, which is an even more complex concept. So, let us first explain insurance and reinsurance through a car insurance and reinsurance example before discussing its importance for India's economic growth until 2050.

Risk is a fact of life. Every individual and firm faces risks of different kinds. From carrying an umbrella to managing the risk that it might rain to buying insurance to protect against the risk that a storm might damage the house, individuals and firms manage risks as a part of their day-to-day lives. Risk management involves identifying risks and selecting how much of each risk to reduce, how much to retain, and how much of each risk to transfer. Insurance is a particular method of transferring risk to a third party. Insurers specialize in providing this service to multiple parties. It is mandatory by law to have car insurance to drive a car on Indian roads. The insurance policy must at least have 'third-party liability' (TPL) cover.

It is mandatory by law to have insurance so that if you hit another car, the insurance policy will pay for any damage charges claimed by the other vehicle's owner. Unless this cover is available to every driver, the 'risk environment' will not be conducive enough for people to drive confidently. The 'risk environment' keeps changing through innovation in cars and changes in rules and laws regarding the responsibilities and liabilities of car owners. For example, as vehicles become more and more autonomous, the risk environment changes, impacting the features and prices of insurance policies. Sometimes, some risks increase while others decrease.

If there are enough buyers of car insurance policies, insurers can provide coverage on their own. However, some risks may be difficult for the insurer to bear. If an insurer wants to buy insurance cover for some risk that it faces from the cars it has insured, it needs to buy a reinsurance policy. For example, the insurer may issue car insurance policies with theft cover and third-party liability covers. If they find that car theft risk is higher than they would like to bear, they can buy reinsurance cover for car theft risk from a reinsurer. The reinsurer will issue reinsurance policies to the insurer, which work in a manner very similar to insurance policies.

People find it easy to understand that economic growth requires putting financial capital at risk in the form of debt and equity. However, they struggle to understand why reinsurance is critical for India's economic growth. Reinsurance is much too abstract, and its importance for the country's economic growth is not understood adequately, even by well-educated Indian people. Let us explain. As India grows economically, Indians will start and grow many different types of businesses. Every business faces many risks and needs to manage/reduce them and transfer the rest using insurance.

Reinsurance allows businesses to take these risks because the cost of insurance depends on the cost of reinsurance. If reinsurance and insurance are not available, the cost to the business of bearing these risks may be very high and make the business unviable. As Indian businesses continue to grow, they will need to use multiple lines of insurance. High-quality and cost-effective insurance needs high-quality, cost-effective reinsurance.

The Indian economic growth has resulted in many products and services for the Indian and global markets. Much of the Indian economic exports over the past few decades have been through services, where personal/group policies for health, life, and pensions have been more important, along with property insurance related to the infrastructure growth they triggered. Meanwhile, large industrial groups like Tata have expanded globally through acquisitions in different parts of the work, which has led to an increased need for non-life insurance and reinsurance. Building on this, the Indian start-up focus is generating new products and platforms, which is expected to drive economic growth over the next few decades by establishing more India-based platforms and multinational companies.

Companies that create products and platforms face several risks in their operations and supply and distribution chains, which require directors' and officers' insurance, property insurance, business interruption insurance, directors and officers (D&O), product liability insurance, etc.

For product and platform companies, preventing knowledge leakage to third parties is critical. Suppose Indian reinsurers and insurers provide high-quality and cost-effective reinsurance. In that case, they will retain strategic knowledge about the risks faced by Indian businesses within India and leverage the country's significant cost advantages against comparable competitors' costs. While this is done, the cost of managing/reducing and transferring the residual risk to insurers and onwards to reinsurers needs to be kept in line with similar costs faced by competitors around the world, who may leverage deeper expertise in risk management and transfer available in their local insurers and reinsurers.

In certain regions of the world, such as the US, local insurers have begun denying insurance to homeowners and corporations that own properties in those parts of the world. This is because the potential losses from natural catastrophe insurance in these places have increased due to climate change caused by floods and hurricanes. As a result, reinsurance is not available for such insurance policies placed in such regions. Due to the lack of insurance and reinsurance, obtaining mortgages is also problematic in these places.

People living in such places are forced to bear their losses due to natural disasters or move out to other safer places. The number of such places is rising. As more and more places become less habitable, economic activity in those places decreases, impacting local citizens and governments. In some cases, the impact of climate change in a particular place impacts citizens and governments in faraway countries due to the globally interconnected nature of the world, i.e., through supply chains. For instance, some countries like Israel are much less dependent on other countries for their food needs, while others like the UK are much more reliant on imported food items. In some parts of the world, climate change has changed the local weather patterns, causing significant damage to agricultural output. Extreme/unseasonal rain, hail, and extremely hot or cold days can damage crops and/or reduce yields from agriculture. Similar challenges also affect industrial output due to natural disasters. As a result, individuals and firms in countries like the UK face price and volume risks when procuring food and other items from other countries.

For example, families may find key food items more expensive or unavailable and must adjust their budget and/or nutrition appropriately. Food processing companies may find that the inputs they buy are expensive or unavailable, forcing their factories to stop working for periods of time. Such impacts are caused by supply chain disruptions or problems in supply at the points of origin. These problems are not limited to the food industry but extend to other industries, such as semiconductors. Measuring and managing supply chain risk (including buying insurance) is now a critical capability for corporates.

The frequency and intensity of natural disasters in India have increased due to climate change. Owing to the low penetration of insurance among its people and firms, either the people or firms must bear the losses caused by these natural disasters, making their lives like the 'snake and ladders' game, or the government must bail out people. Currently, insurance is available for most parts of India and will likely need less reinsurance. The reason for this is that due to the sheer size of India, natural disasters are never pan-India. If insurers have carefully ensured adequate diversification within their insured people and firms across the country, they can manage with less reinsurance.

However, as climate change increases the frequency and intensity of natural disasters, India will need more reinsurance. The country periodically experiences shortages of various food items that are essential for families and firms in regions or across regions within India due to challenges in supply at the point of origin or disruptions in the supply chains. Indian corporates must measure and manage supply chain risk. This needs high-quality and cost-effective reinsurance. Reinsurers and insurers, as well as brokers, provide risk advisory services that can help Indian corporates manage risk better due to natural and human-made disasters locally or in places from where they source or in places where the supply chain passes through.

The primary types of trade between countries include goods and services, finance and investment, and reinsurance. All these are denominated in different currencies, and one primary reference currency globally is the US dollar. The Indian public is reasonably aware of the goods/service inter-linkages, and the Indian government and press regularly report about foreign direct investment (FDI) into India and gross domestic product (GDP) as crucial metrics of the Indian economy. However, much less attention is paid to interlinkages in terms of reinsurance. As climate change decreases the attractiveness of specific regions for businesses, insurance, and finance, financial/investment reinsurance capital may flee from these regions as it is needed more within the countries of its origins or its 'preference'. Thus, geopolitics driven by climate change and technology change triggers changes in global finance and reinsurance flows. These flows are interlinked. Reinsurance capital flight can easily make a country unattractive for financial capital. The reverse is not true. Withdrawing reinsurance from a country can deprive it of precious reinsurance capital. Replacing 'skilled' international reinsurance capital with 'unskilled' local reinsurance capital means 'ignorance buffers', which increase the cost of risk-bearing and, therefore, the cost of goods/services. Reinsurance enables the reduction of risk-bearing costs by selecting and pooling risks from multiple insurers to generate diversification benefits. It also leverages its understanding of risks to work with insurers and businesses to keep risk within control limits.

Insurers and reinsurers get to know a lot of things about the products and services as well as business practices of the businesses they insure. So, developing 'skilled' reinsurance capital needed for its own economy is one of the most important strategic steps any superpower and aspiring superpower can take. Becoming less vulnerable to the flight of reinsurance capital from India is a strategic imperative. And as India grows its influence worldwide, the capability to provide reinsurance to its allies will be strategic. This can be done by developing a robust local reinsurance market and actively managing the strategic vulnerability to geopolitics generated by international reinsurance contracts, which are steps that such an aspiring superpower should take. Beyond superpowers and aspiring superpowers, we contend that this type of national decentralized reinsurance marketplace system will be mandatory for every country. The ability to bear one's risks with minimal dependency on others is hardly optional for countries.

The Indian government wants to make India a reinsurance hub. This means that Indian insurers will continue to leverage international reinsurers beyond the mandatory reinsurance they must place with the Indian national reinsurer General Insurance Corporation (GIC Re). It also means that Indian reinsurance entities, particularly Indian national reinsurers, will increase the provision of reinsurance to insurers in many friendly countries. As India seeks to grow its global influence, the ability to provide reinsurance expertise and capital is a strategic geopolitical capability. Insurers and reinsurers get to know many critical things about the businesses they insure and develop expertise in managing the risks related to the businesses they insure. Growing reinsurance capability within India will enable it to keep the knowledge about Indian business within the country. In a sense, nothing is surprising about this behaviour by India as the global risk environment changes due to climate and technology changes, making reinsurance a strategic capability for aspiring superpowers like India. Most large insurers and reinsurance companies already have large Indian units focused on India and global service organizations. The human resource capability for India to lead in reinsurance is growing rapidly. Strategic facilitation can enable Indian reinsurers to compete with global reinsurers.

It is estimated that India's GDP will rise dramatically by 2050. This will attract global reinsurance capacity, expertise, and best practices and further retain local talent. Advanced technical expertise brought in by foreign reinsurers in areas like risk assessment, pricing, claims management, and underwriting will expose local talent to these practices, enhancing their skillsets and knowledge base. The benefits of such a global reinsurance hub will further extend to product innovation. Joint ventures and partnerships between local players and foreign reinsurers can foster an environment for exchanging ideas and leveraging each other's strengths.

We already have a few success stories as evidence: TATA AIG, Bajaj Allianz, ICICI Lombard, etc. This cross-pollination can spark creative thinking and lead to the development of new insurance products that cater to segments and risks of all nature. With the availability of capacity and expertise through a modern reinsurance hub, India will be equipped to cover conventional risks and new-age risks emanating from climate change, emerging technologies, social unrest, and global political uncertainties.

Home-grown reinsurers and foreign reinsurers will compete and further collaborate in the Indian global reinsurance hub, leading to the development of reinsurance skill sets in India. This will boost the confidence of local regulators to allow the inflow of local capital to the reinsurance sector instead of the usual inflow of foreign capital. Indian investors will grab this opportunity with both hands, ensuring there is no shortage of capacity within India's reinsurance needs and, in turn, reducing dependence on foreign capacity.

A self-sustainable, well-capitalized reinsurance hub, aided by an able local workforce, will not only compete with Lloyds of

London or large reinsurers of the world but also act as a catalyst for India's success story. With the availability of capacity and expertise through a modern reinsurance hub, India will be equipped to cover conventional risks and new-age risks emanating from climate change, emerging technologies, social unrest, and global political uncertainties through product innovation.

Blockchain also is an important variable in reinsurance. The benefits are 100 per cent auditable; what you see is what I see, and what I see is what you see operations (i.e., 100 per cent reconciliation), which reduces costs and increases compliance. More importantly, the use of blockchain makes operations resilient. Creating a global insurance market is possible using blockchain technology. This can help to meet the Indian government's vision of making India a global reinsurance hub. We believe that a blockchain-based reinsurance hub (market) will emerge in each country over time due to the benefits listed above.

And international reinsurance markets will be headquartered in countries that are global leaders. As an emerging superpower, India should seriously consider creating a blockchain-based infrastructure for its local and international insurance operations. As explained in this essay, this will help India build strong relationships with its allies by becoming the friend in need. Along with this, if Indian reinsurers gain knowledge and capital to bear a larger proportion of Indian risk, then India will become less vulnerable to flight of reinsurance capital. India can become a large global reinsurance hub this way, and this will help it become a much more stable superpower. We hope India actualizes its potential for this.

Notes

Chapter 2: India, the Irreplaceable Giant: Serendipities Leading the Way

1 The Hindu rate of growth is defined as the sub-4 per cent real economic growth (considered sub-power) that was witnessed by India between the 1950s and 1980s.

Chapter 4: Does India Have What It Takes to Be a $30 Trillion Economy by 2050

1 The Economic Times, 'PTI India to Become $5 trn Economy Early in Amrit Kaal: Fin Min', *The Economic Times*, December 03, 2023, https://economictimes.indiatimes.com/news/economy/indicators/india-to-become-5-trn-economy-early-in-amrit-kaal-finmin/articleshow/105725439.cms?from=md

2 IBEF, 'India is Expected to Become a US$30 Trillion Economy by 2050: Mr. Atanu Chakraborty', IBEF, October 12, 2023, https://www.ibef.org/news/india-is-expected-to-become-a-us-30-trillion-economy-by-2050-mr-atanu-chakraborty

3 Deepa Vasudevan, 'In Charts: Unlocking India's Sort Power Potential', *Mint*, October 02, 2023, https://www.livemint.com/politics/indias-soft-power-can-we-make-it-count-11696221303614.html#:~:text=In%202023%2C%20India%20was%20ranked,up%20from%20its%202022%20rank.

4 Peter Zeihan, 'India's Counter-Piracy Operation: A Geopolitical Wormhole', YouTube, January 25, 2024, https://www.youtube.com/watch?v=lc22QxlThKg

5 Christina A Wood, 'Services versus Manufacturing: Which Matters More for Growth and Jobs in MENA?' World Bank Blogs, October 01, 2011, https://blogs.worldbank.org/arabvoices/services-versus-manufacturing-which-matters-more-growth-and-jobs-mena

6 Department of Economic Affairs, Monthly Economic Review – April 2024 (New Delhi: Government of India, 2024), https://dea.gov.in/sites/default/files/Monthly%20Economic%20Review%20-April%202024_0.pdf

7 Vivek Kaul, 'Manufacturing Is Key to Creating Jobs in Services', *Mint*, September 13, 2020, https://www.livemint.com/news/india/manufacturing-is-key-to-creating-jobs-in-services-11600013164168.html

8 Shiva Rajora, 'Services Sector Firms Led India Inc's Job Creation in FY23, Says Study', *Business Standard*, June 06, 2024, https://www.business-standard.com/economy/news/service-sector-firms-led-job-creation-in-corporate-sector-in-fy23-study-124011900965_1.html

9 The Mad King is a venture by Remi Tetot, one of the co-founders of Real Vision and former Head of Research at Global Macro Investor (GMI), mentored by Raoul Pal, aimed at providing insightful, analytical write-ups in the financial domain.

10 The Mad King 'Macroeconomics, Finance, Business and Technology', The Mad King, 2023.

11 Manya Rathore, 'Dependency Ratio India 2013-2022', *Statista*, December 14, 2023, https://www.statista.com/statistics/1323770/india-dependency-ratio/#:~:text=The%20dependency%20ratio%20in%20India,stood%20at%20approximately%2053%20percent.

12 EY India, 'Size and Age of Workforce of India Will Play a Significant Role in its Economic Growth in the Coming Years', *EY India*, April 11, 2023, https://www.ey.com/en_in/india-at-100/reaping-the-demographic-dividend

13 Sameer Mehta, 'With More Local Value Additions, Electronics Manufacturing Sector to be Worth $115 bn in 2024', *The Economic Times,* January 1, 2024, https://retail.economictimes.indiatimes.com/news/consumer-durables-and-information-technology/consumer-electronics/with-more-l

14 Press Trust of India, 'With Localisation, Electronics Manufacturing to be $115 Bn in 2024', *Business Standard*, December 31, 2023, https://www.business-standard.com/pti-stories/national/with-more-local-value-additions-electronics-manufacturing-sector-to-be-worth-us

15 Grand View Research, *India Consumer Electronics Market Size, Share and Trends Analysis Report by Product (Mobile Phones, Televisions,*

Refrigerators, Digital Cameras, Air Conditioners, Washing Machines), And Segment Forecasts, 2023 – 2030 (San Francisco: Grand View Research, 2022)

16 Nicola Cantore, Michele Clara, Alejandro Lavopa, and Camelia Soare, 'Manufacturing as an Engine of Growth: Which is the Best Fuel?' *Structural Change and Economic Dynamics* (2017): 56-66

17 Nicola Cantore, Michele Clara, Alejandro Lavopa, and Camelia Soare, 'Manufacturing as an Engine of Growth: Which is the Best Fuel?' *Structural Change and Economic Dynamics* (2017): 56-66

18 Peter Zeihan, 'India's Counter-Piracy Operation: A Geopolitical Wormhole', YouTube, January 25, 2024, https://www.youtube.com/watch?v=lc22QxlThKg

19 Hitachi Energy India Limited 'Hitachi Energy India Limited announces Q2FY24 results: Energy transition and climate action plans driving order growth', press release, November 06, 2023, https://www.hitachienergy.com/in/en/news/press-releases/2023/11/hitachi-energy-india-limited-announces-q2fy24-results-energy-transition-and-climate-action-plans-driving-order-growth

20 Statista, 'Twenty Countries with the Largest Population in Mid-2023', 2024, https://www.statista.com/statistics/262879/countries-with-the-largest-population/

21 Standard Chartered, 'India's Energy Transition: A Major Economic Opportunity', *Standard Chartered*, November 22, 2022, https://www.sc.com/en/news/industries-in-transition/indias-energy-transition-major-economic-opportunity/

22 Ministry of Power 'Power Sector at a Glance ALL INDIA' May, 31, 2023, https://powermin.gov.in/en/content/power-sector-glance-all-india

23 Ministry of Petroleum and Natural Gas, 'India's 4-plank energy security strategy is based on diversifying supplies, increasing E&P, alternate energy sources and energy transition through a gas-based economy, Green Hydrogen etc.', Press Information Bureau, January 10, 2024, https://www.pib.gov.in/Pr

24 Niharika Mandhana and Newley Purnell, 'Modi's Vision for India Rests On Six Giant Companies', *The Wall Street Journal*, June 21, 2023. https://www.wsj.com/articles/modi-india-economy-reliance-industries-adani-group-tata-d2c4f89e

25 The Economic Times, 'India Plays an Integral Role in Boosting Supply Chain Resilience through Friendshoring: Yellen', *The*

Economic Times, July 17, 2023, https://economictimes.indiatimes.com/small-biz/trade/exports/insights/india-plays-an-integral-role-in-boosting-supply-chain-resilience-t

26 Statista, 'Total Contribution of Travel and Tourism to GDP in India 2013-2021', Statista, https://www.statista.com/statistics/313724/total-contribution-of-travel-and-tourism-to-gdp-in-india-by-segment/

27 Invest India, 'Tourism and Hospitality', https://www.investindia.gov.in/sector/tourism-hospitality

28 Mahesh Nandurkar, Abhinav Sinha, Nishant Poddar, and Kevin Verghese, India Strategy : Ayodhya – Unlocking India's Tourism Potential', *Jefferies Asia Equity Research,* January 2024.

29 Rajesh Magow, 'India's Travel and Tourism Sector: Steering towards a Brighter Future', *The Times of India*, December 9, 2023, https://timesofindia.indiatimes.com/blogs/voices/indias-travel-and-tourism-sector-steering-towards-a-brighter-future/

30 Press Information Bureau, 'Record Growth in the Number of Airports in India', Press Information Bureau, April 23, 2023, https://static.pib.gov.in/WriteReadData/specificdocs/documents/2023/apr/doc2023423184101.pdf

Chapter 6: Human Capital Can Continue to Be India's Superpower

1 Jean-Marie Huriot, 'Towers of Power' *Metropolitics*, January 25, 2012.

2 CBC News, 'Skyscraper Boom Heralds Economic Downfall: Barclays', *CBC News*, January 11, 2012

3 FRED, 'Constant GDP Per Capita for India', FRED.

4 Forbes India, 'GDP of India: Current and Historical Growth Rate, India's Rank in the World', Forbes India, May 7, 2024.

5 Wikipedia, 'List of Countries by GDP (PPP)', Wikipedia.

6 Justin Sandefur. 'The Great Indian Poverty Debate, 2.0', Centre for Global Development, April 19, 2022.

7 University of Oxford, 'Poverty Rate in India Was Slashed, Says Report, But Globally 1.2bn Still Poor', University of Oxford, October 17, 2022.

8 Shiva Rajora, 'Indian Middle Class Will Nearly Double to 61% by 2046-47: PRICE Report', *Business Standard* July 5, 2023.

9 The World Bank. 'India's Growth to Remain Resilient Despite Global Challenges', press release, October 3, 2023

10 BRICS, 'BRICS Portal', BRICS, BRICS portal (infobrics.org)

11 I2U2, 'I2U2 Portal', I2U2, I2U2 - United States Department of State

12 The White House, 'FACT SHEET: In Asia, President Biden and a Dozen Indo-Pacific Partners Launch the Indo-Pacific Economic Framework for Prosperity', press release, May 23, 2022, FACT SHEET: In Asia, President Biden and a Dozen Indo-Pacific Partners Launch the Indo-Pacific Economic Framework for Prosperity | The White House

13 Council of Councils, 'Was the G20 Summit a Turning Point for the Global South?', Council of Councils, September 14, 2023, Was the G20 Summit a Turning Point for the Global South? | Council of Councils (cfr.org)

14 Nicholas Eberstadt, 'With Great Demographics Comes Great Power. Foreign Affairs, June 11, 2019, Why Demographics Will Drive Geopolitics | Foreign Affairs

15 David G.W. Birch, 'India Has a Digital Infrastructure, America Needs One', *Forbes*, November 7. 2023, India Has A Digital Infrastructure, America Needs One (forbes.com)

16 United Nations, 'UN DESA Policy Brief No. 153: India overtakes China as the world's most populous country', United Nations, April 24. 2024. UN DESA Policy Brief No. 153: India overtakes China as the world's most populous country | Department of Economic and Social Affairs

17 CIA, 'Country Comparisons: Median Age', CIA, cia.gov/the-world-factbook/field/median-age/country-comparison/

18 The Economic Times, 'India Tops Global Remittance Charts at $125 Billion in 2023', *The Economic Times*, December 18, 2023, https://economictimes.indiatimes.com/nri/invest/india-tops-global-remittance-charts-at-125-billion-in-2023/articleshow/106087493.cms?utm_source=contentofinterest&utm_medium=text&utm_campaign=cppst

19 Swati Dayal, 'Flipside of the Coin: Indian Unicorn's Foreign Destinations', TICE, April 23, 2023, Flip Side of the Coin: Indian Unicorns' Foreign Destinations (tice.news)

20 John Calabrese, 'India-Gulf Migration: A Testing Time', MEI, April 14, 2020, India-Gulf Migration: A Testing Time | Middle East Institute (mei.edu)

21 The Economic Times, 'Share of Agriculture in India's GDP Declined to 15% in FY23: Govt', *The Economic Times*, December 19, 2023, https://economictimes.indiatimes.com/news/economy/agriculture/share-of-agriculture-in-indias-gdp-declined-to-15-in-fy23-govt/articleshow/106124466.cms?utm_source=contentofinterest&utm_medium=text&utm_campaign=cppst

22 C. Peter Timmer, 'The Agricultural Transformation', *Handbook of Development Economics* (Amsterdam: Elsevier, 1988).

23 Mudit Jain, 'Here Is Why Indian Manufacturing Is Struggling', Fair Observer, July 24, 2023.

24 Wikipedia. Gender Development Index, Gender Development Index - Wikipedia

25 OECD. India, Education GPS - India - Overview of the education system (EAG 2023) (oecd.org)

26 Lauren Frayer and Raksha Kumar, 'It's a Mystery: Women in India Drop Out of the Workforce Even as the Economy Grows', *Goats and Soda*, January 16, 2023, Why women in India drop out of the workforce even as the economy grows : Goats and Soda : NPR

27 LiveMint, 'India among Top Countries with High Income, Wealth Inequality: UNDP Report', *LiveMint*, November 6, 2023, India among top countries with high income, wealth inequality: UNDP report | Mint (livemint.com)

28 Jeff Foust, 'India Returns Chandrayaan-3 Propulsion Module to Earth Orbit', *Space News*, December 4, 2023, India returns Chandrayaan-3 propulsion module to Earth orbit - SpaceNews

29 The Economic Times. 'Malnutrition in India: A Comprehensive Strategy to Combat for Better Future', *The Economic Times*, December 26, 2022, https://economictimes.indiatimes.com/news/new-updates/malnutrition-in-india-a-comprehensive-strategy-to-combat-for-better-future/articleshow/96518242.cms?utm_source=contentofinterest&utm_medium=text&utm_campaign=cppst

30 Ashoka Mody, 'Unlike China, India Cannot Be an Economic Superpower', *Project Syndicate*, July 28, 2023.

31 Aaron O'Neill, 'India: Youth Unemployment Rate from 1999 to 2022', *Statista*, December 2023, India - youth unemployment rate 1999–2022 | Statista.

32 Krishna B Kumar, 'Crisis Beyond the Crises', *Horizons*, Spring 2020, no.16, bf5c9aad1b6efe556da5ac74bab8e8f15e3d483d.pdf (cirsd.org)

33 https://www.pbs.org/wgbh/commandingheights/shared/minitextlo/tr_show03.html#8

34 The World Bank. Government expenditure on education, total (% of GDP) – India. The World Bank, https://data.worldbank.org/indicator/SE.XPD.TOTL.GD.ZS?locations=IN

35 The Economist, 'India Has Made Primary Education Universal, But Not Good', *The Economist*, June 8. 2017.

36 The World Bank, 'The Current Health Expenditure (% of GDP)', The World Bank, April 15, 2024, Current health expenditure (% of GDP) | Data (worldbank.org)

37 Akila Radhakrishnan, 'Leveraging Social Mobility: What India's Schools are Missing', The Hindu Centre, January 29, 2023.

38 Bibhudatta Pradhan and Vrishti Beniwal, 'Worthless Degrees Are Creating an Unemployable Generation in India', Bloomberg, April 18, 2023.

39 The Times of India, 'A Robust Vocational Educational Ecosystem Is Being Created in Several Schools', *The Times of India*, November 5, 2022.

40 Mudit Jain, 'Here Is Why Indian Manufacturing Is Struggling', Fair Observer, July 24, 2023.

41 Rahul Kapoor and Chris Rogers. '"Make In India" Manufacturing Push Hinges on Logistics Investments', S&P Global, August 3, 2023.

42 Ana Revenga and Anabel Gonzalez, 'Trade Has Been a Global Force for Less Poverty and Higher Incomes', The World Bank, February 2, 2017.

43 The Economist, 'Opening the Floodgates', *The Economist*, May 7, 2009.

Chapter 7: Aspirational India Chases a $10 Trillion Dream

1 UNDP India, 'National Multidimensional Poverty Index: A Progress Review 2023', UNDP, https://www.undp.org/india/national-multidimensional-poverty-index-progress-review-2023.

Chapter 12: Tradition as a Remedy to Religious Polarization: A Harmonious Bharat @ 2050

1 Saumya Dey, *The Seedbed of Pakistan: Cultural Conflicts, Elite Muslim Anxieties and the Congress 1885–1906* (New Delhi: Vitasta Publishing, 2023) 9–10.
2 S.N. Balagangadhara, *Generating a Scientific Hypothesis about Religion: A Preliminary Attempt* (Gent: University of Ghent), 10.
3 S. N. Balagangadhara, *Generating a Scientific Hypothesis about Religion: A Preliminary Attempt* (Gent: University of Ghent), 11.
4 S.N. Balagangadhara and Jakob de Roover, 'The Secular State and Religious Conflict: Liberal Neutrality and the Indian Case of Pluralism', *The Journal of Political Philosophy*, 15, no. 1 (2007): 76.
5 S.N. Balagangadhara and Jakob de Roover, 'The Secular State and Religious Conflict: Liberal Neutrality and the Indian Case of Pluralism', *The Journal of Political Philosophy*, 15, no. 1 (2007): 76.
6 S.N. Balagangadhara and Jakob de Roover, 'The Secular State and Religious Conflict: Liberal Neutrality and the Indian Case of Pluralism', *The Journal of Political Philosophy*, 15, no. 1 (2007): 77.
7 S.N. Balagangadhara and Jakob de Roover, 'The Secular State and Religious Conflict: Liberal Neutrality and the Indian Case of Pluralism', *The Journal of Political Philosophy*, 15, no. 1 (2007): 77.

Chapter 18: Brand India to Brand Bharat

1 K.B. Kansupada and J.W. Sassani, 'Sushruta: the father of Indian surgery and ophthalmology', *Doc Ophthalmol*, 93, no. 1–2 (1997):159–67, https://pubmed.ncbi.nlm.nih.gov/9476614/#:~:text=In%20particular%2C%20Sushruta%20describes%20what,a%20testament%20to%20his%20virtuosity
2 Britannica, 'Aryabata: Indian Astronomer and Mathematician', *Britannica*, https://www.britannica.com/biography/Aryabhata-I
3 Radhika Madan, 'AI in India: History and Evolution', *Medium*, May 3, 2021.

Chapter 19: Argument I: Reimagining the Political Economy with Twenty-three Dreams for a Better Republic@2047

1 Nikhil Inamdar, 'Covid Accelerates India's Millionaire Exodus', *BBC News*, April 13, 2021.

2 The Economic Times, 'Over 87,000 Indians Gave Up Citizenship till June This Year', *The Economic Times*, July 23, 2023

3 The Times of India, 'Why India's millionaires are ditching Indian citizenship', *The Times of India*, April 19, 2018, https://timesofindia.indiatimes.com/business/india-business/why-indias-millionaires-are-ditching-indian-citizenship/articleshow/63830380.cms

Chapter 20: Argument II: Protecting the Indian Republic: Threat Identification and Action

1 Rediff.com. 'China has captured 60 sq km of Indian land!', Rediff.Com, June 8, 2020.

2 Mint, 'West Bengal: ED Officials Attacked During Raids at TMC Leader's House; BJP Says "democracy failing again"', *Live Mint*, 5 Jan 2024

3 The Hindu. 'Income Tax Officials Attacked During Searches on the Premises of Tamil Nadu Minister Senthilbalaji's Brother', *The Hindu*, May 26, 2023.

4 Nuclear Monitor, 'The Computer Infection of Kudankulam and its Implications', *Nuclear Monitor*, February 02, 2020

5 Time, 'Is India Headed for an Anti-Muslim Genocide?', *Time*, October 4, 2021.

6 Amit Kelkar, 'Islamists Kill Another Hindu Man While Journalists Try to Paint Mohammed Zubair, Who Triggered the Islamists, a Victim', OpIndia, June 28, 2022.

7 OpIndia, 'How Can Poor Brown People Make Good Vaccines? FT Peddled Lies Claiming PM Modi May Have "Secretly" Taken a Foreign Dose', OpIndia, March 12, 2021.

8 Aakriti Sharma, 'Has India Finally Acknowledged that Chinese PLA Used Microwave Weapons against Indian Soldiers In Ladakh?', *The Eurasian Times*, January 6, 2021.

9 The Disinfo Lab, *The Invisible Hands of Foreign Interference in Indian Election 2024*, https://thedisinfolab.org/wp-content/uploads/2024/06/The-Invisible-Hands-Foreign-Interference-in-Indian-Elections-2024-Disinfolab-Report.pdf

10 Jhankar Mohta, 'From Ram Navami to Durga Visarjan to Hanuman Jayanti: List of attacks carried out by Islamists against Hindu processions from 2019 to 2022', OpIndia, April 23, 2022, https://www.opindia.com/2022/04/list-of-attacks-carried-out-by-islamists-against-hindu-processions/; *Organizer*, 'Hindu Festivals

Under Attack: Instances where Islamists launched assaults on Holi celebrations this year', *Organizer*, March 27, 2024. https://organiser.org/2024/03/27/229576/bharat/hindu-festivals-under-attack-instances-where-islamists-attacked-holi-celebrations-this-year/

11 South Asian Terrorism Portal, 'NIA Raids Suspected Maoist Camps in Kerala, Karnataka and Tamil Nadu', South Asian Terrorism Portal, October 13, 2021, https://www.satp.org/terrorism-update/nia-raids-suspected-maoist-camps-in-kerala-karnataka-and-tamil-nadu

12 Mangalore Today, 'Wikileaks: Kerala, TN are training hubs for Lashkar', *Mangalore Today*, December 06, https://www.mangaloretoday.com/headlines/Wikileaks-Kerala-TN-are-training-hubs-for-Lashkar.html

13 Tech Informed, 'Leaked covid test data largest breach in India's history', Tech Informed, October 31, 2023, https://techinformed.com/icmr-data-breach-one-of-largest-in-indias-history/

Chapter 24: Healthcare in India of 2050

1 The dependency ratio is an age-population ratio of those typically not in the labour force (the dependent part ages 0 to 14 and 65+) and those typically in the labour force (the productive part ages 15 to 64). It is used to measure the pressure on the productive population.

References

Business Standard 'India's Image Portrayed as "Land of Snake Charmers" Even After Decades of Independence: PM Modi Takes Swipe at Priyanka Gandhi.' *The Business Standard*, May 3, 2019. https://www.business-standard.com/article/news-ani/india-s-image-portrayed-as-land-of-snake-charmers-even-after-decades-of-indepedence-pm-modi-takes-swipe-at-priyanka-gandhi-119050301139_1.html

Business Standard. 'Services Sector Firms Led India Inc's Job Creation in FY23, says study.' *The Business Standard*, January 20, 2024. https://www.business-standard.com/economy/news/service- sector-firms-led-job-creation-in-corporate-sector-in-fy23-study- 124011900965_1.html

Cantore, Nicola, Michele Clara, Alejandro Lavopa, and Camelia Soare. 'Manufacturing as an engine of growth: Which is the best fuel?' *Structural Change and Economic Dynamics* 42 (2017): 56-66. https://doi.org/10.1016/j.strueco.2017.04.004

EY. 'Size and Age of Workforce of India Will Play a Significant Role in its Economic Growth in the Coming Years.' Ernest Young, April 11, 2023. https://www.ey.com/en_in/india-at-100/reaping-the-demographic-dividend

Government of India. 2020. 'Digital India Programme.' https://www.digitalindia.gov.in/

Grand View Research. 2022. *India Consumer Electronics Market Size, Share & Trends Analysis Report By Product (Mobile Phones, Televisions, Refrigerators, Digital Cameras, Air Conditioners, Washing Machines), and Segment Forecasts, 2023 - 2030*. San Francisco: Grand View Research, 2022. https://www.grandviewresearch.com/industry-analysis/india-consumer-electronics-market.

Hitachi Energy India Limited. 'Hitachi Energy India Limited announces Q2FY24 results: Energy transition and climate action plans driving order growth.' Hitachi Energy press release, November 06, 2023. https://www.hitachienergy.com/in/en/news/

press-releases/2023/11/hitachi-energy-india-limited-announces-q2fy24-results-energy-transition-and-climate-action-plans-driving-order-growth

IBEF. 'India is expected to become a US$ 30 trillion economy by 2050: Mr. Atanu Chakraborty.' IBEF, October 12, 2023. https://www.ibef.org/news/india-is-expected-to-become-a-us-30-trillion-economy-by-2050-mr-atanu-chakraborty

India Today. 'When Media Was Muzzled: History Retold.' *The India Today*, August 3, 2018. https://www.indiatoday.in/india/story/when-media-was-muzzled-history-retold-1304069-2018-08-03

Invest India. 'Tourism and Hospitality.' Invest India, December 14, 2023. https://www.investindia.gov.in/sector/tourism-hospitality

Ministry of Petroleum and Natural Gas. 'India's 4-plank Energy Security Strategy Is Based on Diversifying Supplies, Increasing E&P, Alternate Energy Sources and Energy Transition through a Gas-based Economy, Green Hydrogen etc.' Press Information Bureau, January 10, 2023. https://www.pib.gov.in/PressReleasePage.aspx?PRID=1889967

Ministry of Power. 2023. 'Power Sector at a Glance ALL INDIA.' 12 Jun. Accessed Jan 27, 2024. https://powermin.gov.in/en/content/power-sector-glance-all-india

Magow, Rajesh. 'India's Travel and Tourism Sector: Steering towards a Brighter Future,' *The Times of India*, December 29, 2023. https://timesofindia.indiatimes.com/blogs/voices/indias-travel-and-tourism-sector-steering-towards-a-brighter-future/

Mandhana, Niharika, and Newley Purnell. 'Modi's Vision for India Rests On Six Giant Companies,' *The Wall Street Journal*, June 20, 2023. https://www.wsj.com/articles/modi-india-economy-reliance-industries-adani-group-tata-d2c4f89e

Mehta, Sameer. 'With More Local Value Additions, Electronics Manufacturing Sector to be Worth $115 bn in 2024,' *The Economic Times*, January 01, 2024. https://retail.economictimes.indiatimes.com/news/consumer-durables-and-information-technology/consumer-electronics/with-more-local-value-additions-electronics-manufacturing-sector-to-be-worth-115-bn-in-2024/106431746.

Ministry of Electronics and Information Technology. 'BharatNet: A Project of National Importance.' 2018. https://www.bharatnet.gov.in/

Nandurkar, Mahesh, Abhinav Sinha, Nishant Poddar, and Kevin Verghese. 2024. 'India Strategy: Ayodhya – Unlocking India's Tourism Potential.' *Jefferies Asia Equity Research*, January 2024.

NITI Aayog. 'National Strategy for Artificial Intelligence.' 2018. https://niti.gov.in/

PIB. 'Record Growth in the Number of Airports in India.' Press Information Bureau, April 23, 2023. https://static.pib.gov.in/WriteReadData/specificdocs/documents/2023/apr/doc2023423184101.pdf

Press Trust of India. 'With Localisation, Electronics Manufacturing to be $115 bn in 2024: Report.' *Business Standard*, December 31, 2023. https://www.business-standard.com/pti-stories/national/with- more-local-value-additions-electronics-manufacturing-sector-to-be-worth-usd-115-bn-in-2024-123123100479_1.html

Press Trust of India. 'India to Become $5 trn Economy Early in Amrit Kaal: FinMin.' *The Economic Times*, December 03, 2023. https://economictimes.indiatimes.com/news/economy/indicators/india-to-become-5-trn-economy-early-in-amrit-kaal-finmin/articleshow/105725439.cms?from=mdr

Rajora, Shiva. 'Services Sector Firms Led India Inc's Job Creation in FY23, Says Study.' *Business Standard*, January 20, 2024. https://www.business-standard.com/economy/news/service-sector-firms-led-job-creation-in-corporate-sector-in-fy23-study-124011900965_1.html

Rathore, Manya. 'Dependency Ratio India 2013-2022.' Statista, December 14, 2023. https://www.statista.com/statistics/1323770/india-dependency-ratio/#:~:text=The%20dependency%20ratio%20in%20India,stood%20at%20approximately%2053%20percent

Sharma, Shivam. 'Shivam Sharma.' Twitter.Com, January 21, 2024. https://twitter.com/upshivamsharma/status/1748977487479271539/photo/1

Standard Chartered. 'India's Energy Transition: A Major Economic Opportunity.' Standard Chartered, November 08, 2022. https://www.sc.com/en/news/industries-in-transition/indias-energy-transition-major-economic-opportunity/

Statista. 'Total Contribution of Travel and Tourism to GDP in India 2013-2021.' Statista, January 26, 2024. https://www.statista.com/statistics/313724/total-contribution-of-travel-and-tourism-to-gdp-in-india-by-segment/

Statista. 'Twenty Countries with the Largest Population in Mid-2023.' Statista, January 23, 2024. https://www.statista.com/statistics/262879/countries-with-the-largest-population/

Studocu. 'Indian Media System During Emergency.' Studocu. https://www.studocu.com/in/document/dr-hari-singh-gour-university/corporate-law/indian-media-system-during/30944633

Tetot, Remi. 'The Mad King 2023 Macroeconomics, Finance, Business and Technology.' The Mad King, 2023. https://www.grant-williams.com/wp-content/uploads/2023/02/From-Babies-To-Boomers.pdf

The Economic Times. 'India Plays an Integral Role in Boosting Supply Chain Resilience through Friendshoring: Yellen.' *The Economic Times*, July 17, 2023.https://economictimes.indiatimes.com/small-biz/trade/exports/insights/india-plays-an-integral-role-in-boosting-supply-chain-resilience-through-friendshoring-yellen/articleshow/101814084.cms?from=mdr

The Quint. '1975 Emergency: Kuldip Nayar and the Struggle for Press Freedom.' The Quint, June 25, 2022. https://www.thequint.com/news/politics/1975-emergency-kuldip-nayar-indira-gandhi-press-freedom#read-more

Vasudevan, Deepa. 'In Charts: Unlocking India's Sort Power Potential.' *Mint*, October 02, 2023. https://www.livemint.com/politics/indias-soft-power-can-we-make-it-count-11696221303614.html#:~:text=In%202023%2C%20India%20was%20ranked,up%20from%20its%202022%20rank

Wood, Christina A. 'Services Versus Manufacturing: Which Matters More for Growth and Jobs in MENA?' World Bank Blogs, October 04, 2011. https://blogs.worldbank.org/arabvoices/services-versus-manufacturing-which-matters-more-growth-and-jobs-mena

World Bank. *World Development Report 2019: The Changing Nature of Work*. (Washington, DC: World Bank, 2019). https://www.worldbank.org/

Zeihan, Peter. 'India's Counter-Piracy Operation: A Geopolitical Wormhole.' YouTube, January 25, 2024. https://www.youtube.com/watch?v=lc22QxlThKg

About the Editor and Contributors

Karan Mehrishi is a journalist by day and an economist by night. For almost two decades, he has been passionately covering the Indian economy, dedicating his whole life to understanding the concept of India as a society and a nation-state. In his current avatar, he is an economics columnist and writes on whatever he deems fit for public deliberation. He specializes in central banking.

Yeshi Seli is a senior editor in *The New Indian Express* and writes on foreign policy and diplomacy. She has been a journalist for over two decades and has worked with leading news organizations. She holds an MPhil in history from the University of Delhi.

Pankaj Murarka is the founder of Renaissance Investment Managers, an 'alternate investment manager' in India. He has over twenty-six years of experience in fund management and has worked as the head of investments for some of the leading domestic and international organizations. He has been consistently recognized as one of India's leading fund managers with a consistent track record of long-term fund performance. He is a regular contributor to various media publications on his outlook for financial markets. He is a member of the ICAI.

Lt Gen. Arun Sahni, PVSM, UYSM, SM, VSM, is a cerebral military leader who retired as an army commander from the Indian Army with immense operational experience. He has incisive strategic insight into geo-strategic and security issues. He is an avid speaker at various forums and writes extensively on a wide range of issues. He is currently mentoring start-ups and is an advisor to a reputed corporation for their make-in-India defence initiative. He also steers a policy think tank on climate change and environmental issues.

Ritesh Jain is a seasoned trend watcher and macro investor, and steers a global asset allocation fund under the Pinetree Macro umbrella. As the founder of Nrizen, he pioneers a platform connecting NRIs with investment opportunities in India. As an independent board member and strategic advisor to a leading wealth management firm, Ritesh's influence earned him a top 3 ranking in the world of economy and finance on LinkedIn in 2019. In early 2024, he was featured among the top 100 in finance in North America by the *Top 100* magazine. In his earlier role, he was a chief investment officer at a major asset management firm in India, where he was involved in overseeing a substantial $8 billion in assets under management.

Maneesh Dangi, a seasoned macro investor with a wealth of experience in guiding clients in strategic asset allocation between stocks and bonds, is a key figure in the financial world. As an independent director at a major financial firm and a board member of IIM Udaipur's Centre for Financial Research, Maneesh brings a unique perspective to the table. His previous role as co-chief investment officer of a notable asset management firm, where he managed over $25 billion in assets, further underscores his expertise.

Krishna B. Kumar is an economist by training. He is the executive vice president of research at NORC, a nonprofit, nonpartisan research organization, at the University of Chicago.

Sutanu Guru is the a veteran journalist and author with thirty-five years of experience leading media platforms in India. He is also the executive director of CVoter Foundation.

Prerna Tambay is a senior academic at Kingston Business School, London, UK. She holds a PhD in management from Birkbeck College, University of London. She teaches and researches HR analytics, mobilization theory, the future of work, digital HR, and other related topics.

Pratap Tambe is a consulting partner at Tata Consultancy Services based in London, UK, and a business advisory board member at Anglia Ruskin University, UK. He has over twenty-five years of experience working in Indian IT companies for global customers. He is well known for his thought leadership in insurance, sustainability, blockchains, and cybersecurity.

Hemang Jani is the senior advisor to the executive director for Bangladesh, Bhutan, India, and Sri Lanka on the World Bank board. He is an international development and public policy practitioner. He has significantly improved public service delivery using technology, designed national-level governance and innovation frameworks, and enabled private sector development at the state, national, and international levels.

Nupur Sharma is a lawyer and a former spokesperson for the Bharatiya Janata Party. She holds an LLM from the London School of Economics and Political Science and was the president of the Delhi University Students' Union in 2008.

Shweta Kothari is a journalist and news anchor. She is an avid reader and a student of public policy and political economy. In her spare time, she teaches journalism students at Jamia Millia Islamia.

Kartik Malhotra is a journalist and executive producer with two decades of experience across India's foremost newsrooms. He is an alumnus of IIM Lucknow. He enjoys being a parent to Kyra.

Yashowardhan Tiwari is a research fellow at India Foundation and an active member of its Centre for Constitutional and Legal Studies. He is primarily interested in constitutional law, modern Indian history, and decolonial studies. He received his LLM from Jindal Global Law School (JGLS) with a silver medal.

Shivani Badgaiyan is a research fellow at the India Foundation. She previously worked as a senior research assistant at the Prime Ministers' Museum and Library and holds an MA in political science from the University of Delhi.

Niranjan Hiranandani is the chairman of the National Real Estate Development Council, a pioneering first-generation entrepreneur, and the founder of the renowned Hiranandani Group. With a visionary approach, he has played a pivotal role in shaping the real estate landscape, demonstrating exceptional leadership in the industry. His commitment to innovation and sustainable development has left an indelible mark on the community, underscoring his dedication to uplifting society through transformative initiatives.

Rajeev Pawar is one of the country's leading fixed-income investors. He is a banker with more than two decades of experience and has held leadership positions at domestic and international banks across Southeast Asia, India, the Middle East, and Africa. He is deeply interested in and understands rates, credit, and FX markets.

Sankar Chakraborti is the founder and chairman of ESGRisk.ai, India's first ESG rating provider. He is the MD and CEO of Acuité Ratings & Research, an Indian credit rating agency promoted by large Indian banks. He is the chairman of SMERA, the world's first SME-focused rating agency, an initiative of the Government of India. He is also the founder and director of the industry body Association of Indian Rating Agencies.

L.C. Trivedi is an Indian Railways visionary with forty years of experience in the field. He served as the principal chief mechanical engineer at ICF, Chennai, where he headed the production team of Vande Bharat Express and other high-speed coaches. He superannuated in 2021 as the general manager, East Central Railway, Hajipur, Bihar. Previously, he also held critical positions as divisional railway manager in Bilaspur, India's coal capital and highest revenue-generating unit of Indian Railways, and chief safety officer of Northeast Frontier Railway, Guwahati. He is an alumnus of Carnegie Mellon University, Pittsburgh, and the HEC Paris, and advises top management on railway-related projects.

Sankalp Mathur serves as the research director at the Centre for Advanced Financial Research and Learning (CAFRAL), an institution established by the Reserve Bank of India. He earned his PhD in economics from the University of Florida.

Amim Ahmed is the co-founder of VoiceWhat Consulting, one of India's leading branded content and sports companies. He is a brand expert and has given strategic consulting to many leading brands. He is the man behind India's first true marketing magazine, *4Ps*.

Benn Kochuveedan is a financial journalist who has spent over thirty years equally between New Delhi and Bombay. From 2009 to 2024, he headed the premier wire agency *The Press Trust of India* in the Maximum City and is currently with *The New Indian Express*.

Debdeep Sengupta has no military background. He reads the news and tries to piece together apparently disjointed threads of information, relying on his memory. Debdeep has an MBA from IIM Lucknow.

Pallavi Nahata is a journalist. She is a reporter and anchor at NDTV Profit and holds an MSc in banking and finance from King's College, London, and an MSc in economics. In addition to all things economic, she loves fashion, architecture, and history.

Roopak Gupta earned his MBA from Columbia Business School and is a technologist with over twenty-five years of industry experience. He has built several successful businesses in the technology space, and mTap was born out of his quest to make networking easy. As the co-founder and CEO of Hureka Technologies, he leads a team of 50+ application developers and digital marketing specialists.

Sharmin Nisar Chougule is a doctoral researcher in civil law and constitutional legality in Italy. Her current research interests pertain to novel issues of IoT and distributed ledger technology (DLT) in smart contracts. She is currently a visiting researcher at UNIDROIT, Rome, and at the Centre for IT and IP Law (CiTiP), KU Leuven, Belgium.

Vinay Singhal did his bachelor's in mechanical engineering from BITS Pilani in 1965 and attended the Advanced Management Program (AMP) at Harvard Business School in 1995. He has worked at Shriram Rayons, Hindustan Unilever, JK Synthetics, and Fortis Healthcare, retiring in 2003. He then switched over to the Clinton Foundation as the India director and represented Partners International (hospitals of HMS) in India from 2003 to 2016. He is currently the director of the ISLE senior citizen project and director of the UK company IUIH in India. Vinay continues to work in the healthcare and social fields.

Rahul Ugile has a diploma in insurance from CII, postgraduate diploma in insurance management from the National Insurance Academy, Pune, and a BE in computer science from Pune University. He is a fellow at the Insurance Institute of India. He has worked in various capacities in reinsurance, such as treaty underwriting, facultative placement, claims management, and technical accounting. He has also formed and operated the India Nuclear Insurance Pool. He was the chief technology officer of GIC Re South Africa Ltd, a subsidiary of General Insurance Corporation of India, where he led the digital transformation and innovation initiatives. He handles cyber and liability underwriting lines at GIC Re, Mumbai, India.